THE COMING
AMERICAN
FASCISM

AMS PRESS
NEW YORK

THE COMING AMERICAN FASCISM

By

LAWRENCE DENNIS

Author of "Is Capitalism Doomed?"

HARPER & BROTHERS PUBLISHERS

NEW YORK AND LONDON

1936

Library of Congress Cataloging in Publication Data

Dennis, Lawrence, 1893-
    The coming American fascism.

    (Studies in fascism)
    1. Fascism--United States. 2. United States--
Economic policy--1933-1945. 3. Capitalism. 4. Libera-
lism--United States. I. Title.
HC106.3.D367 1972   335.6'0973   73-180397
ISBN 0-404-56118-7

Reprinted by arrangement with Harper & Row, Publishers, New York

Reprinted from the edition of 1936, New York
First AMS edition published in 1972
Manufactured in the United States of America

AMS PRESS INC.
NEW YORK, N. Y.   10003

CONTENTS

v

INTRODUCTION

THIS book is addressed to the thoughtful who are not frightened by new and unpopular terms and concepts. If liberal capitalism is doomed, a fight for a lost cause will impose on mankind the most futile sort of suffering. The British Mercantilist System of the 18th Century and the Southern Planter-Slavery System of the pre-industrial-revolution period each fought on American soil an utterly futile and foolish war to save what was doomed by the inevitable and irresistible trend of social changes. If the present system, or more particularly, those features of it which are challenged by current trends be doomed, the longer and harder the fight waged to preserve it, the greater will be the suffering and losses of the people. Assuming that the old system is doomed, the basic premise of this book and an assumption which current events surely render probable enough to be entertained as an hypothesis in exploratory thinking about the near future, What are the possible alternatives to ultimate social disintegration and chaos? Most intelligent observers of the changing scene, whatever their personal preferences and prejudices, are agreed that, in the event the present system is not soon made to work better, the alternatives fall into the broad classifications of fascism or communism.

Precise definition of these two terms, now on every one's lips, should give us little concern. Officially, communism is whatever the latest encyclical from Moscow says it is, while the fascism of every fascist country is whatever its authorized fascist exponents proclaim it to be. Actually, of course, terms like communism and fascism, just as terms like Christianity, Americanism, or due process of law, must mean many different and often mutually exclusive things to different people. It is always possible to sustain two or more sides to an argument about the precise meaning of terms which, in the nature of things, cannot have a fixed definition like that of an English yard or a French metre. Still, if we are to have intellectual discourse, we must use terms like Christianity, fascism, socialism and so forth, in the expectation that other parties to the discussion will accept such terms in the sense in which they have come to be currently used and in the broad and almost undefinable sense in which we accordingly use them. Naturally, if a party to the discussion refuses to accept a term in a sense acceptable to the other parties, discussion must end.

In the case of the term fascism as applied to a social scheme yet to be developed in this country or as a term applied to the mere advocacy of such a scheme, it should be clear that no argument about the correct use of the term fascism can now be settled by an appeal to authority. Certainly Signor Mussolini, Herr Hitler or an American college professor who has written a book against fascism cannot be appealed to as an authority to define what fascism for America would be like. Obviously the official definition given the coming American fascism will be that of its authorized party exponents. This definition is not likely to call the American fascism by that name. It is much more likely to include an emphatic denial that the new American fascism is fascism. And it is fairly certain, if it follows the precedents of other important party platforms and propaganda, to say that the official American fascism, probably called by another name, is a great many things which it clearly is not.

This book is essentially one man's definition of what a desirable fascism, in his way of thinking, would be like. For obvious reasons, it cannot be a definition of the future American fascism, called by that or any other name. In discussing future social developments we can talk to some point about desirable and undesirable possibilities and probabilities. As these are largely matters of speculation and deduction from the limited field of the known to the unlimited field of the unknown and future unknowable, such discussions cannot deal in certainties nor can they to any good purpose give much time to questions of pure terminology respecting what admittedly lies still in the womb of time.

In this book, the system advanced is the thing, not the validity of the term used to describe or identify it. The reader is asked to remember that Italian fascism and German Nazism are not primarily the subjects of discussion. Correctly or incorrectly, the term fascism has come to identify in most people's minds many things and the general synthesis of ideas here advanced, all with exclusive reference to this country. The term, fascism, is therefore used chiefly as matter of intellectual integrity. I am fully aware and am incessantly being reminded that the term fascism is most unpopular at this time in the United States. I am also told that the thing itself is unthinkable in this country, an opinion which I find naïve. Nothing could be more logical or in the best political tradition than for a type of fascism to be ushered into this country by leaders who are now vigorously denouncing fascism and repudiating all that it is understood to stand for. Dr. Arthur Rosenberg, a communist sympathizer if no longer a member of the Party, points out in his admirable *History of Bolshevism* (Page 98) that the motto of the Bolshevist Revolution was not "The Dictatorship of the Proletariat. Down with Democracy!" but its exact contrary: "Long Live Democracy and Down with Dictatorship." The ideal fascism would be one which was honestly and truthfully presented to the people during its struggle for power. The fascism most to be feared is the fascism sailing under false colors. Such a type of fascism will be the worse for the duplicity of its leaders, and much of the blame will attach to those soft-thinking liberal leaders who have sought to make of fascism a synonym for all that is socially iniquitous instead of a descriptive for a rational and workable social scheme to which they happen to be opposed.

Both fascism and communism should be thought of as formulas of revolutionary social action for those of the underprivileged, dissatisfied and frustrated who have a will to power and a will, through the seizure and use of power, to change a situation they find intolerable, and, of course, to conserve a situation they find more satisfactory. Both fascism and communism are crisis formulas, that is to say, unlike formulas of liberal reform, neither has significance except in so far as it may have a chance of full realization as a new totalitarian or all-embracing social scheme. And, unlike liberal reform, neither has such a chance except in measure as the crisis of the existing system makes an entirely different system the alternative to chaos.

While fascism is to be thought of essentially as a formula for the frustrated in an extreme social crisis, it also has a strong appeal to many whose personal fortunes may still be far from desperate in such a crisis, as well as to national governments which may be interested more in conservation than further acquisition. Such persons, while moved by no feeling of frustration, still do not feel a zest for, or confidence in the outcome of, any fight to the finish under present world conditions between those in the house of want and those in the house of have. Interestingly enough, large numbers of extreme conservatives seem to share the understandable eagerness of the extreme communists for such a fray. The communists are entirely logical and loyal to self-interest in desiring and promoting wherever and whenever possible an intensification of class warfare. From it they have nothing to lose and, as a result of it, a chance to come to full power. The back-to-Hoover Republicans or back-to-Jefferson Democrats who would liquidate the New Deal or the back-to-liberalism British leaders who would liquidate fascism in international war stand only to lose by fighting those in the house of want, be they underprivileged nations seeking a place in the sun or the frustrated élite in liberal countries seeking an escape from the consequences of indefinitely prolonged depression. It is little short of astounding to see how the liberals of Downing Street, Wall Street and the Quai d'Orsay have been welcoming the comradeship in sanctions and arms of communist Russia against fascist Italy. (The fountain head of liberalism in America is really Wall Street or the eastern plutocracy, with its endowed and kept agencies of liberal indoctrination, the leading colleges and metropolitan newspapers.) These moneyed liberals who are seeking to use communist Russia in a war against fascism are singularly blind to their own interests, since they can never be comrades of communists. The liquidation of fascism where it is in power could only mean the succession of communism, and that could only mean the liquidation before a firing squad of property owners. And it is not to be supposed by the liberals of England, France, or even the United States, that they would long be safe in a world half-communist. The fact, of course, is that the liberals and conservatives, really two terms for the same people nowadays, as a whole, are still not sufficiently worried over the implications of present trends or over the ability of the system to stage a come-back. To those still in the house of have who are worried and humanely disposed at the same time, fascism makes an appeal which communism cannot make. Fascism does not expropriate all property rights or effect a wholesale liquidation of the owning and managing classes of the present order. And fascism does not mean a dictatorship by the leaders of the Marxist parties, falsely called by the communists a dictatorship of the proletariat.

Fascism is being widely denounced by liberals in the house of have and by their paid propagandists in the United States as being irrational as well as wholly evil. This book is an undertaking to rationalize fascism before it becomes an accomplished fact in the United States. The point of view from which the subject is discussed is that wherever fascism has happened, there has been reason for its occurrence and that wherever it survives, there must be reason in its use of power. Whether one wishes to go with and try to guide an important social trend, the ruling motivation in the writing of this book, or whether one wishes to oppose the trend, one can only profit from an attempt to understand it as a rational pattern of human behavior. It can serve no useful purpose, either of guidance or opposition, to pronounce fascism madness and fascists madmen.

As for the attempt to make fascism out to be a manifestation of mob madness or social irrationality, let it be borne in mind that fascism and communism, respectively, present a new social order, each with its own synthesis of values or ends and each with a highly rational scheme of social means to these ends. Each system of operating fascism and the Russian system of communism will be found to contain much that will be rejected by most Americans and much that would be inappropriate or down-right impracticable in this country. But it has to be recognized by any intelligent person that, so far as ends are concerned, the fascists know what they want, something which cannot be said of many liberal statesmen and something which is not rationally to be called a sign of insanity or irrationality. And, as for means to these ends, it can hardly be denied that fascism has had considerable success in fitting means to ends or in getting things done the way the leaders of action have willed. As much cannot be said of many liberal statesmen and as much cannot rationally be said of any one who is correctly defined as a lunatic or a moron.

Indeed, as to rationality, or fitness of means to ends, it has to be recognized that both fascism and communism are gigantic undertakings or adventures in what might be called sociological rationalization, corresponding to the sort of thing that has been carried so far in the advanced industrial nations in the fields of technology, having been given in Europe the name of industrial rationalization. Whether one starts out from the premise that the liberal ends, such as a chicken in every pot, equal justice under law, personal freedom, etc., etc., are well enough but that the social means to these ends are proving hopelessly ineffectual, or whether, like the communists, one starts out from the postulate that the ends of liberal capitalism are all wrong, the formula resulting from any thinking through of current problems of social ends and means is certain to be revolutionary. And in this fact resides the truth of the thesis of John Chamberlain's brilliant and inevitable "Farewell to Reform."

It seems likely that it will be as a radical program of sociological rationalization to bring our social machinery up to date or to make social and institutional means fit ends, that fascism will exercise a strong appeal in the United States. After many of our discontented and frustrated have experienced a few more disappointments with monetary schemes, economic specifics, and largesses of the public treasury to minority group interests, it is likely that they will see the logic of fascism as the only rationalized scheme of social means and ends, other than communism, which promises success. There can be but one refutation of the charge that the present system won't work and that is to make it work. Those who have been driven by the experiences of economic defeat and frustration to challenge the present system and seek a substitute cannot rationally be expected to respond to appeals to help make the system they are attacking work better. In other words, any rational discussion or analysis of fascism has to be conducted primarily from the point of view of the frustrated with a will to power and of those who feel neither able nor disposed to fight them and who also question the ability of the social order to buy them off indefinitely with government gifts financed by borrowing. Discussing fascism in other terms or from other points of view may faithfully and gratifyingly express one's own feeling about the matter but, so to relieve one's feelings about fascism will not throw much light on the logic of the situation as it must appear to those who will make an American fascism a reality, if it becomes a reality. And it is as a possible reality in the United States that fascism is most worth while discussing.

THE COMING
AMERICAN
FASCISM

CHAPTER I

THE CRISIS OF A SYSTEM: IT WON'T WORK

EVERY social situation has an unlimited number of aspects. Unworkability of the existing system is the particular aspect of the present social situation in the United States which, to the fascist way of thinking, seems most challenging to thoughtful analysis and immediate action. It is the unworkability of a given social system in a changed set of conditions which is most responsible for revolutionary social change. Feudalism, for instance, gave way to modern capitalism, not because any number of the people at any given moment decided that they would prefer a new social order, but because a series of discoveries of new lands and inventions of new machines and techniques created new conditions, among them the rise of a new business class, in which the feudal system could not work. This is not to state a thesis of rigid economic determinism or an exclusively materialistic interpretation of history. It is to recognize that changes in things act on preferences as well as changes in preferences on things.

It seems a fairly sound generalization to say that no social group, after debating the merits of the existing order versus those of a possible successor, proceeded to scrap the old and adopt the new as long as the old system was maintaining a semblance of order or working. Indeed, it is a part of the process of maintaining order and making a given social system work to see to it that the people like what they have. In measure as defenders of a system deem it necessary to argue with the people in favor of the preservation of the old system, they really admit and advertise its doom. There is no doubt but that the continuous attacks on fascism and defenses of the present system featured by powerful publications like the *Saturday Evening Post*, and in the public utterances of influential citizens like Mr. Hoover, do more to advertise and further fascism than almost any other factor calling fascism to the attention of the American people. A social system is either on the offensive, or it is doomed.

There is little point to drawing conservative inferences from the fact that the people are attached to their Constitution and nine elderly exponents of it, to their king and his nobles or to the Druid priests and their human sacrifices. The people are always attached to their leaders, institutions and folk customs, no matter how absurd or barbarous these latter may appear from other points of view. If and when, under changed conditions, the old system proves unworkable, or fails adequately to meet its imperatives, the undermining and upsetting of it are always directed by a small minority of the discontented or frustrated élite who may be divided into several groups but who, in some one minority group, gradually roll up enough mass following to achieve their ends. The defenders of the old system have to learn that the only good argument for the old system is to make it work. And this means, among other things, taking care of those élite who otherwise become discontented and ultimately revolutionary.

The usual defense of the system made today by its supposed friends, however, consists mainly in apologies for the system's unworkability and in appeals for loyal support no matter how it works. There is a typically liberal naïveté in appealing to Y's reason to be loyal to a system which still suits X, but which is not working so well for Y. That kind of loyalty is not born of reason but habit, early conditioning and wholly unreasoned impulses. One of the earliest proofs of the unworkability of a system, after its failure to care for the élite, is its failure to maintain the suitable mass conditioning for the system's survival. But of this we shall have more to say under another heading.

In the fascist view of the situation, the unworkability of the present system is the starting point in social thought and action. It is also the most vulnerable point for attack—and the fascists are attackers. Taking this particular view of the system's crisis or slow decline does not mean that a fascist-minded

person sees nothing else in the situation but mechanical defects or that he minimizes other aspects of the situation. That
the injustices of the present social situation, in which millions
suffer hunger and privation while productive instruments, like
human hands, land, and factories, remain in enforced idleness,
are a crying shame, the fascist fully recognizes. That Father
Coughlin and his League for Social Justice should emphasize
this phase of the situation and demand its correction is both
humane and helpful. But, if an individual or a group sets about
the correction of these injustices, the first order of problems encountered will be found to lie squarely in the fields of social
mechanics or government and management in the broadest
sense of these terms.

These problems are matters of getting things done rather
than of formulating moral judgments. It is well to say what
ought and what ought not to be, but satisfying any given moral
or ethical imperative about social conditions is largely a matter
of using the coercive force of government and the resources of
technical management of the social and material factors determining social conditions. In other words, while the impulse
to get something done may spring from wishing to have it
done, getting it done is not exclusively a matter of imagining
or wishing it done.

The voice of the prophet, which is the voice of conscience
denouncing sin and extolling righteousness—word these phenomena as you will and let them take the personal and institutional forms and expressions they will in different ages and
cultures—has been a moral force in every civilization. But, after
conscience or the prophet has denounced a condition and demanded its correction in the name of some metaphysical value
or social myth, without which no social scheme has ever operated, there always remain the governmental, managerial and
technical tasks of getting it done. Today these tasks are more
complex and inter-related than ever.

In ancient times and even down to the opening of the industrial revolution towards the close of the 18th century, the period
when most of our American social concepts, norms and insti-

tutions were supposed to have reached their final and definitive form for all time, it was ordinarily enough for some measure of correction of an evil to have the voice of conscience, through the prophet or priest, convince the Prince, or small group of head men, that it ought to be done—provided, of course, the prophet whipped up some enthusiasm for the correction by a little effective indoctrination of the people. In those bygone, pre-capitalistic, pre-industrial days, it could reasonably be expected that satisfactory improvement of a social situation would result from an effective pointing out of the evil and a fairly general observance of certain rather elementary rules of personal conduct such as are to be found in all the world's great moral codes.

Before division of labor had been carried very far, or before the industrial revolution, and as long as people lived in simple, closed and self-sufficing economies in which the members of one small group produced about everything they consumed, the chief moral imperative was doing the decent thing by one's neighbor—in other words, President Roosevelt's "good neighbor" philosophy. The "good neighbor" code was still fairly adequate in the comparatively recent days of our frontier rural communities, long after the drafting of the Constitution. There were no really significant divergences between the moral imperatives for good neighbor behavior as laid down by Hammurabi, Moses, Buddha, Socrates or Jesus. In the days of simple social organization and simple economic arrangements, the problem of public order was largely one of having the king or leader listen to the voice of conscience and having the subject fear God and obey the king.

It is amazing how many otherwise intelligent people still imagine that, in our complex modern society, public order can be maintained by having certain elementary rules of conduct appropriate to simple rural communities followed by millions of individuals. These latter are in fact grossly unequal in economic power, and each individual, or legal person, including the billion-dollar corporation, is left free to interpret the Constitution for himself, and to hire as many lawyers as his means will allow to champion through endless litigation his particular interpretations. Only the lush opportunities of the opening of the earth's largest and richest area for appropriation and settlement could furnish enough to be grabbed off by almost every one to make it possible to maintain public order under such a régime, which Thomas Carlyle once characterized as anarchy plus a constable.

In taking the traditional attitude towards social evils and social reform, 19th century reformers have rarely made an attempt to think through the social mechanics of getting any desirable social situation achieved. Where the reformers of the era of modern capitalism have essayed to do a little thinking through of the problem of correcting a social evil, they have usually confined their thinking to one rather narrow field of social institutions or phenomena such as taxation (Henry George), currency (William Jennings Bryan), or business regulation by law making and law enforcement (Theodore Roosevelt and Woodrow Wilson).

Broadly generalizing, one may say that, in modern Christendom, only reformers thinking in the framework of the Roman Catholic faith, and the various schools of modern fascist and communist thought, have consistently and seriously attempted to work out social solutions in terms of an all-embracing social synthesis. It is interesting to note in connection with this generalization that the distinguished jurists and, especially, the economists of modern capitalism, have all been fairly radical and daring in their thought or really of a definitely reforming kind. Blackstone, for instance, wanted to reform the absolutism of the Stuarts; John Marshall wanted to go much farther than the writers of the Constitution in strengthening the Union and centralizing social control—not in the Federal Executive or Legislature but in the Federal Judiciary; while the much venerated (and now considered conservative) Adam Smith, in the gloomy field of economics, was nothing short of a radical for his time, because he assailed the eminently respectable theses of applied 17th century mercantilism and demanded a régime of economic laissez-faire such as the world had never known before and such as it is not going to know again for a long time.

Now, it is a distinguishing characteristic of practically all the builders of the liberal capitalistic scheme of concepts, norms, and social institutions that they have tried to restrict their social thinking to some one field, like law or economics, and that, even within these already narrowly delimited fields, they were apt to specialize in one particular subdivision. This, doubtless, was a part of the separation of powers and division of labor ideals of the late 18th century. The jurists and statesmen assumed that no economic development could ever prevent the enforcement of the Constitution and lawful contracts, while the economists and business men took it for granted that no political or legal development could seriously or for long interfere with the free market, the laws of economic supply and demand, or the fixation of wages and prices in free competition by freely contracting legal parties.

They did not foresee billion-dollar corporations as parties contracting with fourteen-year-old children. The rise of the modern trust has upset their premise of a market free from monopoly, restraint of trade, and innumerable sorts of present day economic coercion. Specifically, they assumed that a mortgage could always be foreclosed, and that hunger could always be relied on to make a man work for the highest bidder however low the bid, but that no one would be coerced by combinations and conspiracies in restraint of free trade.

The political and economic systems thus fully, ably and separately expounded by a long line of legal and economic rationalizations, were assumed to be permanently workable and both fool and disaster proof, each functioning in its own watertight compartment. These compartments, of course, were kept water-tight from time to time by the definitions of legal decisions and the pedantic treatises of writers on the various social sciences. There was supposed to exist a series of perfect institutional harmonies, and it was a pious dogma that democracy was fool and disaster proof. The 19th century cultural leaders of liberal capitalism, though innovators, reformers, and improvers, as well as rationalizers, rarely thought in terms of a universal or even a national synthesis. Indeed, most of the 19th century socialists were incapable of such thinking.

The reason why Karl Marx towers among all the prophets and reformers since Luther and Calvin is that his was the first influential mind after the industrial revolution to try to think things through in connection with the denunciation of what he considered evil and the advocacy of what he considered righteousness. Marx, in his prophecy, did not proceed on the assumptions that the social evils he deplored were in the nature of defects rather than properties of the prevailing system, and that social justice, as he idealized it, was something obviously attainable within the framework of prevailing institutions, provided the people so willed it. He worked out a theory of the existing system to explain the evils he deplored— the exploitation and misery of the workers; a theory of a new system to realize the ideal he cherished—a classless, stateless, governmentless society of workers enjoying the highest standard of living which available resources could afford; and a program of action to effect the transition to this ideal order—the transitional program being the dictatorship of the proletariat.

I am inclined to find in his explanation of the existing system and its inevitable course to collapse many flaws in logic and science. I find the ideal of a classless, stateless, governmentless society of workers enjoying social order and material abundance fantastic and unattainable. It appears unattainable for the reason that social order requires government and administration by a ruling class or power-exercising class which must always be an aristocracy of management, however selected, operating through some set of mechanisms of social control, economic as well as political. Incidentally, it is to be remarked and even stressed that communist Russia, no less than the fascist countries, the billion-dollar capitalist corporation, or the efficient army in the field, meets with extreme thoroughness and rigor these universal imperatives of social order and administrative efficiency. The communists will, of course, admit this fact but try to convince the non-communist as well as themselves that these features of contemporary Russian communism are peculiar only to the present revolutionary phase, and that when revolution is finished, i.e. when the communist millennium comes, the state, government and the dictatorship of the proletariat will be sloughed off. The noncommunist with a realistic turn of mind will find this prediction of a coming millennium lacking in plausibility.

Incidentally, one of the important points of difference between fascism and communism is that fascism is singularly free of millenarianism. Fascism is without the naïveté peculiar to the belief that we today can have in the mind's conception an ideal social pattern for all time or for the people living a hundred or a thousand years hence. The only social patterns a hard, realistic mind can find useful in the enterprises of life are those of immediate organization and action, either to conserve what we now have and like, or to change from what we now have and do not like to something different which we can never accurately foresee but which we hope will be more to our liking. The social end must always be composed largely of the means of its achievement, which is to say that social ends and means are much the same things. Social ends and means are not only parts of a whole but, if they are to have any meaning, they must be parts of a whole which is realizable in a lifetime.

There is something vicious in the wish to impose on future generations our scheme of values. The fascist proposes only to give posterity a heritage of achievements and instruments of achievement, not a heritage of eternal truths and values to which it must slavishly be bound. The egotistical wish to define the values of future generations is common both to the liberal constitutionalists and the communist believers in the classless society of the future. What right or logical reason can we possibly have to take it for granted that our values or ideals will be acceptable to future generations or appropriate to their material situation? Only the belief that we have received a revelation of eternal truth can rationalize such a pretentious assumption. Interestingly enough, Russian communism, as an operating fact, is essentially a phenomenon of one five-year plan after another, just as capitalism, as an operating fact, is a phenomenon of one boom-crash-depression-recovery cycle after another.

The chief end of communism, regardless of its rationalizations, has to be considered the successful execution of one five-year plan after another. Of course, it is not material whether the duration of the plan be five years or ten years, but it is fairly certain that it cannot be for more than a comparatively short period like five years. Certainly, a fifty- or hundred-year plan would neither make sense nor serve any useful purpose. The chief end of communism is the success of the present five-year plan, which is to say, the success both of the ends and the means of that plan. The millennium of a classless society cannot be an end, nor a governmentless society a means, of any five-year plan—including that of 1935.

It may, of course, be thought to serve the purpose of enlisting supporters for a social program to project a far-off millenarian ideal, but projecting such an ideal will not help the solution of any immediate problem. And, sooner or later, it will prove a nuisance to have deluded a large number of people with an ideal which never comes any nearer to realization. The truth is that men want leadership in creative adventure and not leadership to a promised land which their descendants, but not they, shall enter. Indeed, men as a whole have never really wanted to be finally settled in a promised land flowing with milk and honey, with no further adventure left except that of growing fat on the milk and honey. It is the process of leaving Egypt and wandering through the wilderness in search of something new and different that men enjoy. It was this motivation that settled the new continents and produced modern capitalism. It is the same fundamental motivation that is producing the planned economies of fascism and communism.

As for the Marxian means to the impossible end of a stateless, classless society of workers—free of a governing class, of course—I find the means actually in use, namely, a dictatorship of the aristocracy of the Communist Party, grossly misrepre-

sented when called by Marxism a dictatorship of the proletariat. The dictatorship of the higher-ups of the Communist
Party is no more a dictatorship of the proletariat than the di-
rectorate of a billion-dollar corporation is a dictatorship of the
stockholders, or than the general staff of a great army is a dictatorship of the soldiers. Of course, it may be argued that, in
each of the three hierarchies just named, the rank and file can
change the ruling class if they so will. But this argument must
be based on assumed combinations of circumstances which
occur too rarely to constitute the basis of a generalization. In
the case of the Communist Party, the American Telegraph and
Telephone Company, or the French army, the dictatorship, as
a practical matter, is a self-perpetuating dictatorship of management—management which is answerable mainly to itself so
long as it is efficient and successful. Of course, an essential element of success is a large measure of efficient and loyal service
to the best interests of the Communist Party rank and file, the
stockholders of the A. T. & T., or the soldiers, as the case
may be.

Aside from the logical inconsistencies implicit in the alleged
end of a classless society and the means of a so-called dictatorship of the proletariat, there are innumerable values in the
communist scheme which I find unacceptable for wholly subjective reasons. But these faults in logic, these vices of intellectual dishonesty, and these unmentioned features of communism which I do not like, do not take from it a merit which
is not found in the social philosophies of the liberal reformers
from Adam Smith to the embattled bondholders of the National Liberty League of 1935.

This merit of communism is a program or a theory of action
which, given a possible combination of favoring circumstances,
can be followed with success. Marxism has this merit solely
because it is a totalitarian social philosophy which, by reason of
its totalitarian character, must insure adequate provision for
meeting the imperatives of order while its cherished set of objectives is being pursued. There is nothing original in Marx's
theorizing about the nature of the State, the mechanics of

power over men or the political process. His thought derived largely from that of profounder thinkers about these phenomena: Darwin, for the struggle for power and the survival of the fittest, and Kant and Hegel for the philosophy of the State, to mention only three of Marx's sources.

What was original or distinctive in Marx as a 19th century reformer pursuing a social ideal was his recognition of the State, government, or quite simply, power and its efficient instrumentalities, as parts of any given social scheme, and the maintenance of order under that scheme. From this recognition logically flowed the conclusion that meeting the crisis of any given social system or correcting any of its evils must necessarily be an exercise in the use of these instrumentalities for the end sought. Marxism, of course, could never have become a social reality, as it has become in Russia, but for a highly favorable combination of circumstances, one of which was an acute degree of collapse of the old régime in Russia. But the idealisms of liberal reformers of the 19th century could never be realized in the event of any considerable degree of breakdown of the social order, the reason, of course, being that liberal idealisms, when realized, have to be crumbs from a bountiful capitalist table and not creative achievements of liberal reformers in power.

These qualities of Marxism, original for the 19th century social idealist and reformer, are not the peculiar properties of his brand of socialism but merely the imperatives of good logic, or clear thinking, for a man who would meet a major social crisis, correct grave social evils, and realize certain important social ideals. To wish the realization of a social ideal without attempting to understand and without wishing to command and appropriately use the essential instrumentalities, may be said to amount to willing the end but not the means, or to giving evidence of a soft mind and a weak will. No second lieutenant of the U. S. Marines placed in command of an area in occupation by our troops would be likely to display such softness of thinking and lack of will. For instance, if put in command of a district during our occupation of Haiti, he would not have left in the hands of avowedly hostile persons instruments of power which might be used disastrously against our forces, as did the socialists in Germany and Austria when they had opportunities to establish their political control.

There is nothing peculiarly Marxian, fascist, Roman, German or European about good logic. Nor is bad logic good Americanism. These post-war experiences merely go to show that liberalism is logical, effective, and successful only so long as capitalism is a system in expansion or prosperous, or so long as liberal ideals can be conveniently financed out of a good business surplus. As a formula of social unity and action, or merely of good government to meet a situation in which business is not making a surplus, liberalism is simply futility and empty verbiage.

So far, in this chapter, no attempt has been made at direct proof of the specific assertion that the existing system in the United States is unworkable. That kind of proposition can never be argued to any point against a contrary conviction. No doubt both Charles I of England and Louis XVI of France, up to the moment their heads fell on the block, believed that their respective systems were workable. It can always be argued that a system will work if only certain things are done, and it is usually futile to try to prove conclusively that those things cannot be done, given the will to do them.

For the purposes of reasoning to a useful conclusion as to the workability of a given social order, it has to be assumed that if a social system can be made to work it will be. This assumption is tenable, if not indispensable, for many reasons. For instance, the old system, especially in the early days of its decline, always has the preponderance of factors with it—the best talent, command of most of the available resources, and prestige. If the defense fails, it stands to reason that it had an impossible system to defend. Whether the defense could have held out a little longer, and how much longer, are, of course, always open to question. But it hardly makes sense to say that persons with the initial resources of Lenin, Mussolini and Hitler could have overthrown anything but unworkable systems. The term workable, as applied to a social system, has little sense if it means a system that fails to survive. If it works, it survives, and if it survives, it works.

CHAPTER II

CAN WE RETURN TO THE PRE-WAR BASES?
THE SOCIAL MECHANICS OF AN EXPANSION ERA

THE only conclusive test of the workability of a social system must be that of survival. But if one is to help choose the successor system and to shape transitional developments, one must recognize the beginning of the end long before the end is a demonstrable fact. Whatever may be said in derogation of the accuracy of Marx's predictions of the doom of capitalism, it must now be admitted that those predictions were a useful formula in preparing hard-minded Marxists like Lenin and his best associates for effective action in such a social crisis as that through which Russia went in 1917.

On the other hand, it now seems evident that the best liberal teaching of two centuries had not so prepared Kerensky and scores of other liberal leaders of the post-war era. Mussolini was well prepared for social crisis by a mental formation in the thought of philosophers like Nietszche, Sorel, Marx, and Pareto, none of whom could claim Mussolini as a disciple and no two of whom were at all alike in their philosophies except, possibly, as to a general rejection of the assumptions of liberal philosophies. And so it may be said that while one can never prove in advance of the event the final collapse of a given social order, one does get a splendid preparation for the event, whenever it occurs, if one has previously formulated a clear hypothesis of trends which always move in that direction long before the event takes place.

The case for the unworkability of the liberal capitalist system can be built squarely and securely on any honest attempt to answer certain questions which I shall try to state and discuss in this and the next five chapters. The first question, or group of questions, and the subject of this chapter, is: Can we return to the pre-War formula of settling new territory with a million European immigrants a year, preëmpting vast natural resources for the sale of which there is an assured world market, and capturing new foreign markets for a steadily expanding output of manufactured goods?

That, in the thesis of this book, is the only sound or workable liberal capitalism, and that, it is held, can be workable only during the comparatively limited period of a century or so, while the settling, grabbing and conquest of new resources and markets are possible.

A second question is: Can we, in lieu of being able to finance expansion of the pre-War type, resume the—roughly—1915-1929 formula of financing consumption—consumption of munitions to kill people, or consumption of innocent and desirable things, like better homes and automobiles for people who have not enough money to pay for such things under the system when soundly run? In the thesis of this book, financing consumption of things by states, cities or individuals for which they haven't the money to pay, although it produces a happy state of affairs while it lasts, cannot be a workable formula for liberal capitalism.

A third question is: Can we go on under some depression formula (Great Britain has been on one since the War) of supporting from a fourth to a third of our working population in unproductive and discontented idleness, and thereby preventing a financial and social crash, by means of huge yearly governmental deficits or by means of sufficiently heavy taxation to avoid the deficits? (Great Britain reduced her deficit by repudiating her obligations on her sterling debt and by defaulting on her obligations to our Government.)

A fourth question is: Can we effect a sound world economic reorganization so as to put the old system in a better position for a fresh start, assuming satisfactory operating conditions are attainable? That is to say, more concretely, Can we reduce debts to manageable proportions without causing too much of an upset through the results for the creditors? Can we restore comparative freedom of international trade and investment,

restore confidence in future credit contracts by currency stabilization on a permanently sound basis, and liberate such things
as prices, wages, supply and demand from disturbing political
interferences, which are destructive of sound capitalism, without being constructive of a workable socialism?

The question whether we can go back to the 19th century or
pre-War formula, of expanding population and exploitation of
new territory and markets, is obviously answerable only in the
negative. Developing the answer must be largely a matter of
explaining the laws of population growth, for capitalism is as
population grows.

With a rapidly expanding population, serious political obstruction of capitalist ways, or attempts at maintenance of
wages above a given minimum at which production is profitable, cannot prove effective. The rapidly expanding labor supply
flouts all such attempts. The fact that real wages rose during a
period of large labor supply and comparatively little political
interference, though there was some unimportant labor union
interference with wages, is easily explainable by the accompanying facts that, during the same period, the supply of good land
and natural resources for exploitation, as well as the efficiency
of the techniques of production, were increasing more rapidly
than the supply of labor. Briefly, then, the supplies of labor and
natural and technical resources for capitalistic exploitation were
increasing at a rate to make capitalism workable, which is to
say, profitable; and the supply of natural resources and productive techniques were becoming available fast enough to insure
steady improvement in the lot of labor. The capitalist thrived
and the worker was content not to interfere seriously or politically with the system.

What has made capitalism a workable system has never been
stability or slow growth. Capitalism has worked only to the
extent that it has been able to grow in geometrical progression
or at compound interest. The possibility of compounding the
return on the total investment is necessary in order to keep up
continuous reinvestment in capital goods. Continuous reinvestment in new capital goods is necessary, in turn, in order to keep

up employment if certain receivers of income receive more than enough for their current consumption. Every intelligent exponent of the present system, whether a practical business man or a professional economist, has only to offer, as the way out of the depression, a revival of new capital investment. There are wide differences of opinion as to what are the best policies for inducing an increase in new capital investment but never as to the necessity for such investment.

It is not recognized that in the present depression we may be facing the challenge of a physical or mathematical law which, at last, is becoming operative in respect of the growth of capitalism. The ideas that, according to mathematical and physical laws, every quantity which grows by geometrical progression or at compound interest must in a comparatively short time reach the top of its growth curve, and that the total volume of capital invested for a return is a quantity which has to grow at compound interest if the capitalist system is to work, have simply not been tolerated in any respectable body of theory or teaching about our present social order. For over a century of rationalizing capitalism, these simple and obvious ideas have been rigorously excluded from every important body of social doctrine except, of course, that of Marxian communism. Even the harshest critics of modern capitalism have never for a moment questioned its ability to go on growing indefinitely in geometrical progression. During the past six years of the depression, even, it is little less than surprising that reforming liberals of the *Nation* and *New Republic* types, or avowed socialists of the Norman Thomas type, have continued to assume that recovery from depression is well nigh automatic and virtually inevitable.

Now, the laws of mathematics and physics as to every compound interest growth curve flattening out and turning downwards at some point, do not indicate that this particular depression must be the last in the history of modern capitalism. But these laws do prove that there must be a last depression, and that its coming cannot be a matter either of millenniums or centuries. With this fundamental proposition established as a basis for discussion, instead of the classical assumption that, as human wants are insatiable and as physical resources for their satisfaction are far from being fully used, capitalistic investment the world over can continue indefinitely to compound as it has done for a century or so, it becomes a relatively easy matter to deduce from many of the signs of the times that the culminating point in the growth curve of capitalistic investment has been, or is now being, passed. The simplest and most obvious fact indicating this deduction is that of the failure of vast accumulations of current savings, or of immense credit potentialities of our banking systems, to make new investments.

The point of this chapter is that liberal capitalism, involving among other things, as it does, a quantity of profit-yielding investments, furnishes no exception to the mathematical laws of growth. Liberal capitalism has not the quality of being able to go on growing as nothing else on this planet can go on growing. If any one is inclined to question that liberal capitalism was ever supposed to be an exception to this rule, let him but read either the dry-as-dust economic texts or the bigger and better business propaganda of any period during the past hundred years. This contrary-to-fact assumption of the possibility of indefinite growth for capitalism was never expounded with more confidence, absurdity, or scholarship than during the five years just preceding 1929, all of which merely proves that the social sciences are merely the sciences of propaganda, and operation of the existing system, and never sciences of detached observation and description of the existing system.

Mathematicians and natural scientists have understood the laws of growth for generations. It is taking the world crisis, and Lenin, Mussolini, and Hitler to teach the social scientists of liberalism that this old law of growth applies to accumulations of income producing investment as well as to everything else that grows in quantity. It is the same law that explains why the descendants of two flies, two guinea pigs, two fish, or bacteria spores, do not and cannot cover the face of the earth in six months or some brief period of time, according to the initial rate of reproduction. If one cent had been put on compound interest, annually at one per cent by a Garden of Eden Investment Trust 6000 years ago, the present fund would be large enough to make every one of the two billion inhabitants of the globe worth about a half a quadrillion dollars. The total wealth of the globe probably does not exceed two trillion dollars, as values are now computed.

Two rather simple series of events prevent the multiplication of any biological species in geometrical progression or at a compound interest rate: The first of these events is the failure to find enough food (in the case of reproductive capital the failure to find profitable markets). The rapidly multiplying creatures soon begin to eat each other, die of starvation, or get eaten by other creatures who find themselves up against the same survival difficulty. The second of these events is auto-intoxication. As the members of the rapidly multiplying colony attain a certain density of population, the poisons which their life processes generate kill off multitudes of them.

The laws of growth can be found in any number of works on natural science, an excellent discussion of the subject being contained in Raymond Pearl's recent *Biology of Population Growth*. He points out that the laws of growth can be expressed in recondite statements or in mathematical shorthand. They amount to saying about this, "Growth occurs in cycles. Within one and the same cycle, and in a spatially limited area or universe, growth in the first half of the cycle starts slowly by the absolute increment per unit of time, and increases steadily until the mid point of the cycle is reached. After that point, the increment per unit of time becomes steadily smaller until the end of the cycle." It is self-evident that this generation is living in a period which marks the turning point in the curve of population growth of the capitalistic nations. The significance of this fact for the capitalistic system is, of course, the central idea of the present chapter.

It is seldom that people stop to think, in discussing the workability of the present system, that in the hundred and fifty odd years of the system's modern operation, or since 1780, the population of this country has grown fiftyfold, or from 2,200,-

ooo in 1780 to 123,000,000 in 1930. The populations of the preeminently capitalistic countries show a similarly geometric progression in population growth, Britain and Germany for instances. All that is needed to give a clear and quick view of the significant population trends for the United States since 1780 is a glance at the curves of total population and percentage of yearly increase in population, respectively. Such a tableau may be found on Page 2 of *Recent Social Trends*, in the article on the "Population of the Nation" by Warren S. Thompson and P. K. Whelpton. The population curve, after over a century of rise, is beginning to flatten out in the 20th century, and the percentage of increase has been steadily going down since the 1830's. During the sixteen decades from 1710 to 1860, the average increase per decade was 34 per cent. In the period 1860-1910 it averaged 23 per cent per decade. In the two decades 1910 to 1930 it has dropped to 15 per cent per decade. By the end of the decade 1930-1940, it will have dropped to 8 per cent per decade.

Writing on "The Population Question Restated," Mr. Roberts, in the *New Statesman* of June 16, 1934 says "At the present time every four female children born in England and Wales leave on the average but three female descendants. In other words, if the present birth rates continues, the number of potential mothers will diminish by one-quarter in every generation. Assuming no further fall in the birth rate, Dr. Charles says that, once a stable age composition has been reached, the population of England and Wales will in 200 years have fallen from 35,000,000 to 6,000,000 (where it was in 1830). Should the net reproduction rate fall to two-thirds of its present figure, our total population would in 300 years drop to 45,000." Kuczynski, an American authority on population, points out in *The Balance of Births and Deaths* that "According to the fertility and mortality in western and northern Europe in 1926, one hundred mothers gave birth to ninety mothers only. With the fertility of 1926 the population is bound to die out unless mortality of potential mothers decreases beyond reasonable expectation." He predicts that population will reach its maximum in France in 1937, in Germany in 1946, in the British Isles in 1942, in the United States, a maximum of 142 million by 1960. Russia is the one large country in Europe with a rapidly increasing population. There, 100 mothers are giving birth to 165 potential future mothers.

These population figures show that even if we had not stopped three-fourths of the pre-War yearly immigration by new restrictive legislation just after the War, the time would soon have come—it is here now—when our annual quota of immigrants must be reduced to a small fraction of what it was before the War. Actually, during the past three years we have been losing more people by emigration than we have been gaining by immigration. The chief reason, of course, for the end of our population growth by immigration, even assuming no restrictive legislation in this country, is that the European countries, with the exception of Russia, no longer have a rate of population increase which affords them an export surplus.

Capitalism, as a working system, requires opportunities for profit-making. Profit-making requires the use of factors of labor and natural resources in a situation of rapidly expanding demand for their products. A growing supply of workers is not the only essential for capitalist prosperity, but it is one of the absolutely indispensable essentials. It would be difficult, for instance, to measure how much capitalistic prosperity in this country for a hundred and fifty years has owed to rising land values produced by nothing so much as rapid population growth. Many a unit of a basic industry, like farming, railroading, merchandising or amusement, has been operated inefficiently and at a loss but shown a net profit over a number of years, due solely to the sale of real estate that had doubled and trebled in value while in use. To restore this element of capitalist prosperity, rising land values, we must reverse the present trend in population increase. And none of the would-be saviors of liberal capitalism are even suggesting such a remedy. On the contrary, most of them support the demands of labor for immigration restriction and the demands of many for birth control.

The pre-War pattern of capitalism called not only for plenty of cheap labor to exploit, but also for plenty of cheap and good land, and plenty of rich but cheap natural resources to preëmpt and exploit. It was the cheap labor that made the resources valuable, and the cheap resources that made the cheap labor valuable. And it was an unusual combination of circumstances which made a market for the products of these combined factors of production. It should be obvious that the happy combination of factors making for an increasing volume of production and of market demand for the product could not be indefinitely maintained. The iron laws governing the phenomena of compound interest will not allow such geometrical progression to infinity.

Indeed, a stable market, or even a market whose demand increases by arithmetical progression or at a simple interest rate, would not make capitalism workable, for such a market would not provide the necessary incentives for the investment of the surplus. No; the market demand required for the healthy working of capitalism must expand at the same rate of compound interest as savings, which rate, even if it were only one per cent, would turn one cent into two billion times a trillion dollars in 6000 years and would turn the present capital of the world into some equally fantastic quantity in fifty years. Modern capitalism does not mean merely ownership of the instruments of production or private management of production. It means that ownership may take as large a cut as it can get, and that it may or may not reinvest its surplus as the prospects of profits are thought to indicate.

The feudal lord of the manor was quite as much a property owner as the millionaire under modern capitalism. He had property rights in the tools of production, and often directed some of the processes of production. But, unlike the man of property under modern capitalism, he could never make a decision in respect of his property rights one of the results of which would be widespread unemployment and destitution, for, as a practical matter, he could not expel the serf from the land or deny him the use of the land and some elementary capital for the production of food, shelter and clothing.

Modern capitalism is the first important system of property rights to allow property owners to make decisions which result in large scale unemployment. The much vaunted freedom of modern capitalism is largely a matter of the freedom of property owners from social responsibility for the consequences of their economic choices. It is a matter of the freedom of property owners not to invest their savings if the profit incentive is not considered sufficient. To say that it is also a matter of the freedom of the worker to abstain from work is to utter a shallow mockery of human necessity. The rich man is, in a practical sense, free to withhold his savings from investment. The poor man is never free in any but a legal and absurd sense to withhold his labor from the highest bidder, however low the bid, if, as the principles of sound capitalism require, so to withhold his labor is to starve. At the present time, one of the fundamental rules of sound capitalism is being violated by the payment of the dole, which prevents a man from starving and thus enables him to withhold his labor from the highest bidder if the bid is not materially higher than the amount obtainable from the dole.

Of course, the chief assumptions on which liberalism, in contradistinction from feudalism, has accorded the prevailing measure of economic freedom to capital and labor are that the profit incentive will always suffice to insure a full and voluntary use of savings and available credit in new work-making investments or enterprises, and that hunger will always insure the acceptance by labor of the highest bidder for labor. Both of these assumptions are knocked into a cocked hat by present facts. The latest figures on unemployment and the hoarding of bank credit and private savings suffice to prove that the profit incentive is not forcing idle funds and credit into new investment. And an almost universal dole is preventing the hunger incentive from driving the unemployed to accept the market wage which might be as low as, or lower than, the dole.

The point of this reference to the difference between feudalism and capitalism is not to argue any proposition as to the relative merits of the two systems and certainly not to plead for a return to feudalism. The point merely is that property rights are not synonymous with modern capitalism, or that a régime respecting private property rights can also impose social responsibilities and discipline on property owners which our good liberal system and American Constitution expressly exempt property owners from bearing. The point may also be put in this way: Whereas modern liberal capitalism requires a market expanding in geometrical progression for its successful operation, other systems maintaining property rights did not require any such rate of market expansion.

If modern capitalism simply meant private ownership and management of the factors of production with a view to yielding owners and managers a return for ownership and management (such return to be fully consumed by the recipients, put into necessary capital replacements and even into some expansion of production as well as use property in arithmetical progression or at simple interest, without any considerable compounding of profits) there is no iron mathematical law which would doom it to collapse in some comparatively brief period of feverish operation. That sort of system of private ownership and management could be made stable and workable, given good national planning and good government. And that sort of system fascism envisages. But that sort of system is not capitalism, nor is it workable within the framework of the present system. If profit-yielding investments cannot be piled up in a compound interest or geometrical progression ratio, capitalism does not work. It will, of course, be asked by many, Why not?

The constant cry of the liberal reformers is for a readjustment or revamping of the present system to get rid of some of its contradictions or mechanical defects. Why these readjustments cannot be made within the framework of the system is really one of the larger themes of this book, and cannot be covered fully in any one chapter. Suffice it to say at this point that the fundamental reason why a stable system of private ownership and management cannot be operated under the present system is that any stable system would have to include a large measure of state planning and state imposition of many features of the unique national economic plan, all of which the State is now, by Constitutional inhibitions and a lack of necessary mechanisms, prevented from realizing.

In short, no return to the 19th century pattern of expansion is possible today. Possibly, a thousand or more years hence, after the world's population shall have been reduced from two billion to a few score million, and after the Americas shall have been returned to a mere handful of nomadic aborigines, a new liberal, capitalistic culture may arise from the ruins of decadent planned economies and flourish while the new continents are being settled, and while population is being increased several thousand per cent in the course of a few brief decades. The break needed for a revival of liberal capitalism is the starting point of 1775 or even 1840. For a cycle of expansion, or growth in geometrical progression, nothing matters so much as the starting point, whether it is a case of multiplying flies or productive capitalistic plants. You can start a rapid growth cycle quite easily with two flies—but not with several quadrillion. You can start a rapid growth cycle with several million dollars seeking profitable investment—but not with several hundred billion. Most of the pleas by liberal economists and sound business men for a revival of capital investment, and most of the recommendations as to the ideal conditions to provide for such a revival, entirely ignore all this. The starting point for the expansion cycle is the thing.

That, briefly stated, is the dilemma of modern capitalism in 1935 as it faces a world of closing markets and the inevitable corollaries of rising fascism and communism. Since 1914, broadly speaking, the two prevailing formulas for the operation of the system have been the financing on credit of consumptive expenditures and/or the financing of pure depression relief, equally on credit. In the United States financing consumption on credit with great accompanying prosperity, was the formula from 1914 to 1930, except for a minor set-back in 1920. And financing on credit relief for banks, railroads, farmers and the unemployed has been the formula from 1930 to date. The questions whether we can resume the consumption credit financing of the boom days or go on with the relief financing of the New Deal, will be discussed in succeeding chapters.

CHAPTER III

CAN WE RESUME CONSUMPTION FINANCING ON CREDIT?

IN THIS chapter I shall take up the question, Can we resume the financing on credit of large scale consumption? In the next two chapters we shall continue the discussion, with attempts to answer the questions, Can the present system go on carrying the depression? and Can we effect reorganization under the present system?

As to whether financing consumption on credit is a workable formula, it should be enough to state the question to have answered it in the negative. But, thanks to the material achievements as well as the fallacious propaganda of the late new era, and thanks also to the numerous and influential money and credit management schools of thought, the consumption-credit formula needs refuting. The case for the consumption-credit formula is made appealing by the statement of three indisputable facts: The first is the enormous increase in our material equipment and productive capital between 1914 and 1929; the second is a great increase in the productive efficiency of man and machinery; and the third is a rise in the average standard of living and a 32 per cent increase in the real wages of the employed between 1914 and 1928.

These achievements were, of course, marred by a slow but sure growth of technological unemployment and an increasing tendency for real wages to lag behind the rise in productive efficiency and the total output. But these defects, which the Technocrats and most schools of social critics used as good talking points against the system, did not suffice to discredit it greatly with the masses or to prove it unworkable. The only thing effective that can be said against the prosperity of 1915 to 1929 is that it could not be kept up.

President Hoover's Committee on Recent Economic Changes, in a report drafted in 1929, just before the crash, reassured the country that as human wants were nearly insatiable, we should be able to keep up and even enlarge indefinitely our production. But the depression has taught that the insatiability of human wants has little to do with the volume of effective demand for goods and services.

After the insatiability of human wants, the excellence of the latest financial machinery and techniques was generally supposed to constitute the next best guarantee of continued prosperity under the formula of credit financed consumption. Yet all that the excellence of the financial institutions and their operation served to do was to enable a bigger inflation bubble to be blown than the world had ever seen before, with this difference between the ensuing sequel and that of all previous bubbles—when the bubble burst the explosion was bigger.

Before 1929 it would have seemed necessary to argue the point that the volume of production could not be maintained indefinitely by lending people money to pay for consumer goods which they could not otherwise afford to purchase. This argument, stated more fully in my previous book, *Is Capitalism Doomed?* (see pages 17-30), runs somewhat as follows: First, the buyers whose added consumption is financed are, in a short time, borrowed up to their limit, and thereafter they are forced to buy and consume less by the amount of interest they have to pay than they could buy, pay for and consume had they never borrowed. Second, the receivers of the interest will not consume or reinvest their full interest income because, among other reasons, the payers of the interest are consuming less and so furnishing less incentive for the investment of new capital.

All this has now been demonstrated practically by depression experience. In this connection it is not amiss to remark that Professor E. R. A. Seligman, the dean of American economists, wrote *The Economics of Instalment Selling* at the peak of the boom, this work being subsidized by General Motors Finance Corporation, as an objective study of consumptive credit. The most interesting thing about this voluminous work was that it devoted less than a page to the barest mention of the only important feature of instalment buying, namely, the interest cost to buyers and its implications. Professor Seligman might have shown, but did not show, that instalment buyers never pay less than fourteen per cent interest, and in some cases pay over fifty per cent. The high actual interest charge, of course, is somewhat concealed by a nominal rate like six per cent on the initial amount borrowed, which may amount to an average of fourteen or eighteen per cent on the money actually in use, for the borrower goes on paying six per cent on $100 for ten or twenty months, though he may have that amount of debt outstanding only during the first month.

Today, the simple plea to lend people money to pay for goods they cannot afford, though common enough, is less often heard than during 1914 to 1929. The consumptive credit fallacies are by no means dead, but they are less blatantly proclaimed. The main reason, probably, is that so many influential people, including notably the rich and the bankers, are now preaching economy, retrenchment and a balanced budget to the richest government in the world, all of which makes it a little inconsistent for them publicly to exhort poor people and poor cities in the next breath to buy and spend on credit.

The most appealing current arguments for an attempt to resume the consumption-credit formula for capitalistic prosperity come from the money and credit cranks, and are strangely interwoven in their various schemes of inflation, managed money and managed credit. In effect, what they say amounts to something like this "You have had your fingers burned playing the Wall Street and high pressure sales schemes of credit uses. Now try our new system, which can't lose. It is different."

Some of these apostles of more money or cheaper money or lower interest rates by the Central bank are eminent, erudite and disinterested believers in their scheme. Keynes, Cassel and Irving Fisher may be named as distinguished examples of this sort. The vast majority, however, have a personal interest to serve, even if it is only reëlection, in getting the government to buy silver, gold, cotton, wheat, government bonds, commercial bank paper, preferred stocks of banks or anything else with paper money at a price in excess of market value. The simplest set of interests served by the inflationists is that of the Congressman who wants the votes of the people to whom the Government gives the money, as well as the votes of the people who don't want to put up this money in additional taxes.

Practically all the money and credit panaceas involve an increase in the quantity of paper money or central bank deposit credit, on the following line of reasoning: The central problem of any depression is getting more goods paid for; getting more goods paid for is a matter of getting more money spent; getting more money spent is a matter of getting more money into circulation; getting more money into circulation is a matter of getting more money printed by the Government printing press or created by the Federal Reserve Banks in the form of loans to member banks of the Federal Reserve System, or purchases by the Federal Reserve Banks with their simple notes or credit of gold, silver, bank paper or anything else Congress, by law, may authorize them so to acquire.

These reasonings, of course, completely disregard many simple and obvious facts. First, there is always enough money in circulating currency, plus bank deposit credits, to permit enough buying to put every idle man to work on overtime and to keep him busy indefinitely, provided there were the requisite disposition to keep on spending and investing. There was no decline in the total volume of bank deposits in the United States until the third year of the depression. As for currency circulation, its total volume has varied little except during the run on the banks in the early part of 1933.

Second, money does not get spent or invested merely by reason of being deposited in banks, whether by the Government depositing newly created money or whether by private individuals depositing their genuine savings. If the banks do not find that the state of business justifies lending out the money deposited with them, or, rather, using such money as a reserve base for the creation of new loans and deposits, the banks can receive no end of new money from the Government, or savings from private individuals, without, in consequence, increasing total deposits or loans. This statement is now established as a fact by the holding of nearly three billion dollars of surplus reserves by the banks of the United States, or reserves enough to support thirty billion dollars of new loans and deposits, the investment of which in new capital goods would give us a boom for four or five years.

Believers in money and credit panaceas generally fail to perceive that the uses made by the banking system of genuine savings and the instrument of bank credit determine more than any other group of factors the beginning, duration and end of a depression. It is the use and not the quantity of money savings or money reserves that counts. And quantity of money does not determine its use. In the case of a vast majority of the people, sheer need determines the use made of 100 per cent of the money which passes through their hands—this money gets spent by them as fast as received. If the poorest half of the population received ten per cent increase in money income, they would, it is fair to assume, spend the entire ten per cent. But if the richest two per cent of the people received ten per cent increase in money income today, it is fair to assume that hoarding would be increased to this extent. In the case of the surplus money held by those who can save, or the surplus money held by banks, quantity has little to do with use. Only the general business situation, or the prospects of making a return with safety for the principal, determine the bulk of decisions made either by banks or individuals as to the use made of surplus money.

Only during the past year or two have professional economists come to recognize that a dollar saved and deposited in a bank is not, necessarily, a dollar invested in new capital goods. Up to five years ago, it was dogmatically asserted in every respectable economic text book that a dollar saved was, necessarily, a dollar invested. Making this assumption served a useful purpose as propaganda. For instance, extreme conservatives could reason from this premise or axiom that the greater the inequalities in income, the larger would be the savings and, hence, the greater the increase in productive capital for the general enrichment of mankind. With this fallacious axiom firmly planted at the outset of the discussion, any attempt to open up the question of the effects of unequal distribution of income could be completely crushed.

It is from this same fallacious premise that the money and credit believers, and the quantity-theory-of-money believers, have invariably reasoned to the conclusion that more money, rather than merely more money for people who have not enough for decent living, is the acute need. The crux of the problem, so far as getting money spent is concerned, is that two-thirds of our savings are made by 2.3 per cent of the families of the country, or those having incomes in excess of $10,000 a year, and that our total savings do not get invested in new capital goods as fast as accumulated.

It is not the fact that savings are made, but the fact that savings are not promptly converted into demand for new capital goods that is responsible for the initial decline in total production and consumption. The reason why savings are not continuously and fully invested, of course, is that consumption does not increase fast enough. And, one of the chief reasons why consumption does not increase fast enough is that so much of the national income is being withheld from consumption or saved. This dilemma is fully explained in the series of the Brookings Institution, on *America's Capacity to Produce, America's Capacity to Consume,* and *The Formation of Capital.* The dilemma is in no sense a monetary one.

The monetary and credit theorists never propose anything quite as simple as having the Government print and give away so much money to so many poor people just for the sake of getting the money spent. If they did, their case would be much stronger in logic though not in political discussion. And, of course, they never propose anything as obvious and sensible as having the Government take so much money from so many people who are not spending or investing it and give that much money to people who are so poor and needy that they would be sure to spend any money they received as soon as they got it. It takes a mind as intelligent as that possessed by the late Senator Long to think of anything as simple and sensible as that—simple and sensible if the real purpose is to get more money spent.

No, the monetary and credit crank schemes work on a theory which is much more complex and silly. The basic assumption is that the whole system works inevitably, and would work better if it got a little monetary or credit shot in the arm. The Government accordingly puts out more money, or causes the Federal Reserve Banks to put out more money—which is the same thing. This is done in such a way that the Government is said to be giving no one something for nothing. And no one is having anything taken from him for nothing. Everybody, including Uncle Sam, gets his money's worth. When it is all over, there is supposed to be more money and more goods to buy with that money.

Most of these money theories and policies for getting more money into use (or really into the banks) have been, and are actually being, tried out by the Roosevelt Administration. Chief among these policies is that of having the Government offer to buy in theoretically unlimited, though in practically quite limited, amounts 22 grains of fine gold for $1.67, whereas it used to pay $1 for that much gold. Thus, the Government puts out $.67 cents more for the same quantity of gold, which it does not have any earthly use for, as it already has more gold than it requires. But almost every monetary theorist felt that if the Government paid $.67 cents more for a given quantity of gold it did not need, prosperity would follow. This measure was also supposed to help the debtors, who, obviously, have no gold and who have had just as hard a time getting a paper dollar since 1933 as they had before. Of course, had the yearly gold output of the United States been increased several thousand per cent as a result of the higher buying rate for gold, the Government could have put out a great deal more money.

But doubling the American yearly output of gold for the

new price would not mean putting out much more than an extra hundred million new paper dollars, a mere trifle for a Government which is spending six times that much paying the C.C.C. boys to chase caterpillars and play around in the woods. If the inflationists had only authorized the Government to buy all the peanuts tendered at sixty-seven per cent above the market price of June, 1933, we might by now have half the United States in peanuts, with a resulting crop that would take several billions of paper dollars to pay for, thus giving the country a real dose of inflation. Moreover, the peanuts so produced in car loads might possibly find uses which the gold being acquired by the Government and buried again under the earth certainly does not find.

It is only fair to the monetary and credit believers to say that their theories, as well as the underlying assumptions as to a dollar saved being a dollar invested, and as to banks being forced by increasing reserves to increase loans and deposits—assumptions common to orthodox economics as well as heterodox monetary systems—did not appear as mad in the 19th century, or even up to 1929, as they now seem. During the 19th century there were usually more good borrowing risks at high interest rates than the banks had reserves to take. And so it happened, to cite but one conspicuous instance, that in 1879, following several years of depression, recovery was greatly assisted, if not actually started, by a few hundred millions of dollars being added to our cash and gold reserves by reason of the happy combination for the United States of a bumper wheat crop and a drought over the major wheat producing areas of Europe. Today, pumping two or three billion dollars of new money into the money stream or the reserves of the banks, may be compared to forcing heavy doses of food on a man whose chief complaint is an inability of the stomach to retain or digest food.

Banks do not lend money, or use their surplus cash reserves to increase loans and deposits, merely because they have such surplus cash. Banks lend money only if they see a good chance of getting it back with interest. Making money easy, cheap or abundant, as one may care to word it, does not, of itself, create the conditions which make a profit possible. The liberal economists have assumed, always without proof, that such conditions are inherent in the natural order of things. This assumption merely adds proof that liberal economics was essentially a system of propaganda, for, as far back as recorded history can enlighten us, it has been the custom of the rich to hoard their wealth in gold, precious stones, and treasure rather than to invest it in new capital goods.

It has only been a feature of a special world situation to have surplus income or wealth continuously reinvested in more productive capital. If there is a natural order in respect of saving, it would appear to call for hoarding what is saved, as is now being done and as was done for thousands of years. The return to hoarding is a return to what was traditional for thousands of years in all parts of the world. The return to hoarding is something to be explained not as unusual or extraordinary, but merely as a sign that the era of modern capitalism is approaching its end and that we are getting back to a normalcy with respect to the disposition made of surplus funds which prevailed for thousands of years all over the world.

Inflation, of course, if and when carried far enough to induce a state of panic about the future value of the currency (as happened in Germany in 1923 and 1924) certainly does stop money hoarding by producing a flight from money to goods. But, while acute inflation stops money hoarding, it intensifies credit hoarding. This is true because, while inflation makes the holders of surplus money want to exchange it for goods, inflation certainly does not make any one want to exchange money or create new bank credit money for promises to make future payments in money which will be worth less.

Now, if one stops to reflect that the supply of currency is around six billion, whereas the supply of bank deposit money has been reduced during the six years of the depression by over twenty billion through the curtailment of bank loans, one must see that an acceleration in the velocity of spending of the forty billion of bank deposit money still outstanding, plus the six billion of currency money in circulation, would have to make up for the loss of twenty billion of bank deposit money extinguished since 1929, plus the further loss of now outstanding bank money which would follow the outbreak of a real inflation panic. There is no doubt, however, that a real inflation panic could, for a brief moment, accelerate spending to such an extent that all our stores and warehouses might be emptied overnight of goods, so to speak. But it could not last.

The dilemma of inflation is that it must either stop, thereupon leaving the patient worse off than before, or else lead to disaster. The boom on rising prices can last only as long as the purchasing power of the currency can fall, and this can only fall to zero. Many reputable economists and statesmen have been preaching the fallacious doctrine that conditions can be improved and stabilized at a higher level of prosperity simply by having prices stepped up so much and then stabilized at a higher level. Prices can be put up but they cannot be stabilized.

Simple logic as well as the most exhaustive study of economic history indicate that if all prices are moved up so many points and kept there, no one is any better or worse off, and that, if certain prices are raised more than others, certain persons will profit on the losses of others. It is, however, always easy to whip up enthusiasm among farmers and business men for a price rise, because through it they can at once figure on a quick and sure money profit. They do not pause to reflect that the profits from such price rise must be lost when they turn around to restock or to consume their wealth. A study of price movements over a hundred-and-twenty-year period shows an almost even division of total number of years into years of rising prices and years of falling prices. Good times, of course, went with rising prices, and hard times with falling prices. These periods of rising and falling prices resulted from the play of relatively freely acting economic forces and not planned price manipulations.

Nothing in sound theory or actual experience warrants the hope, on which the early New Deal philosophy leaned heavily, of attaining anything like price stability under the present system. Nor is there any reason to imagine that price stability is ever desired by business men as a whole. The price raising advocates never say to the people "We offer you a limited period of rising prices and good times which must be followed by" either (1) "an approximately equal period of falling prices and hard times such as characterized our 19th century business cycles" or (2) "a disastrous currency and credit smash when our inflationary bubble bursts as occurred in Germany in 1924." On the contrary, they say, "We offer you immediate profits and increased business on the price rise and stabilized prosperity when we get prices where we want them."

The first four months of Mr. Roosevelt's administration were brightened economically by a mild flight from the dollar to merchandise and manufacturers' inventories of goods and speculative holdings of securities at higher prices. This flight from dollars to goods or securities was induced by the devaluation of the dollar—first by the *belief* or *rumor* that devaluation was intended, and then by the *White House announcement* that it was intended. Devaluation was stage managed with perfect technique to secure the desired effect. The same measure of devaluation could have been carried out in our situation without affecting prices if no prior announcement of it had been made and if it had been suddenly proclaimed to be an accomplished fact. Every one then would have had exactly as much money the day after as the day before, as of course actually happened in 1933, except the few people who had gold coins or bullion—not much over $500,000,000 at the time. And no one would have had any good reason to act differently as a result of the devaluation except owners of gold mines.

Of course, the Federal Reserve Banks, after the devaluation, could lend more paper dollars and so enable the member banks to lend a great deal more. But they have done the opposite. The gold reserves of the Federal Reserve Bank since the war have always been far in excess of requirements, and so also have been the cash reserves of the member banks. Foreigners can buy our goods cheaper than before because of the devaluation, but they don't buy more on account of the lower gold price because their tariffs and other economic policies prevent them from doing so. Consequently, the devaluation of the dollar has been a dud as an inflationary measure. We shall get inflation only by reason of direct government spending in excess of revenues. We shall get such inflation by government deficits inevitably but slowly—and with the usual debacle at the end.

No doubt, however, Mr. Roosevelt was relieved that the mild flight from the dollar to goods induced by his announcements of devaluation purposes did not go very far. For, as we have already pointed out, the proponents of deliberately planned policies of price raising always find themselves sooner or later on the sharp horns of this dilemma: Horn one, when prices stop rising the boom collapses; Horn two, if prices don't stop rising, everything collapses. This New Deal dilemma is not the way to avoid fascism, as the New Dealers have hoped, but rather to make it inevitable.

And, even while prices are rising, every one is not on the bandwagon. The high cost of living is not an empty phrase for the worker whose wages do not rise as fast as the food and clothes he has to buy. It is always easy to infer, when one sees newly-rich profiteers on price rises giving champagne parties during an inflationary boom, that all is well. But this inference is only possible if one fails to observe the misery caused by the wage lag behind prices.

The question whether the present system could resume use of the consumption-credit formula of 1915-1929 was posed for discussion in this chapter. The theoretical impossibility of operating on that formula for any length of time, due to the consequences of increasing debt charges, was pointed out, and brief allusion made to the practical demonstration of this impossibility furnished by the depression. Then we took occasion to pay our respects to the monetary cranks who would increase the supply of money in the hope that the newly created money would get spent and lent. We have seen that new money gets spent and lent when Government actually spends or lends it, but that it does not get lent or spent merely by reason of being put in the banks, whether by direct Government loan or gift to the banks, or by deposit by private individuals. The banks could today use their surplus reserves to make large loans to consumers for consumption. Such loans are rightly deemed unsound by the banks and are not being made. This banking judgment pretty well answers the question whether we can restore prosperity by financing additional consumption on credit—if it needed any other answering than that furnished by good theory and the post-war experience with spending beyond income.

This conclusion, however, must not be mistaken to involve in any way the notion that, during the credit boom, we were spending or consuming too much. On the contrary, we were not spending on consumption goods enough to provide a market for the capital plant we were then expanding, which, as we have already seen, was the reason why the further expansion of capital goods was checked, this checking of new investment constituting the depression. We were not consuming enough, but we were consuming too much on credit. To be self-sustaining, consumption must be on a pay-as-you-go basis. And, obviously, production can only be sustained in a volume equal to that of consumption. The best interests of ownership and management now require a new formula which is antithetical to that of modern capitalism. The new formula must recognize that ownership and management can take a cut of total production as a wage of management, or a reward for saving, if such a reward be found necessary, only for use and not for compounding the investment. The new formula will seek maximum total production and consumption with long-run stability. The new formula will, therefore, make no use of credit financing of consumption.

CHAPTER IV

CAN THE SYSTEM CARRY PERPETUAL DEPRESSION?

THE wording of this question may be considered invidious, since no defender of the present system admits that the present depression is anything more than a temporary or emergency phase. The assumption that the depression is an emergency, and that recovery must be around the corner or already in progress, is fast becoming untenable. Towards the middle of 1935 there had become quite pronounced in conservative and even radical circles an optimistic reporting of signs of world-wide business recovery. Maxwell S. Stewart, a representative liberal critic of economic conditions, gives expression to this idea in a contribution on "The Facts: Employment, Standards of Living and the National Income," to a symposium on *Economic Planning* edited by Mary L. Flederus and Mary Van Kleeck, when he says that for two and a half years business conditions throughout the world have been definitely on the upgrade. Similarly optimistic statements about the business trend can be found prominently emphasized in the public utterances of publicists like Walter Lippmann or representative spokesmen of business conservatism, all of whom cite this business recovery as the major reason for letting up on the reform features of the New Deal and allowing a larger measure of economic freedom both to private initiative and to the unemployed to find jobs or starve.

These optimistic findings of business recovery throughout the world are based largely on misleading citations of statistics which show greater economic activity or steadiness in 1934 and 1935 than could be seen in 1931 and 1932. They take little account of the New Deal in the United States, a major war of conquest being waged by Japan for the past two years,

40

a national government in Great Britain engaged in all sorts of enterprises of state intervention in the economic process, and with fascism or communism in full blast in the other larger nations except France, where admittedly there is an economic crisis unmodified by what even an optimist would call business recovery.

The indices of industrial production, for instance, taking those of the Federal Reserve Board economists for reference, show an improvement from a low of 64 (1923-1925—100) for the year 1932, to 76 for 1933, 79 for 1934, and 89 for April, 1935. It is not considered how much of this increase in industrial production is due to deficitary government spending, inaugurated as a continuing policy since 1932, or to the Japanese war, or to war preparations all over Europe, and in this country, which have expanded enormously since 1932.

The principal index or group of indications seized upon by the optimist of 1935, of course, may be said to lie in the field of psychology. There is more confidence in banks and a better feeling among the better-off about the general state of economic affairs—all reflected in higher security price levels. It is not considered how much this improved feeling is due to the fact that everyone now believes that Government will allow no further deflation or large scale liquidation, that the business enterpriser and the gambler on price changes have done extremely well, with some exceptions, on the government's price and currency manipulation policies, and that it is generally thought that the areas of social unrest are now being satisfactorily relieved by the dole. It is forgotten that increased production and better feeling have not reduced unemployment or increased new capital investment.

If the term business recovery has any useful meaning, the trend called recovery must be characterized by an increase in new investment and by a decrease in unemployment. As for unemployment, the figures of the International Labor Office of the League of Nations may be taken for the world at large, or the figures of the American Federation of Labor for the United States. Whatever the figures taken for the trend in employment during the two years preceding June 1, 1935, they will not show any marked change for the better in the number of the unemployed. Production has been increased since the bottoms of 1932 were touched, but employment has not been increased accordingly.

As for bank loans to private enterprise, they have declined in total volume by about fifty per cent, or over twenty billion dollars, during the six years of the depression, and they have declined slightly since 1933. Their shrinkage continues in 1935 in spite of a mild inflation of prices. From June, 1934 to June, 1935, bank loans declined by about a billion dollars. Perhaps the most conclusive index of business conditions is that furnished by the amount of money going into new capital issues of bonds and stocks to finance private enterprise. These figures are easily obtainable, and are compiled and published monthly by the *Commercial and Financial Chronicle*. If more money is being put by investors into industry and trade to create new productive plant or working capital, then there is recovery. If not, it cannot be said that there is any recovery in progress. Let the following table tell the story of new investment before and during the depression up to the middle of 1935:

NEW CAPITAL GOING INTO CORPORATE ISSUES OF STOCKS AND BONDS

(The remainder of the new capital issues total is taken up by governmental and foreign issues.)

The figures indicate units of one million dollars.

	1935	1934	1933	1932	1931	1930	1929	1928
For the entire year.....		178	160	325	1,763	4,944	8,639	6,079
For the first 6 months of each year...........	100	99	59	160	1,311	3,666	4,698	3,967

	1927	1926	1925	1924	1923	1922	1921
For the entire year.....	5,391	4,357	4,100	3,322	2,702	2,335	1,823
For the first 6 months of each year...........	2,825	2,522	2,129	1,709	1,539	1,388	921

New capital going into private investment is the surest index of business health. Such investment, as is seen from the preceding table, averaged over three billion two hundred million during the first six months of each year during the five-year period 1925-1929. For the same six months period during each of the years 1933-1935, the corresponding figure has averaged eighty-six million, or one hundred million for the first six months of 1935. The difference between three billion two hundred million and eighty-six million is some measure of the distance recovery has to travel from the middle of 1935. The difference between fifty-nine million for 1933 and one hundred million for 1935 gives some idea of the progress recovery has made. It seems a safe generalization to say that there can be no recovery until new capital going into corporate investments exceeds six billion a year, as occurred in 1927, 1928 and 1929. For the year 1935 new capital for private enterprise through the issue of securities bids fair to remain below two hundred million dollars.

The question posed for discussion in this chapter is not whether the well-to-do still have the means to maintain their living standards or to make new investments. In France, during the French Revolution, the privileged classes maintained their standards up to a few days before they went to the guillotine. The question is whether the system can carry the present and slowly increasing overhead costs of the depression with the present level of produced income and new investment. The question, Can the system carry the depression? may be divided into the questions, Can the system carry the depression until we enter the next big war? Can the system carry the depression and keep us out of the next war? and Can the system survive our participation in another war?

Back in the halcyon years between 1923 and 1929 it was the custom to boast that American workmen had too much self-respect to accept the dole and that American capitalists had too much spunk to stand for British taxation. After England went off the gold standard in September, 1931, American conservatism still found occasion to give thanks that we were not as other men were: our Constitution would not allow us to go off the gold standard. In 1935 the American Tories are pointing to the British situation with its unstable currency, huge dole, high taxes and crisis-coalition government as a model of recovery.

The fact, of course, is that the British have stabilized hard times better than any other large industrial nation. This they have succeeded in doing because, first, after the United States, they are the richest nation in the world and hence, after us, the best prepared to carry the overhead costs of a long depression; and, second, because the depression settled on England before it gripped any of the other industrial nations. England had no post-war reconstruction or inflationary boom on borrowed American money. She settled down right after the war to the depression and to carrying its liabilities—such as the unemployed. By 1935 she has grown so used to economic hard knocks that whenever there is a slight ease-up, it seems almost like recovery.

From the end of the War to September, 1931, when England went off gold, deflation was in course, but the slight fall in British gold prices had failed to expand British exports to their pre-war volume. Doubtless British export prices, whether on a pre-war sterling (gold) basis or on any devalued basis, could not have been lowered enough to expand British exports to the pre-war volume. Nations all over the world have been bent on increasing their economic independence of British manufacturing monopolies and, accordingly, maintaining nearly prohibitive tariffs against England's basic exports at any possible price, thus dooming British textiles and heavy steel industries to perpetual depression. The British standard of living for the employed on wages and the unemployed on the dole, all necessarily constituting costs of British industrial production, has kept British real costs well above those of foreign competitors like the Japanese and central Europeans maintaining much lower living standards. Since September, 1931, when England went off gold and on the protectionist path, the British have been taking mild doses of trade tonics which cannot prove indefinitely stimulating and which will not square with the imperatives of the British situation. This dubious, though much touted, improvement in British domestic trade, often miscalled recovery, has been engineered in lieu of an unattainable recovery of the British export trade. It has been engineered mainly by fostering wholly new industries through the adoption of protective duties and by financing a construction boom in housing for the middle classes and equipping the new British industries made possible by protection. Britain cannot indefinitely maintain, out of her accumulated but now fast diminishing foreign surplus, the present British standard of living and the costs of imperial defense without the large profits that went with her pre-war foreign trade in which she enjoyed great bargaining advantage over the foreign customer. Once England went protectionist, she thereby admitted final defeat in foreign trade. She also thereby doomed herself to having the world arrayed against her for having closed her markets, just as the Spanish by a similar policy of closed economy for the Spanish colonies arrayed the rest of the world against Spain down to the opening of the 19th century when Spain finally lost most of her colonial empire. Yet the end of free trade and the adoption of protection have been depression necessities for Britain, but they are necessities which spell the doom of a liberal British imperialism. It remains to be seen whether a fascist British imperialism will survive or whether the British liberals will carry the empire down in their inevitable defeat.

Certain it now seems that, with the first war move, England's liberal capitalistic and parliamentary system—the parent model of the system—such as the war has left it, will metamorphose overnight into a new authoritarian system. In this connection the much ignored fact is to be emphasized that the World War brought English institutions de facto far closer to fascism than they were before the war, or than our institutions are today. The post-War trend in England towards the enlargement of the sphere and powers of the executive branch of the government has been the subject of a critical book by the Lord Chief Justice.

If there were not a chance that the United States can stay out of the next world war, as there surely is not for Great Britain, there would be little point to discussing the question whether American capitalism can carry the depression until the outbreak of that coming event. The chances are the next big war will break within five years and the chances are about fifty-fifty that public credit and ballyhoo under President Roosevelt can hold out until then.

What gives most point to this discussion is the consideration that there is a chance—not a good one, admittedly, but still a chance—for us to stay out of the next war. But can we do so and go on carrying the depression as we are now doing? The question really boils down to one of whether we shall get fascism through the war, or fascism before the war and without getting into the war. A fascism we developed before the war would in all probability be vastly better than a fascism we got in and out of a war. As for the question whether an American fascism would help or hinder our entry into war, a question discussed in a later chapter, it need only be said here that the liberal democracies have as bad a war record as, and larger military budgets today than, the fascist countries. There is, therefore, no reason to suppose that the war danger is any greater under fascism than under liberalism or communism.

Assuming that the next war comes within five years, let it be granted, for sake of argument, that the liberal capitalist system in the United States can carry the unemployed and the rotten financial situation until then. Then let us face the questions, first, whether liberal capitalism in the United States can go on carrying the depression and also keep us out of the war, and second, whether it can carry on through and survive our participation in a war, and third, whether it can carry the depression indefinitely if we succeed in staying out of the next war. The question whether liberal capitalism can go on carrying the depression and keep us out of war is the one which merits most careful study. Under any circumstances, the ability of the present system to go on carrying the depression is largely a question of how the institutional or mechanical factors, and how the peculiarly psychological or human-behavior factors, behave under the strain.

In these fields, especially the last named, accurate scientific measurement and prediction of the future are out of the question, but certain probabilities may be deduced from known present conditions and past experiences with similar difficulties.

Now as to the more or less impersonal, mechanical and institutional phases of the credit and business behavior factors, we have the following data to reason from: First, carrying the depression means spending five billion a year on relief in 1935; second, playing good politics for the 1936 elections will mean spending this money without a corresponding rise in taxes; third, playing good politics for the farm vote and support of the business and speculative interests will mean continuing positive policies aimed at price-raising and price-maintaining, such as the subsidizing of agricultural scarcity; fourth, good politics will also dictate all sorts of policies to check a fall in prices or to prevent heavy deflation; fifth, the considerations just mentioned, and others too numerous to mention, indicate a price rise before the end of the next fiscal year, July 1st, 1936, to June 30th, 1937, which will make this fiscal year's volume of relief cost a great deal more next year; sixth, the logic of these considerations is a bigger and bigger public deficit each year as long as the depression has to be financed by a government forced to play politics for reëlection; seventh, the results of this sort of deficiteering must be a currency and credit debacle, the nature of which is too well known from post-War European experiences to need any detailed explanation.

So much for some of the more significant institutional or mechanical factors. The preceding chain of logic and logical sequences grips Mr. Roosevelt like the swift flowing current of a rapids. Only a superhuman effort on his part, or an unlikely series of lucky changes, can rescue him from the course outlined. If Mr. Roosevelt made such an effort, it would be along fascist lines or in the direction of fascism. I call these factors impersonal, mechanical and institutional because they leave Mr. Roosevelt no real choice. Having said A, he must say B, and so on until he has run clear through the alphabet.

As for the more typically psychological or human-behavior factors, we can surely reason from the following premises: First, pressure groups already in existence and yet to form will make bigger and more determined raids on the public treasury. If the government is to remain indefinitely committed to spending money according to the views of a favored few of the President's inner circle, to check deflation, to raise prices, to induce recovery, to relieve suffering groups and interests, and to get votes for elections, why shouldn't any group use whatever means it can command to get some of the easy money, and why shouldn't any individual join as many money seeking pressure groups as he can and support their drives on the public treasury for what he can get out of them?

The question can be worded somewhat differently: If Senator Harrison and Mr. Hopkins (merely to cite at random two names of reputable public men whose counsels the President is understood to seek in money spending matters) have so much to say about spending so much money, why isn't it good democracy to enlarge the list of such counselors and make it include representatives of other groups and interests? Why shouldn't my friends and your friends get jobs as well as Mr. Harrison's, Mr. Hopkins', Mr. Farley's and Mr. Tugwell's friends? Why not, indeed? There is no law against it. And there can be no liberal law against it. Whatever is legal in the pursuit of self-interest or in the exercise of, or threat to exercise, the ballot has to be protected by the system. It is hardly less than funny to hear business men who have lobbied or supported lobbies all their lives for special privilege legislation, such as tariff-raising raids on the consumers, denounce the war veterans or some other group for playing the same legal, democratic game.

Why is it more unpatriotic or less public spirited for war veterans to try to get theirs by hook or crook than it was for the war profiteers during the war? It may be said that two wrongs do not make a right. But here there can be no question of right or wrong outside their definitions in terms of effective law. It is a matter of getting as much as you can within the law. That has always been good capitalism and good liberalism. If that is not considered right, there is no use talking about it, for nothing can be done about it as long as human nature and the law remain unchanged. And one of the values of the liberal-Constitution upholders must be the Constitutional right of minority group pressures to petition Congress and use the ballot as an instrument of coercion over Congressmen.

The disorders which are going first to strain the system to the breaking point in the near future under the present financing of relief will not be functional disturbances or mechanical breakdowns—of which there will be plenty in the institutional or impersonal machinery. They will rather be dynamic contradictions of national or collective interest, such all-too-human contradictions being legally and democratically asserted by minority pressure groups.

The good American individualism which is the boast of the Tories is exactly what is going to plague them most. For the leaders of the frustrated élite, the sinking members of the middle class who are by way of being declassed, are going to show the Tories still at the top that the ruthless, predatory tactics which the founders of most of our great fortunes, colleges and charities used in getting theirs can be used by the leaders of democracy, or of the now fast sinking middle classes, to raid the public treasury, and through it the remainders of the great fortunes. We shall have occasion to revert to this theme, so we need not pursue it at this point through many of its logical interrelations with other social problems under consideration.

The point here is that, while it might be possible within technical safety margins for our currency and bank credit to have the Federal Government run the national debt from its present figure around thirty billion dollars up to a hundred billion before the final currency and credit crash (thus allowing fourteen yearly deficits of the 1935 total to pay for relief

or carry the depression—assuming rising prices did not raise
the ante) the human element is not going to allow money
to be dished out over such a long period in such amounts in
that measured rhythm. The new gold rush to Washington is
just beginning.

It seems a reasonable inference, from all visible indications,
that the chances are about even that liberal capitalism in the
United States may, under the drives of pressure groups, fail to
maintain order and carry the overhead costs of the depression
until our entry into the next war, assuming that event does
not occur for four or five years. It is also a warranted inference
that, in measure as the internal economic strains become
aggravated, an increasing pressure will be put on the President
and his associates, more in the area of the subconscious than
the conscious, to force them to take the country into war as a
face-saving exit from a domestic impasse under the system
they are pledged to support. (They are sworn to uphold and
defend the social theories of a majority of the judges on the
Supreme Court, i.e., the Constitution.) Certainly, the more
unemployed men and slack industries there are, the more
people there will be to hail with genuine relief our entry into
war. For, whatever war might ultimately mean to the individual or group, its outbreak means at once jobs for all the
unemployed.

As for the other question, whether we could fight another
war under liberal capitalism, the answer must be negative, and
its best demonstration found in the present plans of the War
Department for mobilizing industry on the outbreak of the
next war. Of course, the Army is not interested in profits but
in war materials and services for the objective of destroying
the enemy. The Army would therefore approve of, or even
insist on, a wide margin of profit at the outset in order to
insure the best initial effort of management, while the general staff was perfecting its technical control of industry
through the installation of army officers in strategic posts in
industrial and financial management. But the Army would
stand for no nonsense about economic or constitutional free-

dom for individuals to thwart military plans. And as soon as the mechanics of paying the large paper profits allowed at the start proved a difficulty, the Army would end or modify the profit system as the demands of military success might indicate.

Liberal capitalism survived the last War in Britain and France only because the richest country in the world was a late comer into the conflict and threw all its fresh resources into the effort during and after the War to save Europe from chaos and communism and to preserve the integrity of international and domestic credits. It is commonly overlooked nowadays that there is a vast difference between the situation of the international financial system of August, 1914, and August, 1935. No longer can any power in another world war mobilize foreign credits as did the leading belligerents, particularly on the Allied side, at the outbreak of the last War. Mobilizing economic resources today, or rather in tomorrow's war, will not be a matter of quickly liquidating securities and claims for cash or of signing I.O.U.'s to be deposited in some foreign government's treasury (for subsequent repudiation) and drawing against the cash or I.O.U.'s unlimited supplies. No; it will mean establishing a military dictatorship over the factors of production no less complete or absolute than that of communist Russia. The last War found the international bankers ready to make money and lend money. The next war will find the fascist ready to seize power and govern, where they are not already in power. And the fascists of a war-begotten fascism will be men in uniform on whose social attitudes the liberals will be less influential than they might be on the minds of the leaders of a fascism born in peace time.

The question, Could the system carry the depression indefinitely if we stay out of the next war? is fairly well answered by the logic of the answer made to the question, Can the system carry the depression up to the next war and keep us out of it? The only reason for specifically formulating what is almost a foolish question, as to the chances for the permanent stabilization of the depression by liberal capitalism under peace, is that such an achievement is the seriously entertained expectation of innumerable conservatives and liberals.

I cannot share that belief, not so much because of the mechanical or institutional difficulties I see in the way, as because of the faith I share with Mr. Hoover and other individualists in the good American predatory and combative instincts. These instincts, with which the Tories, now trying to conserve liberalism, have always been over-endowed, they are wont to call by such euphemisms as "rugged individualism." My faith in the vitality of American democracy and individualism assures me that we are not going to have any prolonged period of peace with stabilized depression. The democratic movements and pressure groups marching on the public treasury are not, at first, going to fly the banners of fascism or be interested in its values or ideas. So much the worse for the nation at first, and especially for the Tory Constitutionalists and libertarians who will be the favorite targets of these armies of liberty lovers and liberty takers. These movements and pressure groups are going to fly the banners of liberal capitalism, and democracy, Jeffersonian and Jacksonian. And their acts will be in the best tradition of the great empire builders.

In other words, they will be out to crush their opponents and to grab all they can. And how they will uphold their constitutional right to coerce Congress and the constitutional right of Congress to dish out the money of the eastern bondholders who are now so anxious to save the Constitution. States' rights will be very dear to them, especially the rights of the debtor states to tax the property of absentee owners living in the creditor states of the east.

I hail these movements and pressure groups, not because their members are as yet fascist or friends of fascism, but because they are making fascism the alternative to chaos and national disintegration. I also hail these fellow countrymen with pride that there is too much red blood in American veins to allow of peace with stabilized scarcity, misery and frustration. You cannot stabilize a situation in which the middle classes are being declassed and twenty millions are being carried on relief. There is no finer trait in man than that which makes peace with frustration and defeat impossible. If the élite must suffer misery and frustration, they won't have it in peace. In conflict they can at least lift themselves out of humiliation, even if not out of misery. And it is the people to whom self-respect is important who make history. The best hope of the American masses is that the élite don't take it lying down and that the élite are a larger percentage of the population in this country and day than in most others.

CHAPTER V

CAN WE REORGANIZE UNDER THE PRESENT SYSTEM?

WE NOW take up the fourth and last of the main questions set for discussion as a part of our attack on the larger question whether the present system is workable. In one chapter we reached the conclusion that a return to the 19th century, pioneer, frontier, expansion pattern is out of the question, mainly because we have not the requisite starting point. In the next chapter we were forced to dismiss, as highly improbable of realization and wholly undesirable to undertake, any large scale resumption of consumption financing on credit along the lines followed between 1915-1929. And in the last chapter we estimated the chances to be about fifty-fifty that this system can go on financing the costs of the depression until the outbreak of the next war, which seems likely to start within the next five years.

In this and the next chapter we are closing out the attack on the workability problem with a discussion of the chances or possibilities of reorganization within the framework of the fundamental principles and institutions of the present system. It is, of course, one of the premises of fascism that reorganization under the present system is impossible. And it is a proposition about which all sound exponents of capitalism must find themselves in agreement with the fascists—that the present system can only operate successfully (assuming, as the defenders of the system assume and as the fascists deny, that the requisite conditions for operation still exist) if reorganization and readjustment can be effected. The issue is not whether reorganization is necessary, for that is universally conceded, but whether reorganization is possible. So far, the affirmative

54

rests more on hope and prediction than on achievement since the War.

The weakness of capitalism is not the occurrence of mistakes and maladjustments. Nor is freedom from such misfortunes to be claimed as a merit of any social planning so far achieved. The weakness of liberal capitalism in the period since 1914, or really the period which includes not only the War and its sequels but also the irreconcilable conflicts of interest which had to culminate in the outbreak of the War, is that, in this final phase of capitalist decline, capitalism cannot reorganize and readjust in ways essential for its continued operation as a social system. The system has developed organic inflexibilities in the debt structure, the price structure and the volumes of supply and demand. A planned economy can readjust its maladjustments almost as easily as it can make them. It is ever making adjustments and maladjustments at the same time.

A planned economy can be, and probably will be, responsible for expenditures of human effort quite as foolish, harmful and objectionable from almost any rational viewpoint as the construction under free capitalism of several billion dollars worth of office buildings and apartment hotels for which there is no adequate market. But a planned economy does not have to put up with large-scale unemployment as a result of having been responsible for bad investments. War, for instance, can be considered a bad expenditure of effort and resources for one or both belligerents. But France with its devastated regions, the victor, and Germany, with a war tribute to pay, the loser, did not have to suffer depression or unemployment for many years after the War. Why? Because, in both countries, the state intervened to insure after the disaster or blunder of war the benefits of maximum activity. The state can reorganize and readjust after the greatest of social calamities, war, with attending benefits and prosperity for all. As soon, however, as the régime of sound liberalism or capitalism once more becomes fully and normally effective, that is, as soon as the State retires from the enterprises of war and reconstruction, the maladjustments produced by a business boom must persist unless the corrective forces of a frontier expansion can operate to dissipate them in another boom.

At the outset of any discussion about economic reorganization let it be clearly stated that the system is supposed to effect its own reorganizations or readjustments automatically through the orderly legal and economic initiatives of private individuals, each acting in his own supposed self-interest. If it does not so happen, that fact, and that fact alone, suffices to prove the unworkability of liberal capitalism, exactly as the failure of a physical organism to eliminate its own poisons is proof that it is not working and that a condition exists which, if not promptly corrected, results in the death of the organism.

This obvious consideration is persistently disregarded by a numerous school of facile liberal writers, of whom men like Sir Arthur Salter are typical examples. Probably, their best defense is to say that they hope to do for the liberal economic system what the doctors do with insulin for a diabetic system, namely, keep it alive by helping artificially to eliminate its poisons which it would otherwise be powerless to prevent from proving fatal.

The problem of reorganization and readjustment can really be thought of as one of getting rid promptly of poisons in the economic system which the system is supposed automatically to eliminate and which it is not eliminating. After unemployment, the chiefest of these poisons, it will generally be admitted, is debt, of which there is incontrovertibly in this country several score billion unpaid, uncancelled and unrepudiated, but clearly unpayable. Within the scope of this generalization is to be included our two score billions of public debt. The capitalist system everywhere got terribly into debt through the War and its sequels, and, as I pointed out in my *Is Capitalism Doomed?* written in 1931, capitalism during the depression is suffering, not from War losses which have been more than replaced, but from the paralyzing effects on world trade caused by lingering War debts, both national and international. Now that the leading nations of the world are cynically refusing to honor their obligations to our government, now that our government with equal cynicism has repudiated its obligation on its gold bonds, and now that so many slightly less important debtors are in difficulties with their debts, it hardly needs to be argued that debt is one of the major maladjustments of the moment.

The following facts make this clear. The study entitled *The Internal Debts of the United States*, page 10, published in 1933 by the Twentieth Century Fund, gives a fairly good picture of the debt situation:

Class	Amounts in Millions of Dollars. Latest Available Year	Pre-war Year
Farm mortgage debts.........	$ 8,500	$ 3,320
Urban mortgage debts........	27,554	5,151
Railroad debts..............	14,264	11,186
Public utility debts...........	11,225	3,294
Industrial debts..............	10,450	3,738
Financial debts..............	21,919	4,040
State and local debts........	18,685	4,751
Federal debt.................	14,237 (30,000 in 1935)	968
Total reported debt........	126,834	36,448
Total estimated debt.......	134,280	37,989

In addition to this total for so-called long term, or funded debt, there is short term debt to be considered. The difference between what is commonly called long and short term debt is purely nominal, for most of the short term debts are really long term debts. Most short term debt is not paid off at maturity but renewed, if not with the same bank, lender or credit grantor, then through borrowing or obtaining credit from another. A short term loan from a bank is paid off with the proceeds of a new loan from another bank. For the purpose of drawing conclusions about the effects of interest and inflexible money obligations, long and short term debt are practically the same. The Twentieth Century Fund investigators computed our total short term debts as follows: (*The Internal Debts of the United States*, page 301):

SHORT TERM DEBTS IN THE UNITED STATES IN BILLIONS OF DOLLARS

Kind of Debt	End of 1913	End of 1932
Short term business debt..............	$47	$89
Short term personal and household debt	4	14.4
Total short term debt................	51	103.6
Total long term debt.................	37.9	134.2
Total debt...........................	88.9	237.8

Unfortunately, there are no reliable figures showing by how much the total debt structure of the country has changed during the depression, or between 1929 and 1935. Bank loans have decreased during this period by about twenty billions, and it is a reasonable guess that long term debts have been reduced by about ten billions through the processes of bankruptcies, mortgage foreclosures and corporate reorganizations. The amount of net total reduction of debts is smaller than may be imagined, for the deflationary processes have been considerably modified by government action and voluntary agreement between creditors and debtors. And the net reduction of private debts has been offset by the net increase in public debt, aggregating for the first six depression years about fifteen billion for federal debts, and at least two or three billions for state and city debts. So it seems a fair guess that the net total of fixed obligations, bearing interest, has not been reduced by more than ten billions, or five per cent, for both long and short term, during the first six years of the depression. The most significant statistical, or numerical, fact about the debt burden, perhaps, is that while the total national income in 1933 was only fifty-seven per cent of what it was in 1929, dividends thirty-six per cent, rents and royalties fifty-two per cent, wages and salaries, fifty-six per cent, the money lender's portion, or interest, was ninety-five per cent in 1933 of what it was in 1929. This is the feature of loans or interest, inflexibility, which contributes most to producing general maladjustment. Obviously, a five per cent reduction in debts or a five per cent reduction in interest charges, does not correspond to a fifty per cent reduction in production or paid income of the nation.

It is, however, appropriate to mention a certain line of apology for the debt structure, the best statement of which, perhaps, has been formulated by Carl Snyder, an economist of the New York Federal Reserve Bank. This apology is based largely on an analysis of figures showing the rates of growth of debts, total productive wealth and total production for fifty or more years prior to the World War. This analysis will disclose that, leaving out war debts, other forms of debt, including that to banks, did not rise relatively to total wealth or current production any faster during or since the World War than during any other correspondingly long period in the past. That is to say, our productive capital increased as rapidly as our total debts, if war debts be eliminated.

This defense seems impressive if one considers only the statistics given, and if one disregards certain other relevant statistics and considerations. It has two fatal weaknesses: In the first place, any attempt to exclude war debts from the debt picture for a comparison, the avowed purpose of which is to show that the debt increase since 1914 has not been dangerous, is unworthy of serious consideration. United States Government debt contracted during the War lays an interest charge on the people like any other class of debt, and as a credit item it plays a more important rôle in the holdings of banks and institutions than any other class of debt or credit.

In the second place, the main weakness of the apology is the failure to recognize that if it be true that most of the post-War creation of debt has been as well matched by the creation of a countervalue in productive capital as were the debts created in any previous period, there is this vital difference to be noted, which Mr. Snyder does not note: New productive capital created in the 19th century, while smaller in quantity and less efficient in operation, found a larger and surer market for its output than new productive capital created since the War. To be more concrete, it may be true that a twenty-five million dollar block of new mortgage bonds in 1929 was matched by twenty-five or even thirty-five million dollars worth of Fifth Avenue office building, or luxury hotel—at the then cost of construction, which was fifty per cent higher than it would be at present. And, consequently, it may be true that this new debt was as fully covered or secured by a physical asset as was a million dollar block of mortgages used to finance the building of New York City tenements in the eighties or nineties.

But there is this difference to note: Due to heavy immigration, the tenements found a market or tenants at rentals which quickly amortized the construction costs, while many a Fifth Avenue office building or hotel constructed during the boom never had a chance of finding tenants at rentals to carry overhead and amortize construction costs. The same difference holds good in reference to debt incurred to develop the productive plants of basic industries like mining, textiles, farming, and the many steel companies launched in the 19th century, and the debt incurred to finance during the 1920's expansion of production in steel, copper, petroleum or raw and fabricated foodstuffs. In a word, the market for the product is the thing that secures any business debt and not the physical or productive asset created with the proceeds of the borrowing.

To point out the inconsistencies between the usual statement of the productivity theory of debt and a large part of current business practice (leaving out of account entirely consumption loans or war debts) would involve a voluminous analysis of modern business. We may look briefly at some of the facts which are inconsistent with the theory as propounded by the apologists of money-lending. Thus we shall see what fascism has to do to make a system of private ownership and management workable, so far as arrangements involving capital income or reward are concerned. The ruling principle must be that capital and management reward must be kept in continuous and flexible adjustment with economic possibilities, and that legal and institutional arrangements—like loan contracts, bonds, legal concepts of just compensation, due process of law, and confiscation—must not obstruct executive action of government to maintain this adjustment otherwise than by the present devices of bankruptcy, foreclosures, reorganization, and cycles of booms and depressions.

In other words, we know the supposedly automatic correctives or self-adjustments of capitalism for bad debts, and we don't like them. Of this medicine, we may say, "We can't take it." Mr. Hoover, in effect, said this when he launched the National Credit Corporation and the Reconstruction Finance Corporation.

A simple, typical and important example of the inconsistency of debt practice with the productivity theory for justifying debt is furnished by the railroads. According to the best debt theory, the productivity theory, a railroad should incur debt only for the original investment which creates or expands earnings. Replacements and betterments which do not increase traffic or which do not increase earnings by lowering operating costs while traffic remains constant, ought not to be financed by new borrowing but out of income, whether such income be made available by reducing interest, dividends or costs, or whether it be made available by increasing charges. New and more comfortable cars do not necessarily or even ordinarily increase railroad travel. New and more comfortable or speedier transportation may be necessary to meet bus competition. But it is obvious that outlay to enable the railroad to hold its own is not an investment which increases traffic or earnings. Money so spent on new equipment is like money lost by reason of a reduction in rates to meet competition or to increase traffic.

A twenty or thirty million dollar passenger terminal for a large city may add to the beauty of the city and the comfort of passengers, as well as to the facilities of operation, but contributes little or nothing to gross traffic or net earnings. The same number of people will travel, whether the station be a dingy affair or an architectural monument, for the decision to take a train is not influenced by the artistic qualities of the terminal. If a million or two dollars a year of interest charges on the new terminal be added to railroad operating costs, it goes without saying that net earnings will be diminished rather than increased by the terminal. The terminal doubtless should be built, but it is in no sense a capitalistic investment on the productivity theory of loans. The new terminal is as much a socialist investment as a new public library or city hall. It should not be financed by bond issues but out of income or surplus. It is an operation cost and not a capital investment. It is a civic adornment.

Now it is largely as a result of financing replacements and betterments, whether grander stations or more commodious and serviceable equipment, with an increase in railroad debt, that we today have a railroad debt of some fifteen billion dollars and an available net income to serve these capital charges, even if all common and preferred stock were extinguished, which does not allow two per cent on the total railroad debt.

Why were these replacements and betterments so generously made? Answer: Because the managing or controlling bankers were in a postion to profit personally on the building and purchasing contracts. Why were these replacements and betterments financed by such large issues of new bonds and equipment trust certificates? Answer: Because the bankers controlling the railroads are merchants of securities. They are, therefore, interested in having the railroads sell as many bonds and the investors buy as many bonds as possible, regardless of how unsound the bond issues may be.

The average college professor teaching economics will tell his students, out of the depth of his ignorance of business as it is, that the bankers have an interest in selling good bonds, for, if they sell bad bonds, it will react against them, all of which is largely nonsense, for the following two reasons: When bankers sell bad bonds, they make money on the sale of the bonds, and then collect inordinate fees and commissions on the receivership, reorganization and refinancing of the railroad which they have wrecked. Almost every important investment banking house has wrecked and reorganized railroads with more profit on the wrecking and reorganizing than on the original financing. Moreover, no matter how many bad bonds the bankers sell their clients, the latter must go to the same bankers again for further investments when they have funds to invest. To whom else can they go for investment securities but the bankers?

Why were necessary replacements and betterments not paid for out of earnings since the War, especially during the boom years, instead of by new financing? Answer: Because the controlling bankers were not only interested as merchants in the security traffic, but they were also making large speculative profits through the ownership and manipulation of railroad stocks, wherefore they had the roads borrow as much as possible so as to provide a favorable dividend and propaganda picture for the common stocks.

Why did government regulation through the Interstate Commerce Commission, and the state commissions, not prevent the bankers from getting railroad finances into their present mess? Answer: Because of the doctrines, self-contradictory, metaphysical and wholly irrelevant to modern economic problems, which the Supreme Court is allowed to apply to government regulation of railroads and utilities.

There is not space in this book to analyze cases and point out in detail the incompatibility of Supreme Court decisions with the development of any government regulation adequate to insure sound railroad or utility financing and management. Briefly, it can be stated that, in respect of the creation of debt and accompanying capital charges, some totalitarian economic theory has to be followed. And it is of the essence of our judicial and political system that no such theory can be made explicit or effective. The chief purpose of our institutions, so far as law and government administration are concerned, would seem to be that of making explicit and effective a political theory developed in the 17th and 18th centuries and appropriate only to the conditions of those days. About the only economic theory which our courts can be said to follow is that they have the right to pass on each and every specific act of government affecting a property right for the purpose of deciding whether that act involves confiscation without just compensation or is an arbitrary, unreasonable or unconstitutional exercise of governmental power.

This amounts to saying that the only governing economic theory, if economic and theory it can be called, revolves not around present day social means and ends but around the court's definition of the terms "confiscation", "just compensation", "arbitrary", "unreasonable", and "unconstitutional", as well as around the court's interpretation of a voluminous set of facts in each case, the complexities of which the judges usually have neither the time nor the technical competence to master. The average American judge, including the average of those on the Supreme Court, having no adequate training in advanced accounting, is no more able to find his way through the books of account of a modern railroad or utility linked up with an involved system of holding companies and banker relationships, assuming he ever tried to do so, than he would be to find his way through the African jungle. To suppose that a judge who could not possibly give a clear statement of the complicated financial arrangements, practices, and interlocking relationships of one of these modern corporate set-ups can determine equity in a given case involving these arrangements, practices, and relationships, is one of the fictions of liberal jurisprudence.

It would be a comparatively easy matter for a corps of business executives, accountants and economists, assuming they were subjected to adequate superior political dictation, to draft a body of theory, and administer a set of rules of practice, to realize any set of feasible social results. One of these results might be keeping capital charges or debt in a constantly workable relation to earnings or to the part of income safely available for meeting capital charges. Such administration could not guarantee any rate of earnings or return to capital, but neither can the present system of the bankers and lawyers. Such an administration, however, if freed from the 17th century inhibitions and imperatives of the present American legal system, could insure continuous adjustment without the processes of bankruptcy, foreclosure, boom and depression, inflation and deflation, on which the bankers and the lawyers now fatten at the expense of social order and welfare. To maintain such constant adjustment is one of the major tasks of fascism. The services of the financial expert and the legal expert can be used as instruments of a national plan, but not as instruments of individual greed playing an essentially anti-social and economically wasteful game.

But no such financial and economic control or regulation could possibly be devised to square with the doctrines laid down by our Courts, or with the principle of judicial review of final decisions and policies of government. The Supreme Court has even gone so far as to hold a regulatory measure confiscatory because it did not allow seven per cent on an investment. This does not mean that seven per cent is the Supreme Court's official rate for a fair return on utility investments. It merely means that no regulatory agency of government can possibly tell what rate of return the Supreme Court will hold just or what rate it will hold confiscatory, in a given case, until that case has been tried by the Court. Nor is it to be understood that the courts prevent all government regulation. On the contrary, the courts leave a comparatively large area of regulation free from judicial interference or review. No; the courts only intervene, as a rule, where regulation is fraught with important social consequences.

To take, at random, one more important field in which debt abuses have been rampant and on a large scale—guaranteed mortgages—it may be said that the most obvious considerations of public interest would have caused government to prevent these abuses had we a government empowered to deal with such practices. I select this example mainly because it is easy to state briefly and simply the ruling considerations. A company with a capital of twenty million odd dollars would assume obligations to guarantee over a billion dollars of mortgages. Now, to forbid a racket of that sort, it should be enough to show that if the guarantee has any value, the defaults in any given year must be so few, and the amounts so small, as to constitute a risk not worth the premium paid by the assured. And if the defaults in a year ever exceed two per cent, the guarantee will prove worthless for defaults in excess of two per cent. To charge one-half to one per cent a year for years and years for insurance which can only be good for two per cent of the risk assumed is obviously the next thing to robbery. Human mortality risks are calculable on the basis of past experience, and we are authorized to expect that never more than a certain percentage of the insured will die in any one year. Mortality risks on loans cannot be so calculated, because no one can fairly assume that any given percentage of defaults, certainly not the maximum of two per cent, will never be exceeded in any given year. The phenomenon of a business depression may inflict twenty-five or even a hundred per cent loss on loans. No one can set aside a reserve for depressions which will constitute any real insurance, since no one can tell, as this depression demonstrates, what the percentage of economic losses of a depression will be until the depression occurs.

A simple way to illustrate the fraud inherent in the insurance of loans or mortgages is to suppose that a company were to offer insurance of United States Government bonds against loss of purchasing power. Such insurance would be a palpable fraud, or collecting something for nothing, for the following reasons: The Government can, as has happened in varying degrees in most countries, including our own, reduce the purchasing power of its money and, consequently, of its bonds. If the government does not do this, the insurance will not be needed. If the government does this to any considerable extent, or, say, to the extent of more than a ten per cent devaluation, the insurance will be worthless. No insurance company could operate profitably and carry much more than a ten per cent reserve against total risks.

Considerations like these are obvious enough, but they cannot usually be made to sustain regulatory measures of government under our juridical system, in which the courts undertake to fix the limits of government interference with private conduct according to no theory of social welfare relevant to the complex pattern of today but according to theories appropriate only to a 17th century social situation. Our courts can prevent a governmental undertaking to solve a problem, but they cannot initiate or guide the initiation of another and better undertaking to solve that problem. On the contrary, the Supreme Court, as in the case of the N.I.R.A., may for two years contemplate the drafting, enactment, popularizing and enforcing of a law which they know perfectly well they are going to repeal with the judicial veto. The courts can never be constituted to rule, but only to function as an instrument or tool of government. If they function as a check on government, the results are certain to be bad, for government finds enough checks in the difficulties of maintaining order and promoting welfare. Government obviously needs the counsels and loyal coöperation of all its agencies, not their purely destructive criticism and obstruction.

One can multiply indefinitely examples showing the impossibility, under the present system, either of preventing or correcting maladjustments in property arrangements once the dynamics of the frontier do not take care automatically of such readjustments.

CHAPTER VI

DEBT REDUCTION A NECESSARY PRELIMINARY TO NEW FINANCING

Summarily, it may be said that the debt burden must be and will be reduced, and that no reorganization, capitalist, fascist or socialist, is possible which does not include debt reduction. Capitalism, fascism and Russian communism are still demanding savings and offering a premium for their use. Gigantic work providing enterprises, public or private, are among the first imperatives of social order. Financing these enterprises is the only financial problem worth mentioning.

Other financial problems merit urgent attention only as their solution will contribute directly to solving the problem of financing the enterprises which will end unemployment. When the depression first began to receive official recognition at Washington, Mr. Hoover's chief preoccupation, probably, was to preserve the credit structure, as he called it. In the sixth year of the depression, it is beginning to be apparent to a few who are a little ahead of Mr. Hoover in their economic perceptions that the great credit problem is financing new work giving enterprise, and not preserving financial arrangements which provided work and prosperity years ago but do not do so today.

A second point in explanation of the impossibility of saving the present debt structure in its entirety is that these heavy interest charges with which a whole people is saddled are too largely connected with past consumption, including that made on the fields of battle, and past business mistakes. If a person has the means of repudiating a debt, and large numbers will always find the means to do so by political or revolutionary action, he is not going to go on paying interest on money used a long time ago either for an act of consumption or for a bad

68

business venture. It was this consideration, almost alone, which convinced me several years prior to Hitler's advent to full power that his triumph was ultimately inevitable, and it was a consideration which few of my friends, especially some of my German friends (who were vastly better informed about Germany than I and who are now in exile), could possibly see to have any validity.

It is not in human nature to bear indefinitely the charges of an unproductive debt, and Hitler was the only political leader in Germany whose stand on German reparations payments showed clear recognition of this human attitude towards debt. The German people might have paid, as the liberal economists and bankers argued, given a requisite willingness to make the necessary sacrifices. But people won't make the necessary sacrifices. They will rather make these sacrifices for war or revolution. For a man to go on meeting a financial obligation, it must be apparent to him that the obligation is connected with an addition to his present productive or debt bearing capacity. And this seems good ethics and good sense. If it is not good law, then so much the worse for the law.

These two points are too much disregarded by statesmen, jurists, and economists who try to defend the integrity and bearability of present debt charges. It is no final argument for the soundness of a debt or debts generally to prove that the people could afford to pay the interest if they made the necessary sacrifices. Suppose they could, but suppose they cannot afford to pay these charges plus the additional charges requisite for new financing to create work for the unemployed, to clear the slums or, quite simply, to carry the depression. That is the rub. Why are new long term loan funds not flowing in adequate volume into new bonds and mortgages for new construction? It is not chiefly because a few score billions of dollars of bonds and mortgages throughout the world have gone into default or repudiation in one way or another. It is mainly because the lenders cannot see that the possible borrower has a chance of meeting present debt charges plus new charges. Possible borrowers, in the main, do not see that they have this chance either, and, consequently, do not apply for loans. These, obviously, are the main reasons why so many railroads are finding it necessary to do their financing with the R.F.C., and why the total of bank loans to non-governmental borrowers is steadily shrinking.

The doctrine that old debts must be swept away to make room for necessary new debts, after all, is but the essential principle behind the biblical year of jubilee, or the logic of the law of geometrical progression applied to a steady growth of debt. A great many people, whose pietism derives from Calvin, the theologian of the 16th century shopkeepers and money lenders (rather than from Jesus, Aristotle or Moses, all three of whom denounced money lending), will say, "But the debtors hired the money, didn't they?" And with the posing of that question the whole discussion is thrown right back where the canonists left it over four hundred years ago, when the gold rushes to the new countries and capitalism got their start.

In those pre-capitalistic days the issue as to usury was argued somewhat in these terms: Ought a debtor to pay interest because he needed or wanted money for consumption, or because he miscalculated profits on a business venture and because, in either case, due to his necessity or miscalculation, he promised to pay such interest? To the question so stated, pre-Calvin Christianity, Judaism and Mohammedanism gave the same negative answer that Aristotle gave. For fifteen hundred years Christianity said that money-lending was sin, a fact which seems to be little known or appreciated by many present day Christians who make the payment of debts a high ethical imperative. Christianity has changed in this respect, but the words of Aristotle, the Bible or the theologians of the Christian Church for fifteen hundred years remain unchanged on this issue.

Briefly, the old or traditional doctrine of the world's precapitalist exponents of ethics as to interest, stripped of the moulds of thought of Aristotle and medieval scholasticism of the Christian Church, amounts to saying something like this:

An income from property or a usufruct of property is permissible—in other words, both land rental and business profits are permissible, but an income for the use of money by another should not be demandable at law unless the use made by the other person of the money has enabled him to pay the return promised.

This principle, the true doctrine of usury, denies legal enforcement to money-lending contracts where the borrowing has been for outright consumption or bad business ventures. Actually, of course, the lender to bad business ventures rarely gets more than the canonist doctrine on usury would allow him as a mere partner, except where, as in the case of the farmer, the lender can for a time collect his interest out of the living standard of the debtor who has made a bad business venture. The evil of fixed obligations consists not so much in what they take as in the mischief they cause for a time by reason of the effort to take what the economic possibilities and welfare imperatives will not allow. The vice of loan or interest contracts is inflexibility. During the period of modification of the canonist doctrine against usury, under the pressure of the emergent banker and merchant interests of medieval Europe, the theologians of the Church worked out subtle contracts and interpretations of Church law to get around the Church ban on money-lending and yet produce the equivalent of loan contracts. The Calvinist countries, of course, after the Reformation, admitted money-lending to full respectability and legality.

Present day experience with debt is demonstrating the basic soundness of the canonist, biblical or Aristotelian views about money-lending, when such views are fairly stated in terms of present day economic problems. These views, if now given enforcement, would make every contributor of capital to a profit seeking venture, whether of a government, a corporation or a private individual, merely a partner in that particular venture to the extent of his contribution. And these views would bar all loans for consumption. War financing would have to be done by tax levies, or else by following the old

Roman precedent of selling to capitalists shares in enemy loot, if, when, and as captured, rather than by claims on the home folks' future income, as capitalist war bond financing does. Under this rule, the working capital for business enterprises would be supplied entirely by partners, active or inactive, and by shareholders, where the enterprise was a corporation—never by money lenders.

It will surely be asked how, under such investment arrangements, insurance companies and trustees could safeguard the principal of funds entrusted to their management. The notion that in a contract or a legal bond there resides a peculiar security is a fallacy that neither Shakespeare's *Merchant of Venice* nor the default on the Allied bonds to the United States Government seems to have succeeded in debunking. To this question as to security for trust fund investments, I have only to reply, "How do trustees safeguard their investments at present?", and to answer in the same breath, "They don't." Actually, they secure only what the economic possibilities allow—or less sometimes. What of the billions of dollars in railroad and mortgage bonds which were eligible under state laws for trust fund investments and which are now in default, or soon going into default? The investor under any set of conditions can take only what the economic possibilities allow, and any legal contract specifying safeguards to the contrary is just another of the fictions or farces on which our army of superfluous lawyers make a parasitic living.

Legal services in connection with a single corporate bankruptcy, reorganization, or mortgage foreclosure, frequently run up a bill of several million dollars, which usually come out of the pockets of the investors, who have been taught to revere lawyers and their handiwork as the great safeguards of investment and property rights. In practically every instance where the lawyers collect a bill running into millions of dollars, the final settlement or settlements could have been worked out with little expense or difficulty by any small group of honest men, aided only by law clerks, accountants, and other technicians to give practical effect to their agreement. The agreement, if it is to be carried out, should be drawn in terms of economic possibilities which any sensible person properly informed can perceive, and not in terms of legal considerations which only lawyers can understand and which only contrary-to-fact fictions can rationalize. The toll taken by the legal profession from business in the United States in perfectly legitimate ways is one of the least defensible and most anti-social rackets in the country. This vested interest in making economic arrangements in a way to provide work for lawyers is responsible for the propaganda which, in turn, is responsible for the belief of the average American that a legally worded or implemented economic arrangement affords the wayfaring man a protection or an economic advantage not otherwise obtainable. The public has been trained to hanker after the lawyer's wares or services. The chief need of a stable economic order is flexibility. The chief contribution of liberal law to the economic system is inflexibility.

This taste for litigation and complicated legal arrangements, of course, constitutes our cult of the law and the Constitution and, also, the psychological basis of our lawlessness as a people. This cult of the law is exactly the same cult of the law that Shylock had. It is the cult of law either as a means of making a living by its practise, or as a means of getting the better of the other fellow in an economic way. This cult of the law must be smashed in order that a new cult of national interest and social discipline, the only true scheme of law, may develop.

Money-lending, with the idea of a bond being given to furnish a degree of security which the economic results would not afford, is a large element in the American or any liberal cult of the law. Anglo-Saxon liberalism was born in greed and conceived in usury. Since the rise of money-lending to respectability in the 16th century and later, the money-lenders have relied heavily on the law as their instrument of coercion and exploitation. There comes a time, however, when economic events and human revolt prove mightier than the money-lender's law. Then debtors take law into their own hands and repudiate, or the law becomes nullified by economic forces which the courts cannot enjoin.

It is not a lawless thing but a truism to say that contractual stipulation and legal action to enforce it in defiance of economic realities or human needs is anarchy, not law. Facts or economic possibilities are the highest law. Law, the attempted enforcement of which defies facts or realities, is not law but futile nonsense. Making this generalization a little more concrete, it is not a lawless thing to say that most of the law connected with money-lending, when its application is attempted in a period of economic adversity, or after the frontier era, is productive of conditions of economic and social anarchy.

Coming back to the discussion of usury (from which we have digressed slightly to point out the connection between legalism and the notion that a loan contract provides a security for a trust fund not to be had otherwise) it is here also to be observed that most of the theories and sales-talk of the insurance companies and institutional trustees of savings are the purest moonshine, wholly unsupported by historical evidence. That is to say, we can see innumerable examples of large fortunes being conserved for over fifty years in land, as evidenced by the estates of the Astors and thousands of landed families the world over, or in a family-run business like that of the Rothschilds, the Morgans, the Krupps, the Duponts, or the Rockefellers. But it remains for the insurance companies and banks offering the world their services as trustee custodians of investment funds to show a single large private fortune which has ever been conserved for fifty years by an insurance company or bank trustee through continuous investment in bonds or fixed obligations. Let the advertising insurance companies and trust companies cite but one of their clients whose fortune was preserved intact for fifty years through trustee investment in good bonds. We know what has happened to the purchasing power of investors in fixed obligations and insurance in the European countries which have experienced devaluation. We know also that great industrial fortunes in going enterprises have been, for the most part, conserved and many have even increased during this period. The Krupps beat inflation, but the investor throughout the world who sought the protection of a legal contract with a borrower has been expropriated in varying degrees running all the way to zero.

The doctrine of the canonists or Aristotle about usury is coming back into its own in the world-wide collapse of credit, repudiation and devaluation. This doctrine is not opposed to property ownership or business enterprise, but it is incompatible with the spirit and technique of modern finance capitalism. It is a doctrine which fascism everywhere must adopt and follow as rapidly as possible. For the benefit of the professional economists who may be inclined to sneer at any one who reasserts doctrines which they have thought they had disposed of during the past hundred years of rationalization of modern capitalism, I may say that I have read most of the leading theoretical explanations and defenses of interest. I might add that I could, had I time, demolish each of these theories of interest, one by one, with the arguments of another. But what is the use of demolishing with theoretical analysis the academic theories of interest when defaults, repudiation, bankruptcies and successive currency devaluations the world over are doing so much more devastating a job of confuting classical theories of money-lending and interest?

Take, for instance, Böhm-Bawerk's subjective theory of interest, and the many refinements or elaborations of it, which explain so beautifully why people promise to pay interest but do not show how they can pay it, or why it so often happens that they fail to pay it when they have the misfortune to be borrowing in an age and country not enjoying an expansion boom and rising prices. Does any intelligent person need the heavy Teutonic reasoning of the Austrian economists to understand why a prodigal government or individual promises to pay interest, or why a man playing the stock market for a rise promises to pay ten or fifteen per cent on call money? The reason, undoubtedly, is largely subjective, as Böhm-Bawerk points out. The borrower feels the money now is worth a lot more than it will be a year hence, because between now and then he expects to make a killing. But does this subjective theory of interest explain why the market finally beats the traders? Was it ever much of a contribution to useful knowledge to tell us why people borrow money and assume obligations they can't meet?

There has never been propounded a satisfactory theory of interest, or one that can be read without seeming absurd in the light of post-war experience. The productive theory of interest, of course, is the purest romanticizing. For much borrowing has always been done for uses that had no chance of producing the money of repayment, as we have already seen in the preceding chapter to have been the case in financing railroad betterments in this country. Government borrowing, for instance, has been the keystone of credit and lending, and has never, in any substantial amounts, been done for uses which produced the means of repayment. The fundamental thought of the pre-capitalistic exponents of ethics with regard to money-lending, like Aristotle or the Bible, stands far better the test of analysis in the light of present day experience than the economic theories about interest spun during the 19th century, when most borrowers were taken care of by the increasing land values of rapidly expanding colonies and of nations undergoing industrialization and rapid population growth.

While we are on the subject of theories of interest it is not amiss to remark that the professional economists and publicists of liberal and conservative tendencies, with few exceptions, have been favoring either complete cancellation, or considerable scaling down, of War debt, but have had little to say about scaling down private debts. Of course, our professors and publicists who went about making propaganda for war debt cancellation or reduction until the War debtor nations closed the discussion by the *fait accompli* of unabashed default, will, with an air of learned and pained superiority, defend their treatment of War debts differently from privately owed internal debts, on the ground that a transfer problem aggravated by our high tariff interposed peculiar obstacles in the way of War debt payment by foreign countries to our government.

They will then express regret that it has proved so hard to make the American people understand that European debtors cannot pay their debts to us if they are unable to sell us the requisite amount of goods.

Strangely enough, it has never occurred to the advocates of foreign War debt cancellation that every debt presents a transfer problem, and that this problem is fundamentally the same in every case. The debtor, in order to be able to pay the debt, must find a market at a right price for his product or services in the money of payment of the debts. The Iowa farmer, or the home-purchaser-on-the-mortgage-plan anywhere, has the problem of converting Iowa corn or personal services into New York dollars, quite as much as the British Government has the problem of converting British goods into New York dollars. A high tariff may hinder a British debtor from selling British goods for New York dollars to pay a British debt to an American creditor, but a high tariff does not hinder the sale of goods or services produced by the American debtor to the American creditor.

The fact is, of course, that the advocates of War debt cancellation have been furthering the propaganda of the financial community of New York, which would have been glad to have had the War debt slate wiped clean, provided the American internal debts were respected. It is not strange that the American people have received with manifest resentment the propaganda of eastern seaboard capitalists, and their endowed propagandists in the academic world, in favor of War debt cancellation while practically nothing was being said by the same financial or intellectual communities about the debt difficulties of Americans.

Obviously War debts had to be cancelled and, fortunately, the debtors have disposed of this matter for us. It is most unfortunate that the British ever broke the allied front against the American insistence on War debt funding. But if the imperial and royal government of Great Britain cannot keep its agreement and pay its debt because of economic adversity, why should Farmer Brown be held to his agreement when crippled by even greater economic adversity? If one important body of debts, like War debts, must be cancelled or drastically reduced, a similar measure of relief must, sooner or later, be accorded to all debtors. The credit and debt structure of any country is an integrated whole. If the taxpayer of the United Kingdom is given a respite of some five dollars a year through non-payment of the American War debt, why should the American taxpayer be held to pay the interest and principal of the fifteen billions of outstanding War debt owed to American holders of our War debt? The only good argument against further repudiations of public debts must be based on political and social convenience. It would be more convenient and equitable to eliminate our public debt burden by means of a capital levy than by means of repudiation or cancellation through further currency devaluation. But reduce this burden, we must.

CHAPTER VII

A DEBTLESS ECONOMY THE IDEAL FORMULA

IF PRIVATE ownership and management of producers' goods is to be preserved, even in a modified form, it will be necessary to adopt a formula which can quickly straighten out the worst of the existing maladjustments due to the use of fixed money obligations; prevent, as far as possible, the recurrence of these and other types of maladjustment; and correct promptly in the future any maladjustments which occur in spite of preventive measures. So far as debts are concerned, this would seem to demand, first, equitable and efficient means of reducing debt burdens with a minimum of disturbance and a maximum of conformity to economic possibilities; second, a new scheme of legal arrangements to provide for private ownership and management with a minimum of inflexibilities, and maladjustments—this new scheme amounting, as soon as possible, to a debtless economy; and third, a nationalized system of banking which would make bank credit or deposit money, as well as paper and metallic money, a state monopoly.

A debtless economy, free of fixed interest charges and without legal enforcement of contracts which stipulate fixed money payments regardless of economic results, is the only formula of private ownership and management which can be made to work in anything but a frontier era, when lucky strikes and the steady rise in land values can be counted on to make the number of the victims of usury too small to have cognizance taken of them by ethics, law, or political economy. This ideal, debtless economy, cannot be equitably or conveniently initiated by one wholesale extinction of all creditor rights unless the succeeding formula is to be communism. But any sound reorganization must, in the debt field, proceed on the principle that we have to scrap as fast as possible the theory and practice

79

of interest. With the new principle established, or rather the ancient principle reëstablished, the present debt burdens must be drastically reduced in all spheres according to a national formula of equity and redistribution of the debt burden.

More explicitly, an ideal scheme of immediate procedure in debt reorganization might work somewhat as follows: First, state debts would be paid off in full, not with additional issues of paper money of considerably less value than the amount nominally owed, but with good money taken by a capital levy made on the progressive tax formula of the income and inheritance taxes now in force. There would be no liquidation of privately-owned property to provide money to pay this levy. There would merely be an attachment by the State of a certain percentage of privately-owned property, the income from which would go to the State to serve to retire any money issued to purchase the public debt. In this way, many large holders of government bonds would really pay themselves fifty cents of every dollar they were reimbursed on their government bonds. Savings bank and insurance funds, however, would thus be protected one hundred per cent against confiscation. There would be no expropriation, either by honest socialism or dishonest devaluation, except, of course, in so far as taxation may be thought to constitute expropriation.

Second, all private and corporate debts would, so to speak, be laid on one table of a National Tribunal of Debt Conversion, which would carry out a number of different plans of conversion for different types of debts. In the case of the railroads and public utilities, there could be a simple pooling of all indebtednesses, and their assumption by state-administered holding companies for all the railroads and public utilities jointly. Then, whatever was deemed a fair and workable total payment of annual income would be distributed among the bondholders and claimants according to their holdings and claims. This total amount for the railroads and utilities would vary from year to year according to economic conditions and social policy. In the cases of private debts, a great variety of formulas or settlements would have to be worked out, to fit different cases, but always on the principle that the creditor, mortgagee, or bondholder received an interest in obtainable future income in exchange for his old constitutional right of legal action, which gave him power to throw all sorts of monkey wrenches in the economic machinery, from mortgage foreclosure of a poor man's home to plain blackmail suits in all kinds of reorganization or settlement procedures. Another ruling principle would have to be ample provision for new financing to secure needed working capital for operation and replacements. The proposed formula, possible under fascism but not the present system, would really amount to nothing more than giving the average capitalist money-lender or creditor, in a simple, orderly fashion, all that the situation, efficiently and humanely handled, would allow him.

Under the present system that is all he gets, anyway, on the average; and often he does not get that, because of the legal and procedural fees and costs. But, in order to uphold the Constitution and support the largest army of lawyers per capita of any nation in the world, it cannot be done in a simple, orderly fashion. Under liberal capitalism according to the American constitutional formula, government has to guess at the Constitution, and have its guesses argued over by lawyers for years and finally validated or invalidated after years of confusion. There can, therefore, now be no executive readjustment—the only feasible form of readjustment of debt maladjustments.

The foregoing outline of general principles for a program of reorganizing the debt-credit structure is obviously impossible of realization under the present system. But it, or a much better scheme, is workable, under other conditions. Our present theory and practice in regard to property rights, made explicit by the Courts in the interpretation and application of the Constitution and laws pursuant thereto (always in specific litigations), explain why any debt reorganization formula is impossible under the present system. Legal inventiveness, of course, can get around many constitutional difficulties but, as a general rule, only through recourse to devious expedients which can never be resolved into any scheme of national reorganization. Getting around the Constitution usually means or forces the giving of relief in an expensive and impractical manner.

The Supreme Court, in passing the judicial veto on the Frazier-Lemke Bill for farm mortgage relief, made bold to intimate to the Administration that there was open to it a constitutional way of giving relief through allotment of public funds to distressed mortgage debtors. The trouble with the Supreme Court's view of the economic problems of the present is that the Court insists on thinking of the unemployed, the distressed debtors, and the economically crippled generally, as presenting just so many specific cases for public relief, similar in nature to those created by a big fire, flood or earthquake. It is assumed that the depression does not suspend the Constitution, and that within the framework of what the Constitution sanctions any needed remedy can be properly worked out.

The trouble with this view is that the Government cannot, with safety for the entire system, adopt any of the many policies based on this view. It cannot, for instance, indefinitely provide loan funds to make good the deficiencies in income of the farmers due to low agricultural prices, of the unemployed due to lack of work, of the railroads due to innumerable causes, or of the insurance companies due to interest defaults. Nor can the Government make up the deficiencies in present value of bonds, mortgages and notes held by banks, savings banks, and insurance companies. For only a limited time can the Federal Government stave off food riots, farm revolt, railroad bankruptcies and bank runs by rushing funds to bolster up specific situations which are weak.

The reason why depression problems, like debts, cannot be dealt with in the same way as flood or earthquake relief, can be simply stated as being primarily that of the sheer magnitude of relief required for these weak situations of the depression. The Federal Government could always spare a few millions, or even a few score millions, for specific relief. The theory of the Supreme Court, or, for that matter, of the system of which the Supreme Court is a sound exponent, is that relief needs will never require expenditures in excess of what Government can safely appropriate.

Aside from the magnitude of debt relief demands, there is to be considered the fact that the credit-debt structure of the country is really an integrated whole. It is not a series of separate cases—as liberal law and administration would have it. No readjustment can be effective except as a series of coördinated measures.

At this point it is to be reiterated that the present system provides amply and definitely its own formulas for disposing of bad and slow debts, but that the trouble with these legal formulas is that the staunchest believers in the Constitution are even more opposed to their consistent application in the present situation than I am. What better proof of the unworkability of the system could be wanted?

Mr. Hoover, who questions Mr. Roosevelt's interpretation of the Constitution, started both the National Credit Corporation and Reconstruction Finance Corporation, the purpose of which was to prevent the orderly processes of constitutional bankruptcy and bank closure from being carried out, in a legal manner, against certain debtors but not against certain others. (The inequity under liberal, constitutional norms—equal justice for all—of using government money to save some debtors and creditors but not others is too obvious to need argument.) One of the chief articles of Mr. Hoover's economic creed, as we have already seen, was that the Government should do everything possible to save the debt structure involving the big banks and institutional investors. But, as any one who has a nodding acquaintance with the theory of our laws and economic institutions must understand, the system requires that bad debts should be wiped out as quickly as possible by the orderly processes of bankruptcy, foreclosure and reorganization.

In fact, preventing the accumulation of bad debts by the banks is one of the results of correct observance of the system. Impeding these processes has been good Hooverism as well as good Rooseveltism, but it has not been good capitalism. Capitalism, being essentially a complete social system, cannot for its own health put the interests of the lender or unlucky bank creditor and investor ahead of the interests of general financial soundness. But the logic of good capitalism has no way of imposing itself on men in power who are swayed by the logic of good politics or self-interest, as were the Republicans in the palmy, balmy post-War days. It is, therefore, doubtless without point to talk of the logic of a system which makes individual liberty to injure the system one of the values it has to conserve.

In the long run, the logic of the system, brutal and devastating as it might be in action today, and as fatal as its application would be to any politician's reëlection, is better than the logic of the Hoover constitutionalists, who would save debts with government support and yet fail at the same time to end the depression. All of the extraordinary formulas for saving the debt structure are nothing more or less than matters of making bad private debts ultimately bad public debts. The harsh logic of the system says that it is better to foreclose and bankrupt half the people, and maintain the soundness of the credit of the other half and of the State, than to stay the system's processes of debt adjustment, with the final consequence of wrecking public credit and the foundations of the present system.

It may be said that Germany survived the wrecking of her public credit. That is true, but it is true only because the public credit of America and Britain stood firm and was able to finance a fresh start in Germany. When American public credit goes the way of German public credit in 1924, what other great financial power will be able to effect our financial rehabilitation under the old system? The dilemma of the Hoover constitutionalists is really three-horned, for they cannot get votes by giving the Nation the constitutional "works" in the matter of debt adjustment; they cannot carry out any workable reorganization of the debt situation, such as I outline, consistently with the Constitution; and they cannot stave off indefinitely the day of reckoning for the Hoover or Roosevelt policies of saving the debts.

In sober retrospect, of course, it is apparent that a most important deviation from the system's debt theory and practice was made when, during the War, our Federal Reserve Act was revamped to authorize the Federal Reserve Banks to issue money and credit against long term government bonds, instead of only financial and commercial paper payable within ninety days—except for agricultural paper which was allowed to run nine months. A second breach in the system's debt theory and practice came in a long series of failures of national bank examiners to do their duty, presumably in accordance with the instructions of the Secretary of the Treasury. In the period from 1921 to 1929, had bank examinations been correctly made and sound standards for liquidity of bank loans and uses of bank funds been enforced by the bank examiners, the major credit and speculative abuses could not have continued for six months, instead, as they actually did, for nearly a decade. The two largest banks in New York could not have used their own funds for speculative operations in their own bank stocks, for instance, if bank examination had been faithful to public interest. The National City Bank, under correct national bank examination, could not have used twenty-five million dollars of new money from a sale of bank stock to bail out, through the National City Company, a bad loan to a Cuban sugar company instead of writing it off surplus.

As soon as a Congressional Resolution in January, 1933, forced disclosure of the names of the borrowers of the R.F.C., the banks of the country began folding up like jackknives until the bank holiday closed them all. It was asserted in the Myers-Newton article in the *Saturday Evening Post* of June 15, 1935, entitled "The Origins of the Banking Panic of March 4, 1933," that "With the nervous public temper of the time, the publication of these borrowings would be apt to subject these institutions to the suspicion that their borrowing was because they were weak when, as a matter of fact, they were not." The writers, however, adduce absolutely no evidence to support their assertion that the institutions borrowing from the R.F.C. in January, 1933, "were not weak." If they were not weak, why could they not borrow from the large New York banks which had surplus funds and were reducing all the while loans to American country banks, though they had huge outstanding loans to American and foreign speculators who were selling borrowed dollars short or buying our gold for export? What better borrower could a New York bank have than a country bank or insurance company, which is "not weak," than the Dawes Bank of Chicago, for instance, which needed an eighty-million-dollar loan from the R.F.C. and could not get it in New York though it "was not weak" at the time?

No one can convince an intelligent person that any American bank is not weak as long as that bank fails to publish a statement of its security assets at market value, or to make certain statements about the nature of its loans and loan policies. Most of the banks in the United States in January, 1933, were weak, and the best proof of their weakness then, as in 1935, is the fact that national bank examiners allow them to carry in published statements their bonds at cost price rather than market value. Moreover, the examiners allow them to carry frozen loans which good bank inspection would have purged from the bank portfolios years ago.

It is idle even to talk about the possibility of financial reorganization in this country under the old system as long as it is impossible to have the truth published about the condition or operations of the banks without starting a run, and as long as it takes a billion and a half dollars of advanced Government funds to keep them open. It is idle, also, to try to divide the banks into the sheep and the goats, or the strong and the weak. If the Government were to withdraw its support from the weak banks and to impose on them high standards of bank examination, their closing would only precede and precipitate the runs which would close all the banks, as in March, 1933. The banks of the country must stay open or close together. Professor Parker Willis, one of our most influential banking authorities, in an address on June 10, 1935, to the New York

State Bankers Association, advised the member banks to withdraw from the Federal Reserve System in protest against the governmental despotism over banking which he said would be established by the Eccles Bank Bill. This piece of academic advice, of course, was not, and could not be, taken any more seriously than most other advice from similar sources of unrealistic social philosophy. Yet Professor Willis will doubtless prove to be right in his warning that the doom of private banking is spelled out in the Eccles bill.

The debt situation in the United States, however, is such that the banks, the principal merchants of debts, can operate only as long as the people feel that deposits are guaranteed by the Government. This being true, the bankers cannot break with the Government, nor can they allege any good reason for their further existence once they fail to command enough confidence to operate without government support. The only possible reorganization of this debt situation would have to include nationalization of banking, from which, on the Roosevelt itinerary, 1935 is not far removed. With the nationalization of banking in either the United States or England, it can be said that liberal capitalism is at an end. The logic of it all is that the country needs money and credit, and the private bankers have shown themselves incapable both of financing recovery and of administering a money and credit system when times are good, within the framework of liberal law and with common sense and common decency. To substantiate this drastic statement it is necessary only to read from the record of the Senate investigations of Wall Street, whether in 1913 or 1933.

With the debt problem is interwoven the fate of the insurance companies, college and charitable foundations, and life savings of private investors, as well as the fate of the commercial, savings, and investment bankers as a class. Strange as it may appear, it is still true that in high banking and insurance quarters there are many who maintain the attitude that if inflation takes the dollar the way of the mark, the rouble and the franc, it will be a good lesson to the middle classes for having supported Mr. Roosevelt. Little do they realize that the discomfiture of the middle classes can turn into a Roman holiday at which the big bankers will be supplying and not enjoying the fun. The big business leaders and bankers never would be missed, while the middle classes cannot be liquidated. In this moment of crisis, it is amazing that so many business leaders should be rallying around the Constitution instead of around a leader and a workable formula for their own salvation, as well as for the future preservation of social order. But such has been the blindness of the dominant class in more than one crisis of world history.

CHAPTER VIII

CAN WE RESTORE FLEXIBILITY WITHOUT PLANNING?

IT WILL be recalled that in Chapter V we undertook to wind up the attack on the problem of the workability of the present system by posing for discussion the question whether, within the framework of liberal capitalism, necessary readjustments could be made to render it workable, assuming the requisite conditions for further operation are found. And, pursuing this line of inquiry, we discussed in the last three chapters the debt maladjustments. It was pointed out that, in the United States, under the New Deal or under the processes of deflation which have been largely held in abeyance or counteracted by government inflation, we have not, as yet, appreciably decreased our debt total. And it was seen that those countries in which debt burdens have been extinguished by inflation and currency devaluation have gone communist or fascist, or are in acute economic crisis. The present debt burden, we concluded, must be drastically reduced in a more tolerable way than through either the orderly processes of bankruptcy and foreclosure or the disorderly processes of inflation and devaluation. Furthermore, a debtless economy is indicated as, perhaps, the only formula for preserving any measure of private ownership and management. Getting rid of debt burdens in a satisfactory manner, and getting on under a system of private ownership without debts, or with only partners' and shareholders' capital, will require the intervention of a strong executive state.

There still remain to be considered many areas of maladjustments other than debts. To these we cannot devote the space their discussion in an adequate manner would require. We can only mention briefly, with a summary statement of broad principles, the facts that the price structure, supply and demand, and the movement of goods and capital in national and international trade, since the War, have shown increasing inflexibility or failure to find working adjustments, one with the other. Thus, during the boom, the prices of finished goods did not fall as fast as the costs of producing them. Increased use of power and increased efficiency lowered production costs, while increased use of credit by powerful monopolies, in collusion with the bankers (both to hold surpluses off the market and to finance consumption at artificially high prices) served to keep the prices of raw materials and finished products from falling with the fall in production costs.

As a result of the increasingly large spread between selling prices and production costs, so caused, huge business profits were made. These profits gave support to an absurd inflation of market prices of common stocks, real estate, and earning properties generally, such inflation being aided by our friends the bankers through making available for pure speculation on common stock price changes as much as eight billion dollars at one time. In this way the stock market collapse of 1929 was rendered inevitable, and in this way the magnitude of the collapse was determined by the magnitude of the speculative abuses. And thus, since the bubble burst, just as business and financial leaders conspired to keep prices artificially high during the boom, practically every one has conspired during the depression to keep production costs from following the drop in wholesale prices of raw materials and finished manufactures. By production costs I refer particularly to the cost of money for new investment—interest—the cost of government—taxes— and the costs of labor—wages. These production costs have not fallen as fast as selling prices, with the result, naturally, that profits have declined all the way to large minuses or losses in many industries, and with the further result that millions of workers who could not be profitably employed have been thrown out of work and kept out of work. The facts stated are matters of such common knowledge that it seems wholly unnecessary to give figures or elaborate explanations.

Now all literate exponents of the theory of capitalism will

say, in different ways, that a smoothly working capitalism demands flexibility in the movement of prices, costs and wages, quick responsiveness in the adjustment of supply and demand to each other, and fluidity in the national and international flow of goods and investment capital. If exponents of this theory, and business men who voice its dogmas somewhat more crudely than the pure theorists, would only avoid the use of the term and concept freedom, and use terms like fluidity, flexibility, or adjustability, there would be less confusion of thought about these problems. Freedom can mean either easy adjustability or legal freedom to do what, in the circumstances, is practically impossible. Every one with an informed opinion on the subject agrees that many readjustments are now needed and that any social system must give a satisfactory performance in the making of readjustments. And most experts, even those with the most widely divergent interests and purposes, could agree fairly well as to what are the readjustments required to make any given social system work. But how can there ever be understanding, not to say agreement, among persons having conflicting interests and purposes, if some of them insist on using vague terms like freedom or economic freedom? The question, Freedom for whom to do exactly what?, always remains unanswered.

About the only workable definition of economic freedom or political freedom would be what is within the law and within the limits of practicability. And such a definition begs too many questions to be of much use. Whenever the restoration of economic freedom, or greater freedom in price, wage, or international trade movements, is advocated, what is meant is usually a return to some past legal régime and to some past economic situation, in which a great many people were far from free to do many things they considered desirable and wanted to do.

The advocate of more economic freedom may hope to return to some idealized past legal régime by having certain laws, like tariff measures, repealed, and certain governmental policies, such as the dole or various types of recently inaugurated business regulation, abandoned. And he may hope to return to the general economic situation of the past, which he now idealizes, by auto-suggestion, which he calls a restoration of confidence. He rarely recognizes that what he calls confidence is mostly the product of material conditions, and that material conditions are not chiefly produced by states of mind. A certain state of mind may have brought early fortune hunters to the coal fields of Pennsylvania, the gold fields of California, or the cornfields of the Mississippi Valley. But a state of mind did not put the coal and gold there, or make the soil of the Mississippi Valley richer than that of the Italian peninsula or northern Germany. What the intelligent and public spirited advocates of more economic freedom really want, then, whether they stress tariff reform or more laissez-faire in some other respect, is greater adjustability of the economic factors to changing conditions, and better conditions to which to make adjustments.

If terms and concepts like adjustability are used, it will be found that both the fascists and communists also want a high degree of adjustability of economic factors. The problem, of course, is how to get it under the given system in question or in favor. Fascism and communism must achieve satisfactory adjustments or readjustments from day to day largely through State planning and intervention. Liberal capitalism must expect such adjustment and readjustment to happen automatically under a given régime of law enforcement as a result of the play of private initiatives. The question really at issue throughout this book is whether we can reasonably expect that the system will give a better performance in the way of adjustment and readjustment to changing conditions if we modify the legal régime in the direction of repealing or abandoning some of the present laws or government policies of economic interference, or if we modify the present legal régime with different types of intervention, but in a way which leaves the liberal capitalist system substantially intact. In other words, briefly put, Is more or less laissez-faire the way to get better or prompter adjustments? Or, Will the factors of capital and labor, bankers, business managers, investors and wage earners work out better the problems of prompt and successful adjustment if given more legal freedom and if interfered with less by government?

Now it would be ideal for purposes of settling arguments and making scientific observations if the American elections of 1936 were fought on the issue of more or less laissez-faire, and if the winner kept his campaign pledges and really gave the country a stiff dose of laissez-faire. Then we could make some useful comparisons and perhaps draw some instructive and valid conclusions based on pure experimentation. Unfortunately, however, while some Republican arch-conservative may well run on a platform which includes a fulsome homage to laissez-faire to obtain Park Avenue and Wall Street financial contributions, the platform will also include all sorts of vote-catching promises of special favors to regional, economic and class interests, such as the tariff-sheltered American industries, agriculture, the West, the South, the A. F. of L. and the veterans, most of which promises will be inconsistent with laissez-faire.

And whatever the promises of laissez-faire made, the laissez-faire candidate, if elected, which seems improbable, would continue to enlarge the present measure of state interventionism under the pressure of group lobbies and desperate economic and social predicaments. So nothing conclusive, or even instructive, about the merits of more laissez-faire is likely to be proved by any course of events, for the excellent reason that no political party or leader in power, or likely to come into power, is going to give us more laissez-faire.

The advocates of more laissez-faire, however, are a sufficiently important and respectable influence, on the whole, to merit a serious answer based, as it must then be, on theoretical speculation rather than any proof of the pudding by the eating. And it cannot be repeated too often that laissez-faire is the only authentic formula under liberal capitalism for effecting necessary readjustments in the formation of prices, the movements of trade, or the balancing of supply and demand. Adequate refutation of the argument for more laissez-faire would have to include a thorough examination of the basic assumptions of liberal laissez-faire, something which is done sketchily in different connections throughout this book.

A briefer and, it would seem, a fairly impressive refutation of the argument for more of what is commonly called economic freedom, or what is really less government interference with the doing by certain people of certain things as the proper way to insure satisfactory adjustments and readjustments under the present system, is merely to point to the universally admitted fact that the leaders of business and finance were directly responsible for the chief initiatives and policies which caused the maladjustments we are now told can be corrected by giving these same leaders more freedom. The failure of prices to fall as production costs fell during the boom period was one of the achievements of our financial and industrial magnates, and was their proudest boast at that time. Who lent hundreds of millions of dollars for the maintenance of the price of copper, coffee, sugar and innumerable other commodities at prices which did not correspond to the indications of supply and demand? What could be sillier than the attempt to make it appear that tariff interferences with foreign trade are the work of the politicians, when, as a matter of fact, tariffs have always been written at the dictation of the most powerful business or economic interests?

It is an obviously desirable thing to have greater flexibility or adjustability in the price, wage, cost structure, or in the movements of supply and demand. But more laissez-faire or freer trade is not the way to attain it. Neither are the processes of parliamentary democracy. On the contrary, history and present day experience are full of demonstrations that the more there is of what is commonly called laissez-faire, economic freedom, democracy or parliamentary government, the more economic maladjustments there will be, and the more difficult of readjustment they will prove. Not only high finance and big business contributed to the freezing of prices and the maintenance of artificial conditions of supply and demand during the boom; but the masses, through their democratically elected political representatives, and through their labor union leaders, supported in every possible way the perpetuation of all these now universally denounced maladjustments. And during the depression, who has opposed deflation or the adjustment downwards of prices more than the bankers, the landlords, the manufacturers, and the labor union leaders? The so-called deflationists have only advocated deflating the other fellow. Thus the industrialist and banker have quite logically argued for a reduction in wages, but they have combined to support the opposition of the landlord, banker and mortgage owner to a wholesale liquidation of bad real estate loans, which would have brought rent down and thus helped enormously towards making lower wages acceptable.

No one economic or professional class can be given all or most of the blame for the stickiness of prices or the inflexibility of economic adjustments under the liberal capitalist system. All economic classes are offenders. One can only say that the greater the economic or political power exercised at a given time, the greater the blame for these maladjustments. It is on this ground that the bankers deservedly come in for so much blame. But they are quite right in most of their charges against their clients who, in 1929, wanted the follies of inflation and who, in 1935, want the folly of attempting to prevent the necessary scaling down of debts. The industrialists are quite right in most of their complaints against labor leaders for demanding wages which cannot be paid with full employment of now unemployed labor. But to the industrialists attaches greater blame for the inflexibility of prices than to the labor union leaders, because the initial and strongest force in checking a general adjustment downward of prices, including the price of labor, has been, ever since the War, the unholy alliance between large scale industry and finance to stabilize prices and increase profits on bases which were obviously unsound and necessarily impermanent. The labor union leaders merely sought to play the same game, though always with poorer cards. Under the New Deal, the farmers have been playing the same game through the A.A.A., with the farm vote and President Roosevelt's agricultural obsessions as their high cards.

It needs little argument, and no new evidence, to establish the point that all the important economic factors or group interests have, both before and during the depression, used economic and political power equally to prevent the adjustments in prices, supply, demand, and trade and capital movements essential to the proper operation of the system. These interferences contributed to the collapse of the boom, and they are now contributing to the prevention of recovery, not that recovery would eventuate if these interferences were ended.

What, however, does call for considerable argument is the point, one of the major points of this book, that, under the liberal régime and in the present world situation, the economic factors cannot be expected to behave in a way either to prevent or correct unbearable economic maladjustments. It is impossible to show why each and every specific reform proposal would fail to bring about better total adjustment or maintain easier adjustability. The proposals are too numerous and too complicated. Within any brief space, one can only attack the fundamental premises of the classical case for the economic harmonies of the game as it is supposed to be played under the liberal régime, and reiterate the fact that these harmonies are largely either fictions or incidents of a past frontier and pioneer era. The rebuttal of the liberal case in this respect is largely a matter of saying that more of the poison will not eventually prove an antidote.

The strongest case for economic liberalism today is made out by those who are hardly less vigorous than the extreme radical in denouncing the abuses of economic power by monopolies and the financial leaders. This case is well stated in a collection of critical essays entitled *The Economics of the Recovery Program*, published by seven members of the economics department of Harvard University. The essays are extremely naïve and unsophisticated which, of course, makes them the best sort of liberal defense. In the final essay, "Economics versus Politics," the writer strikes a high note in the great liberal symphony when he says (page 176) that "The corner-stone of the 'liberal' program was the law and ethics of property and contract, which in spirit or intention are the law and ethics of common honesty in all business relations, and in the relations between government and business. Honest business is not pursuit of power and advantage over others; [It would be interesting to hear the comments of competitors crushed by the great and now flourishing business trusts on this pearl of academic naïveté. L. D.] it is production and exchange of goods and services on terms of *mutual* advantage to both parties in every transaction."

It is the basic premise of the preceding quotation, which is also that of Bentham, Rousseau, Adam Smith and economic liberalism, which is utterly untrue. And it is the untruth of this premise which explains so much of the absurdity of liberal economic doctrine. If, contrary to these assumptions about successful human beings not loving power, about the nature of the results of success in competition, and about the ways of men in a so-called free market, it happens that monopolies arise and perpetrate great abuses, or that the country as a whole goes on a mad speculative orgy trying to get something for nothing instead of producing and exchanging goods and services in terms of mutual advantage to both parties in every transaction, these good liberals do not reëxamine their premises.

They merely try to bolster them up with even more absurd explanations and recommendations. They will berate the wicked monopolies for their anti-liberal conduct, and talk vaguely about the "curse of bigness," forgetting that some of the best things in our civilization we owe to the technical achievements of monopolies—achievements which small-unit enterprise could never have realized. They will then ask for laws to control these monopolies, forgetting that, under liberal rules, one predatory millionaire bank official and market manipulator will have more influence in the making, interpreting, and administering of laws than all the economics professors and liberal theorists in the country put together. They will try to make it appear that financial abuses or misdeeds are the work of a small minority of the total number of financial leaders, forgetting the fact that the financial and large industrial institutions form a series of closely integrated networks of management and control in which no important policies or acts can be committed by any considerable number of higher-ups without fully engaging the responsibility of all the large financial institutions and industrial corporations, or rather of their heads.

Of course, the responsible policy-deciding heads of the two hundred largest corporations which control over two-thirds of our corporate wealth are very much of a minority of the total number of members of the business community. But if ninety-five per cent of all the business men and bankers are small fry and consequently never in on the promotion of bad financing, the manipulation of stocks (including those of the largest banks in New York) with the aid of the resources of the entire country, or have no share in combinations and conspiracies in restraint of trade and market freedom, it is childish to assume that these misdeeds of high finance and captains of industry are not participated in by the majority of business men and bankers who are small fellows simply because the latter do not approve of such doings.

Nothing better knocks into a cocked hat the liberal assumption about financial evils being largely the work of unscrupulous and irresponsible individuals who temporarily occupy positions of power than the patent fact that the whole country went mad on a speculative orgy in which the chief objective was to get something for nothing. This may be thought of as an abuse of economic power by the mighty or as an abuse of economic freedom to trade by the many. It was both. The number of the actual gamblers was relatively small. John Flynn thinks it was well under a million. But whatever the number, it was too large to be called an insignificant minority. And it was too inclusive of all classes to be called unrepresentative.

Still more annihilating of the liberal assumptions about the economic or social wisdom of the people in the free market is the fact that the foolish and anti-social attempts of several hundred thousands of gamblers on price changes to get something for nothing enjoyed the high approval of the people as a whole, an approval which was voiced repeatedly by almost every important political leader from the President down.

The liberal apology that these nation-wide speculative waves are temporary attacks of mass insanity is too shallow for serious consideration. The fact always is that a boom ends because the operation of mechanical factors over which the speculators and the community as a whole can exercise no staying influence finally forces it to end. The end of the speculative madness is not started through a return of the people to sanity in this respect. The return to sanity begins when a considerable number of the alleged insane perceive that the mechanical or impersonal factors which they cannot control are gradually closing in on their speculative operations.

Then they begin to retreat. Several bear raids on the market were started during the boom, but none of them succeeded in turning the tide of speculative madness until finally, in October, 1929, one of them met with enough support from the mechanical factors which had got sufficiently out of joint to make a further rise in prices on the prevailing scale quite impossible to maintain with the available credit resources. The people do not come to their senses in a speculative boom until material factors knock sense into them. If trying to get something for nothing be madness or badness, hundreds of thousands indulge in, and the nation approves of, this madness and badness as long as the mad, bad speculators can get away with it.

Thus we are warranted in saying that the follies and misdeeds in finance and speculation, or the so-called free market, as well as the abuses of economic power by monopolies, are usual, within the limits of the lawful and practicable, and in no sense the acts of minorities or exceptional individuals. Barring, in the main, acts of common forgery, embezzlement and simple theft, which, on the evidence available from prosecutions, appear to have been committed only by a minority of bank officials, it may be said that acts which were clearly anti-social, abuses of power, and productive of grave economic maladjustments, have been committed with the full responsibility of the partners or directors of every large New York investment banking house or commercial banking corporation.

As for the speculative follies of the masses of stock market gamblers, they must be recognized to have happened on a scale and with social consequences which completely invalidate some of the most fundamental liberal premises about the intelligence and decency of the conduct of the people in the free market under the régime of liberal law. As for monopoly abuses of power producing maladjustments, it seems fair to formulate the following explanations: From the time when a liberal régime began to emerge out of the earlier feudal pattern, economic competition under the liberal capitalist rules—whatever the changes in these rules, and they have been many—has always resulted in a few winners and many losers, with the great masses always remaining in a status of marked inferiority to the wealthy few by reason of the consequences of inequalities in wealth. Money is power.

Human nature has not changed materially under liberal capitalism. The masses have not the intelligence or the humanity, nor the winners the magnanimity, which liberal assumptions have postulated. Economic power is used for oppression and mischief. Economic opportunities in the free market are freely used by the masses in ways to cause grave social maladjustments. Laws and customs, establishing the rules of the game, get made in ways which are wholly different from those posited by liberal theory. Given certain basic liberal principles securing property rights and the enforcement of contracts, the less the amount of government interference, the greater the abuses of economic power and opportunity both by the monopoly and the individual shoe-string trader in the free market.

It is of the greatest importance in this connection to emphasize that the economic winners get the laws they want through financial pressures and lobbies, and, through having the courts packed with judges who were their former employees, they get most of the breaks in interpretation and development of judicial theory which is as important a part of the law as the statutory law. Thus, the economic winners have achieved for the perpetrators of economic or anti-social offenses an almost complete immunity. To illustrate this point, comparison may be made between the law governing the professional conduct of military officers and the law governing the conduct of bank and corporation officials. An army officer is court-martialed for conduct alleged to be unbecoming an officer and a gentleman. If convicted, the lightest penalty must be dismissal. A navy captain is always tried for the loss of a ship, and has the burden of proof to show that it was due to no fault or negligence on his part.

How funny it sounds to talk of trying a bank president who sold his own bank stock short while advising his friends and customers to buy it, on the charge of conduct unbecoming a bank president and a gentleman. No liberal capitalist code or discipline requires or, consistently with our constitutional guarantees, can require a banker to act like a gentleman. How utterly inconsistent with liberal norms of law it would be to put on the responsible heads of banks and big corporations which are wrecked or badly mismanaged, the burden of proof to show that they had not been guilty of negligence of duty.

Even the rules of evidence applied in the trial of economic or anti-social offenses, such as tax evasion or noncompliance with technical banking regulations, follow entirely different theories from the rules of evidence applied in trials of offenses against the person. Every week someone is executed for a murder on which conviction was had on purely circumstantial evidence. But when a millionaire income-tax dodger, or violator of banking laws, or security fraud laws, is brought to trial, circumstantial evidence is not only barred but such standards of proof of criminal intent are set by the courts as to make conviction virtually impossible. The millionaire tax dodger can even have the judge charge the jury that if it finds the unlawful act charged was committed in the belief that it was lawful, such belief being based on legal advice, the jury should not convict. Fancy a judge charging a jury in a murder case that, if the accused is found by the jury to have committed the homicide in the mistaken belief that he was acting in legitimate self-defense, such belief being based on previous legal advice, the jury ought not to convict of murder. Under liberal capitalism, the economic winners largely determine the making, interpreting, and administering of the rules.

The maladjustments caused by monopolies and anti-social uses of legitimate economic opportunities in the free market are due to exercises of liberties granted by the liberal system, and to inhibitions placed by this system on the power of government to regulate economic activity and prevent anti-social conduct. Obviously, anti-social conduct by important economic personalities should be prevented by regulation rather than be prosecuted after commission of the wrongful act. If the laws and administrative practices or customs were determined by the college professors and political and economic theorists, who constitute themselves the authorized exponents of the system, their statement of theory and their defenses of the system might have more consistency with the facts. But laws and administrative customs, under any régime, must be determined by those who have power, and not by those whom they subsidize.

It is not a weakness of the liberal capitalist system that it protects monopolies and permits concentration of economic power in a few hands. For this is inevitable and may have many desirable results; but those allowed such power do not exercise it in a way to meet the imperatives of social order, and cannot be coerced by the liberal state so to exercise such power. A strong authoritarian, executive state, commonly called fascist, has the merit not of eliminating monopolies or trading in the market, but of exercising, with adequate instrumentalities, an ample power over monopolies and the market to enforce a workable scheme of national interest. The authoritarian state can say "Stop" to business or in the market, as the liberal state cannot do. It is an interesting fact that the liberal state can prevent pedestrians and cyclists from using express highways, or whites and orientals from intermarrying, without violating any of the rights of man, but cannot regulate market practices or child labor without running afoul of all sorts of constitutional difficulties.

More liberal liberty merely means more power to the economic winners, who, it should not be necessary to add, are not exactly, "We, the people." Changing the scheme of economic liberties or government interference may also, and incidentally, mean a different set of economic winners. Thus, if we repealed all tariff duties, or completely stopped relief payments to the destitute and unemployed, or abandoned all counter-deflationary policies, we should have a long and bitter economic war, from which would eventually emerge a new set of economic winners—that is, if complete chaos did not supervene during the conflict.

But, after the international trade war following tariff repeal, or after the capital-versus-labor-strike war following a sharp turn to laissez-faire, had been won, the new economic winners would promptly avail themselves of liberal liberties to have laws and administration modified to suit their interests. We should then be as far from story book liberalism as we are now and as we have always been. The same tendency to create maladjustments, and the same inabilities to effect readjustments, would still be manifest.

The obvious conclusion emerging from any searching inquiry into the possibilities of maintaining adequate adjustments and prompt readjustments in anything but a pioneer, frontier economy is that this must be a supreme feat of social management or government. Its performance has to be the function, professional pride, and self-interest of a political leadership of the nation. To achieve readjustability under liberalism we would have to restore the frontier.

CHAPTER IX

PLANNING: A PROBLEM IN VALUE CHOICES

It is hoped that the discussion of the preceding eight chapters leaves the larger question of the workability of the liberal capitalist system as well answered in the negative as it can reasonably be expected that such a question could be answered in a few chapters and in advance of the only conclusive verdict, that of history. After all, the unworkability of the present system is only a premise or a hypothesis which, in the light of current events, seems to have strong probabilities of being proved entirely correct by future events. It is a necessary premise for the building of a successor system, without which we shall be badly off if, and as, the proofs of the unworkability of liberal capitalism continue to accumulate.

Assuming, then, as proved sufficiently for our purpose, the proposition that liberal capitalism is unworkable, or that it no longer meets satisfactorily the imperatives of public order in the present situation, What are the order imperatives to be met by a successor system? and, What are the probable choices in the development of a successor system?

No one idea or principle can be called central or paramount in any enterprise as vast as that of erecting a new civilization on the ruins of an old one. But, for the purpose of making a quick intellectual approach to this enterprise, as a present day undertaking, no word could carry the mind farther than that of planning.

Social planning is the outstanding imperative of public order and material abundance in the present day and in the near future. Of course, nothing makes it certain that the world will enjoy order and abundance in the coming era. Wells and Spengler see chaos ahead. Fascism sees no inevitable millennium but merely says, "Given existing conditions in the leading capitalist countries, here is a formula for order and abundance which can be made to work and which most people can be made to like."

As for the questions, "What is fascist planning?" or "What is the fascist plan?" it must be answered that whatever fascism, or the modern executive state, becomes and does, in any given country and period, results from a combination of the requirements for successful management of the productive and cultural factors, from the ideal of a social scheme cherished by the leaders of the discontented élite who seize political power and, of course, from the play of the innumerable and complex factors of the world situation. This is why one cannot express the fascist scheme in the language either of liberalism, or communism, or any other system based on the assumption that it possesses a monopoly of absolute truth.

The liberal scheme rests on the ideology of supposedly eternal and absolute truths. These truths are but verbalisms, like equality before the law, freedom of contract, democratic self-government, fair competition, just compensation, and so on. They sound impressive to the masses, who cannot possibly explain what these verbalisms mean in terms which harmonize the official definitions with the definitions furnished by daily experience.

The fascist scheme of things is an expression of human will which creates its own truths and values from day to day to suit its changing purposes. The logic of liberalism is that of organizing and conducting society according to revelation. Before the French Revolution and the conquest of English puritan liberalism by late 18th century Continental rationalism, truth was supposed to be revealed by God. Since Rousseau and Tom Paine, truth has been supposed to be revealed by reason. Whereas the medium of God was one's conscience if one was a Protestant, and God's vicar on earth if one was a Roman Catholic, the medium of reason in the American liberal commonwealth has been supposed to be the courts. Like the priests of the ancient cults who were ready to say, what God or the oracle revealed, the American courts are supposed to be ready to say what the Constitution and reason reveal through them to the human mind at large. If five of the nine judges agree on the revelation, that makes it binding.

Fascism, on the other hand, starts out from a situation of fact and a human will to do something about it, whether to alter it or to preserve it. As a triumphant force, fascism is essentially an expression of the human will reacting to the changing situations of life in the eternal struggle for existence. Like all forces which are revolutionary in their beginning, it starts out as an expression of the human will to change a given situation to some other desired pattern. Truth, right, justice, and reason are whatever serves the fulfillment of this purpose.

It may be said that the fascist plan is what the people want or what the leaders want. But it must be said that fascist planning is the way to get it. Fascism triumphs because it is, among other things, a formula of fulfillment, which people are happy to turn to from the liberal formulas of defeat, frustration, and inhibition both of governmental and private initiatives—in the fast crystallizing post-War situation. Liberalism today means millions of individuals who cannot do anything about some of their most vital personal problems, such as finding work and a place in the scheme of things—they can no longer go west or migrate—and governments which, because of legal and customary inhibitions, cannot do anything adequate about these great social maladjustments. Fascism may do the wrong things but it is not inhibited from doing anything. The chief plank in the social or political platform of most of the conservatives today can be summed up in the one word inhibition—inhibition of government, inhibition of the underprivileged, inhibition of anything in the nature of a vital plan of a nation.

To talk fascism, communism, or 19th century liberalism, of course, is to talk a different language in each case. For that reason many people will have difficulty in understanding this book, which does not reason from many customary assumptions. It is written in the sanguine hope that a few people will be able to understand the language of a system of concepts and purposes which, though different from that of their early mental formation, is not in conflict with their fundamental interests. The usual tendency of the mind in this respect is to try to reduce the content of another ideological system, like liberalism, fascism or communism, to the language of one's own system. When this tendency is not successfully repressed, the values of one system get transmuted, by the processes of translation into another language, from virtues to vices, from rationalities to monstrosities.

Thus, in the language of communism, a small storekeeper, or a farmer hiring a few helpers and working twelve or fourteen hours a day to make a pitiful living and raise a family, is a dirty bourgeois or capitalist oppressor. And, of course, the liberal prints these days are full of choice and violent epithets for things and personalities fascist or communist. What fascists regard as an ennobling love of country, translated into the liberal language becomes mass hysteria. What fascists cherish as social discipline, translated into the liberal language becomes tyranny—and so it goes.

Two simple but profound and fundamental notions are essential to any understanding of planning, or fascism, or communism, as well as to the formulation of any new social system. The first notion is that any social system represents a given scheme or hierarchy of ultimate values, or group and personal objectives, the upholding of which is one of the chief duties of man, the State, and social institutions generally. The second notion is that these ultimate values cannot be validated by the processes of logic or by reason. These two notions are especially important in connection with planning, because the important choices to be made lie mostly in the field of ultimate values, or of ends rather than means.

Contrary to much of the current misrepresentation both of fascism and communism, there is, in the matter of techniques or the choice of means, little difference between liberalism, fascism, and communism. This is true because similar tasks, when undertaken in similar situations and against similar obstacles, are pursued under liberalism, fascism, or communism with similar means, techniques, or policies.

The liberal states in time of peace are free of many of the repressive measures of fascism and communism. But, in time of war, they use quite similar measures, and fascist and communist revolutions are distinctly war phases, just as the English, American and French Revolutions were war phases of an emerging liberalism. The liberal revolutions are over—so is liberalism. Cromwells no longer behead kings and sack Dublins, and the guillotine is no longer working out on the public squares of Paris the liberal ideals of Liberty, Equality and Fraternity. The fascist and communist revolutions, however, are still in course, which does make a difference.

It will be found that the techniques of an American, Russian, Italian or German steel-mill foreman, bridge builder, machine-gun company commander, or army air-bomber will vary intentionally very little where the task is similar. These differences, more imaginary than real, are quite like the differences between German and other brands of militarism during the War. The one differs from the other chiefly in that the one is a little more or less efficient. Before the American army went into the trenches in 1917, our officers attended British and French schools in trench warfare, gas warfare, tank warfare and bayonet drill. It never occurred to any sane American to suggest that we show the Germans good American fighting methods of the days of George Washington, Andrew Jackson, or Grant and Lee. The fact that we may have to follow in the present crisis certain European precedents in economic planning, just as we followed European experience in 20th century warfare, will merely indicate that certain European nations got into the economic crisis ahead of us, just as they got into the late World War before us.

Today one may almost say that there are no peculiarly American or European methods of social or political management. There are just good and bad methods, or apt and inept methods, or modern and obsolete methods. There is nothing in the

American tradition to warrant the conclusion that, in meeting the challenge of new conditions, the American way is inept instead of apt, or obsolete instead of modern. In the social or political field we have some vigorous defenders of the obsolete against the up-to-date, but, influential as many of these defenders are, they will have a hard time proving by events that good Americanism consists in being behind the times. America cannot forever remain 17th and 18th century in its law, and political and social theory and practice, while moving in the vanguard of 20th century technological progress. The defenders of 18th century Americanism are doomed to become the laughing stock of their own countrymen. Americans are no more given to conservatism, backwardness, or timidity than any other people, but rather, less, if anything.

What differentiates different social systems, most of which are trying to make the most efficient use of the same machinery and techniques in the maintenance of some scheme of social order, is differences in values, or objectives, or tasks undertaken, with, of course, some differences due to different specific situations, or difficulties to be overcome, in the pursuit of given sets of objectives. There are no real disbelievers in planning—certainly not Mr. Hoover or Mr. Mellon. There are only disbelievers in certain plans and planning by the other fellow.

We have a wide range of values or objectives for national planning from which to make choices. As for techniques or instruments, we are unlimited as to their use except by the indications of suitability to the end. We have less to gain from a study of European precedents in planning than from analysis of our own problems. A discussion of planning for America must assume a set of values, and explore the possibilities of their realization and the possible means to this end. If, in this discussion, it be assumed that one of our values should be a type of racism which excludes certain races from citizenship, then the plan of execution should provide for the annihilation, deportation, or sterilization of the excluded races. If, on the contrary, as I devoutly hope will be the case, the scheme of values will include that of a national citizenship in which race will be no qualifying or disqualifying condition, then the plan of realization must, in so far as race relations are concerned, provide for assimilation or accommodation of race differences within the scheme of smoothly running society.

It cannot be stressed too much that in the field of choices of ultimate values or objectives lie the issues most to be studied, clarified and debated. I have said that ultimate values cannot be validated or proved good or desirable, or the opposite, by the processes of logic. I am often asked why I try to talk or write rationally about ultimate values if they cannot be validated or proved good or bad by reason. My answer is an easy and adequate one to make: Rational statement, analysis, clarification, and comparison of values are useful for two reasons: First, values are realized, made to triumph, or enforced, through the instrumentality of reason. That is, if you know what you want, reason will help you to get it if it can be had. And, second, values can be clarified and compared only by the processes of reason. What many people, trained in 18th century rationalism, cannot understand, is that there is a difference between the rational clarification, comparison and implementation of a scheme of values, and the rational demonstration that that scheme is good or bad.

In connection with the problems of planning, it is important to dispose of the popular notion that social planning is purely an engineering or technical feat which will be ideally performed by experts, if supplied adequately with facts by fact-finding agencies, and with funds by the taxpayers, or by some endowed foundation. This notion of 18th century rationalism not only assumes that reason is normative instead of being merely instrumental, or the tool of the will and of our emotional drives; but it also regards facts as ascertainable absolutes or truths.

Such notions about the nature and function of reason are among the prepossessions of formal logic. The logician is supposed to wait for the scientist to bring him, done up in neat bundles, the facts for his premises. The logician then pours the facts into his little machine and turns the crank, whereupon truth and error, justice and injustice, right and wrong, come out the other end duly separated and graded like different grades of milk and cream issuing from a cream separator. This notion is one of the basic assumptions made by American jurisprudence as to the function of the courts. It also underlies the logical structures of most of the liberal social sciences.

As the scientist well knows, facts have to be selected according to purposes, or preconceived theories and intuitions, or hunches, or, more definitely, according to the conclusion or verdict which it is desired to reach, or according to the hypothesis it is desired to build up. The greatest scientists recognize that there can be no scientific observation without a previous theory or intuition. Furthermore, as we have already seen, facts are merely the ways in which things experienced or observed appear to different persons. And facts have a charming way of nearly always seeming as they should seem in order to prove some given preconceived theory or conclusion.

Then, too, there is the great limiting consideration that, even if several observers see the same data alike, or agree as to what the facts are, and if they are indifferent as to the conclusion (as natural scientists ordinarily are and as social scientists ordinarily are not) it always remains true that no group of observers can ever observe everything or get all the facts about any matter.

Contrary to the charges of many critics (See Bertrand Russell's article on "The Revolt Against Reason" in *Harper's Magazine*, February, 1935), fascism is not anti-intellectual or antirational. On the contrary, it uses observed fact and logical deduction quite as well as liberalism. Fascism, however, unlike liberalism, does not regard the processes of reason as a game which one must suppose to be played in a certain way and which one must play in a different way. The fascist recognizes that when the fact finders have dumped a series of facts about a given matter into the hopper of a law court, a theorist, or an administrative expert, they have merely supplied a limited number of observations selected with some purpose in mind other than that of pure truth—assuming there is such a thing.

Besides, the fascist does not assume that the truth, all the truth, and nothing but the truth, can ever be known about anything. The will that dictates the purpose in the gathering and submission of facts, and in the logical use made of them, must also, grosso modo, determine the conclusion, verdict or result. Thus we see, in communist Russia, that there is one law for the member of the communist party and another law for the capitalist, just as, in capitalist America, there is one justice for the rich and another for the poor in the vast majority of situations in which law is an important factor. Legal advice how to get around the law, or due process of law to beat the law, is to be bought. The more a man can spend on the law and its due process, the less difficulty it will cause him, and the more he can get away with. The social plan expresses the will and purposes of the dominant classes and not the indications of absolutes or abstractions called by names like reason and justice. In a later chapter we shall explore further the power aspects of the social plan.

Reason is useful as a means to an end, and as a selector or clarifier of ends about which one is not clear. Thus, if a man demonstrates to me that he clearly understands a given value or scheme of values which he cherishes, and that he understands all the implications or consequences of that value or scheme of values which I am able to point out to him, and that he still clings to it and is prepared to pay the full price of its pursuit, I, as a rational person, must recognize that there is nothing further I can reasonably say to him to change his mind and purpose in this respect. If I am wholly rational, and not an irrational addict of a certain cult of rationalism, I will further recognize that he may be quite as rational as I in choosing and pursuing a diametrically opposite set of objectives from my own. Nothing raises more doubt of the rationality of liberal rationalists today than the frequency with which they apply terms like mad, insane, and crazy, to persons and things they dislike.

Had I been living in 15th century Spain, with my present religious views, I should have understood the futility of any appeal to reason to dissuade the heads of the Inquisition from their enterprises of religious persecution or purification of Spain of heresy. Their rational capacity was quite as good as mine, and their understanding of the implications and consequences of religious persecution was quite as complete as mine. But their premises and emotional attitudes differed from mine. If they felt that those unpleasant things they did had to be done, or those heavy prices they made Spain pay had to be paid, to save their souls and the souls of most of their compatriots, and that saving souls as they understood it was the most important thing in life (as undoubtedly they felt with all sincerity and deep intensity), what could be said to them in the name of reason to alter their conviction? Obviously, nothing. A really rational mind will size up such a situation as presenting, broadly stated, four possibilities: (1) Become a convert; (2) be a martyr; (3) fight and win; (4) fight and lose. If the decision be to fight, the reason will be found useful as an instrument. If the decision be for conversion or martyrdom, the reason may be found somewhat of a nuisance, though converts and martyrs usually have their reason well under control. The decision will, in any event, be determined by emotional attitudes and impulses rather than the reason.

What is most needed today in the discussion of a plan for America is rational clarification of values or social objectives. Many people who think they cherish a value can be made to repudiate and abhor it completely by being made, through the processes of reason, to see its implications. What most people cherish, after all, is a set of verbalisms, some of which, of course, stand for values they would die for, but most of which are just meaningless symbols to which their emotional responses have been conditioned to react in certain ways, but which their understanding never even attempts to grasp. Thus, if a man says that he is ready to shed the last drop of American blood, including his own, to uphold a decision of the League of Nations, or the World Court, or to maintain the present status quo in Europe, or to keep the Japanese out of the Philippines, I realize that I have nothing to say to him on these questions. If, however, as is most often the case, he is just a muddle-headed believer in international justice and coöperation, or the white man's burden, who has never grasped the consequences of any serious espousal of a cause flying one of these verbal banners, then he is open to an appeal to reason. It is possible to make him reject his value not by rational invalidation but by rational clarification of the value. But some people know what they want and still want it—a fact which many liberals have difficulty in understanding.

What makes so many people tiresome as well as mischievous in the discussion of issues of values is their persistence in attempting to argue on premises the other fellow does not and will not accept. That is their notion of an appeal to reason. Because fascists reject that sort of appeal to reason, they are often accused of being anti-rational or anti-intellectual. Now, a conflict between two nations, or two economic groups, or two persons, can often be averted by making one or both parties see clearly the implications or consequences of maintaining his position. But conflict is rather hastened than averted by one or both parties trying to make the other accept his values or his premises by an appeal to reason.

Using reason to clarify momentous social values and their consequences finally brings the choice of alternatives down to one of fight or make concessions. The attempt to evade this final issue by making the other fellow see that God, reason, justice, right, or whatever else the word invoked may be, is on one's side, never averts the fight but rather exasperates the other fellow, and makes him all the more eager to fight. In the discussion of values or social objectives, it is useful to be clear as to what one wants and what the other fellow wants, and also to find out at what point either party will fight. Taking this view of the issue will usually produce more concessions on both sides than a futile appeal to justice or reason to support one's scheme of values. Certainly, the American Civil War could have been averted had both sides talked constantly in terms of fight or concede. Both sides could have made enough concessions to make fighting unnecessary. But neither side could convince the other that it had God, the Constitution, justice, right, or reason on its side.

In the coming clash between the haves and the have-nots, or between the embattled bond-holders and the frustrated élite of the lower middle classes, a new formula on the basis of mutual concessions is possible. But the appeal by either side to the Constitution, justice, right, reason, or Americanism is not going to avert what must be an irrepressible conflict if neither side is prepared to make concessions. In this issue, obviously, most of the concessions will have to be made by the haves. But they should be reminded that in life-and-death conflicts of interest and principle the final choices are always concessions or throat-cutting. And, before they say their last word against making concessions, they should measure carefully their probable chances in the long run, if conflicts of economic interests finally come to an issue of arms.

CHAPTER X

PLANNING: THE FORCE FACTOR

In the preceding chapter, in opening up the topic of national planning as one of the order imperatives indicated by the present situation, we saw the importance of ultimate values as subjects for discussion, choice, and realization, in connection with any national plan. In this chapter we shall stress the force aspect of national planning. For it is this phase of planning which draws the heaviest fire of critics of fascism, and it is a refusal to see the inevitability of the force factor in the realization of social values which condemns most reformers to futility. A few of the main points of this emphasis may be summarized at the outset.

First, social situations represent always a balance of power, or of the resultants of mighty pressures bearing upon every individual. It may be said that the social situation rests on consent only if it assumed that those who are powerless against the coercion applied consent to what they do not like but cannot alter. Except for marked deviates, who are the exceptional cases, individuals tend to behave as the resultants of force pressures brought to bear upon them may be expected to make them behave in given situations or cases. In other words, there has never been a free society in which men and women enjoyed sovereignty over their choices or conduct. The free society which serves as the premise of so much liberal attack on fascism is the ideal of philosophical anarchy, and not the reality of any society that ever was.

Second, all government, liberal, no less than fascist or communist, has to be a monopoly of force and violence, or, as one great statesman once called it, a perpetual conspiracy of power. The chief objective of this conspiracy is everywhere today, and usually has been in times past, the realization of a given scheme of social values which were both rationalized and cherished by those in power. Much present-day liberal criticism of fascism or the authoritarian State implies, when it does not actually make the charge, that the non-liberal States correspond to no social philosophy, to no moral imperatives, to no collective ideals, but merely to the caprice of the given dictator or governing oligarchy in power.

These implications or charges must seem absurd if one takes a calm view of demonstrations of support given to these governments by millions of people, whom it is not reasonable to assume insane or hypnotized by a single man or a small group of men. It serves no useful intellectual purpose to call what I like liberty, and what I dislike license, or to say, when the law suits me, that there is not coercion but freedom, and, when the law does not suit me, that it is coercive and oppressive. These tricks of argument or propaganda merely amount to saying that government is coercive only when it coerces me or when it coerces others in ways of which I disapprove. If I do not approve of the values or social objectives of a government, why not say so, instead of saying that I do not approve of coercion and that I love freedom? Every one disapproves of certain coercions and wants certain liberties, all of which merely proves that the ultimate value is the thing.

Third, the more complex the technical scheme of social organization, that is to say, the more machines and techniques there are in use, especially in the economic processes, the more of government is required in order to realize the social plan or public order. Robinson Crusoe could enjoy all sorts of liberties from government coercion, but he was deprived of all sorts of advantages which are only possible under a system of complex governmental coercion. Government coercion is not a function of a dictator's caprice or of the malevolence of certain people under any system. It is a function of the complexity and interdependence of the ruling scheme of social organization.

Fourth, coercion of human conduct, whether by organized government or the blind play of impersonal forces and fortuitous events, cannot have a quantitative measurement which is either valid or useful. We cannot demonstrate scientifically that there is more or less freedom or coercion under any one of the three systems, capitalism, fascism, and communism, than there is under the other. Under any one of the three systems we can point out different liberties and different coercions, or liberties and coercions for different classes. But how can we measure the liberties of American millionaires and high ranking officials of the fascist parties or the communist party? And what is the quantity of coercion represented by the plight of twenty-five million Americans who are forced to accept a charity which humiliates them and does not properly take care of them, or of eleven million negroes who are forced to accept a status which is understood not to make them entirely happy, or of an indeterminate number of politically proscribed persons in Germany, Italy or Russia? What is the scientific coercion and liberty meter which gives the American, Russian and German indexes of liberty and coercion? It cannot be the subjective expressions of feeling of those who speak for one class of the proscribed to which they belong and not for all the insulted and injured of the world.

Fifth, it is the total social result or situation, from the point of view of a given individual or a given group, which furnishes the only satisfactory subject for evaluation and comparison so far as social conditions are concerned. The force factors are instrumental in every social scheme.

Sixth, the inevitable uniqueness of a social plan for a given nation at a given moment makes coercion necessary to realize that plan. Many people nowadays seem to reason that, inasmuch as planning is a new discovery—which it is not—and a good thing—which is purely a question of the plan and the point of view—the more plans, planners and planning, the better. In other words, let everybody have a hand at planning. The fact, of course, is that only one social plan can be operative in one country at one time if it is to enjoy public order. If two plans are operative in the realm of deeds, and not merely in the realm of dreams, speculations and wishes—the realm of liberal reformers and socialists—it may be said civil war is either in course or in active preparation. The uniqueness of liberal capitalism as the operating system of one country at one time is best exemplified in the law of property.

The reasons why a given nation can have only one social plan operative at a time seem too obvious, on careful thought, to need any elaboration. Briefly, it may be said that the reasons are much the same as the reasons why traffic must keep either to the right or the left and not follow the individual preferences of drivers. There can be no social order if every individual reserves, and exercises freely, the right to make certain choices according to his own preferences rather than according to the dictates of a unique social plan of the community in which he lives. Our Supreme Court, in ruling on a citizenship case, has held that even a woman wishing to become a naturalized American citizen may not take the oath of allegiance with the reservation that in the matter of fighting for her country she will obey the voice of conscience instead of the voice of the state. Freedom of conscience under liberal capitalism has never been an absolute freedom.

No minority, religious, racial, or cultural, can be allowed to inculcate doctrines or impart social attitudes violently inconsistent with social order. For, after all, social order, and not individual or group self-expression, must be the highest ultimate value of any social plan. Individual or group self-expression in ways incompatible with social order is simply another term for social anarchy. This does not mean that different races, religions, and groups, may not be allowed to flourish and maintain certain group peculiarities, provided none of their peculiarities seriously jeopardize the social plan. To hear many liberals talk these days, one would suppose that the end of social organization was to make the world safe for minority self-expression. Certainly Christianity, when in political control, whether through the Roman Catholic Church or any one of the Protestant sects, has never followed this principle, nor did the Jews when they were a nation.

To say that individual self-expression should be the major objective of the social plan, but that such expression must not infringe any of the rules of the social plan, is merely to say, in different words, the same thing fascism, or, for that matter, every other social order, has said in some form or other. The imperatives of social order always fix the limits of individual self-expression. And the imperatives of social order have always to be interpreted or made explicit by someone other than the person who violates them. Whether a crowned king, a gowned judge or an executive committee, called by whatever name it may be, has the last word as to what the imperatives of social order demand in the way of limitation of individual self-expression, the facts remain that these imperatives always impose restrictions on human conduct, these imperatives are always interpreted by a few persons in power and not by every citizen for himself, and these imperatives are always interpreted and enforced with a view to the realization of some given social scheme.

Liberal teaching constantly raises the question whether the individual may express himself contrary to the order imperatives of the social system, but liberal practice never allows that question to become a real issue. The individual under liberalism, as under every other system, is perfectly free to say and do what may be considered safe by those in power. The only real issue, so far as the concepts of freedom or the right to individual self-expression may be concerned, is one of fact rather than one of principle. It is always an issue how much latitude those in power can and do allow to individual conduct, or how large is the list of safe things to say and do. Contrary to the implications of liberal argument and propaganda, there is no issue between a system which allows what it considers unsafe utterances and acts, and a system which does not allow such utterances and acts. The issue or choice is always between the fact of one ruling class which has one field of safe utterances and acts, and the fact of another ruling class which has another field of safe utterances and acts.

The idea to stress at this time in the interests of larger tolerance or more freedom is that great differences in forms of self-expression are necessary to accommodate widely different human personalities. The case for tolerance is only good when grounded on the factual basis of the widely divergent requirements of different personalities—of personalities whose differences can never be eliminated by education, indoctrination, or any sort of conditioning. It is not necessary in the interests of public safety, and it is altogether bad from the point of view of efficient social mechanics, to try to force an intellectual whose taste runs to unitarianism or some cult of modernist ethical teaching, and another person with a different make-up who finds an elaborate mass or an old-fashioned revival meeting best suited to his spiritual needs, to accept a standardized religious service or to forego any religious service whatever. Nor is it necessary to force lovers of grand opera and jazz, or lovers of Proust and Elinor Glynn, to accept a standard form of dramatic musical or literary entertainment. It is necessary only to prevent the pulpit, the press, or any associational activity, from being used by leaders in ways to defeat the national plan.

To those who boast of the tolerance shown by liberal capitalism to minorities, to different religions or to divergent opinions, it has only to be recalled that we did not tolerate polygamy among the Mormons, and that we do not tolerate thousands of religious practices which are as old as history. Our liberal order tolerates many widely divergent teachings, it is true, but definitely draws the line against many teachings and public utterances. In war time, for instance, it does not tolerate appeals from the pulpit to men in uniform to obey the commandment "Thou shalt not kill." The reasons why utterances or actions dangerously subversive of public order are tolerated nowhere needs no explanation.

It remains to perfect formulas for the tolerance of safe differences of ways, safe preferences and safe expressions of opinion or criticism. And it is desirable, for reasons which the liberals have excelled at pointing out, to have the area of tolerance as broad and inclusive as possible. But there must be no nonsense about tolerance in an absolute or unlimited sense. Such nonsense will not help tolerance today. In times of war and revolution, those in authority often err grievously in exaggerating the requirements of safety. To correct these errors, it will not be found helpful to assert absolutes which are wholly untenable in honest discussion and impossible of application by a social order which aims to survive. It will rather be helpful to the enlargement of tolerance to attempt to distinguish realistically between what is safe and what is unsafe, in a given situation, for the maintenance of a given set of values. It may be safe to allow a fundamental discussion of values which is critical of some of them, or an exposure of evils or mistakes, or the gibe of a vaudeville comedian or a popular cartoonist against the government. It may not be safe, however, to allow ministers of religion to incite to civil disobedience or nonconformity with state-dictated standards of conduct.

The right formula, or the ideal balance between repression and tolerance, can best be sought if the mind is freed of liberal norms, or impossible and nearly meaningless verbalisms, such as free speech, free press, freedom of conscience, and so forth, and if an attempt is made quite simply to determine the minimum of governmental repression compatible with safety for a given plan in a given situation. This formula will have to rely mainly on executive judgment and responsibility rather than on juridical norms and judicial interpretation and enforcement.

For public safety has highly elastic requirements varying enormously according to the place, moment, total situation, and scheme of values, to be realized. Any charter of liberties becomes necessarily an absurdity after a few years, for no plan of public order and means to its realization can long be appropriate to changing conditions. If the theory of verbal norms and judicial interpretation and application be followed, the fundamental law, or the highest social ideals or objectives, will soon be lost sight of in the development of a juridical science or static scheme of ideas and practices which will quickly try to free itself of the nuisances of reality and try to operate entirely within a closed realm of logic—a logic that assumes the realities it requires for its purposes and disregards any refractory realities of experience.

Only an executive can insure the widest measure of tolerance, and he can do this only if he has the widest power to adjust formulas to changing conditions. And, after all, what is safe for the maintenance of public order can only be determined from day to day by a central authority charged with the responsibility of maintaining order. If the lovers of tolerance would only see that tolerance is not an absolute which the state can give or withhold in any quantity it sees fit, quite independently of imperatives of the ruling scheme of values, but that tolerance has always to be fitted into a workable and unique plan of social order, they would concern themselves more with the problems of choosing the plan and making it effective, and less with categorical demands for more tolerance.

The explicitness of government uses of force, and the noticeability of sudden change in the application of force for the achievement of new or different objectives, make state exercises of power, call them what you will, the subject of considerable misrepresentation and misconception where a new social system like communism or fascism is involved. The more governed by political government a community is, the more recognizable will be the force factors, but not necessarily the more coercive. The reason, let it be emphasized, is not that human conduct is more subject to coercion or less free, in the aggregate or on the average, where there is more government or a new social scheme. The reason is that, to whatever extent government purposively coerces to realize given social objectives, the coercion has to be explicit and vested with the personality which attaches to government (e.g. The State versus John Doe). Such coercion is more explicit than that of the pressures of impersonal and anonymous forces over which the individual can have little or no control, and of the operation of which he ordinarily has little understanding.

It may be said that the coercion most keenly felt is the most important or oppressive. To this it need only be answered that where the coercions of government, social custom, or economic necessity, are of long standing and efficient application, the people subject to them are no more conscious of them than habitual motorists are conscious of frustration by traffic lights, or than habitual travellers in the subways and elevators are conscious of claustration in these unnatural and, often, extremely uncomfortable modes of transportation. Those who accept without conscious resentment the discomfort of crowded subways or elevators feel amply compensated by the superior speed and facility of transportation thus afforded them. They do not discuss subways or elevators in terms of claustrophobia, as many liberals discuss government in terms of liberty and constraint, or in terms wholly irrelevant to the points of paramount public interest in the thing discussed.

When the coercions of government or custom take a new turn, as a result of revolutionary change in social objectives, they naturally have the faults of newness, of a new shoe, for instance. To these faults are, of course, to be added those of inefficient and inexperienced application by new personnel in government. A small business or professional man in this country whose very livelihood had always depended on his most servile yessing of his economic dictators in the market, might well consider it an outrageous tyranny if a new set of superiors dictating new social imperatives were suddenly added, by the inauguration of a fascist régime, to those already in authority and power over him. If any one is here disposed to interpose the reminder that under the present system one is free to choose one's boss, one's customer, or one's banker, I can only take time to say in reply, "Tell it to the unemployed and the farmers who are on the dole."

One of the strongest arguing and operating points of liberal capitalism has always been the fact that its most vital and often its harshest coercions, those of economic necessity, under a given régime of property distribution and deprivation, legally enforced with the might of the State, have been applied with impersonality, anonymity, and a large measure of irresponsibility. If a man loses his job, home, or business, through changes he could not control, he is supposed to have no one but himself to blame. For, although the acts of others in power, whether in government or big business, may have contributed largely or almost entirely to his misfortune, there is no one in power with any significant degree of responsibility for the consequences of his economic or political acts. So far as the running of business or finance is concerned, most people today are pretty well disposed to concede this point without argument. For there are few corporation or bank stockholders who are foolish enough to cherish the illusion that their property rights give them any real control over those who manage their property.

So far as the running of government is concerned, however, the delusion of 18th century theories of political democracy, plausible only in the days when the town meeting could be an important factor, still persist. Thus it may be said that the economic misfortunes of the United States were duly charged up to the Republican Party in the results of the elections of 1932. But, if one looks at all below the surface of political changes, one must see that the defeat of a political party or candidate can be called a punishment only in a highly qualified sense. It can never be said to amount to a real conviction of misconduct, negligence, or even bad judgment. In most cases, individuals pass out of political life for reasons wholly unconnected with any expression of public censure, however much their acts may be considered censurable or even censured by a majority vote at the polls. The way the system works, every important political and economic figure has a good alibi for public opinion, and a perfect immunity for legal purposes, so far as the consequences of his acts may be concerned.

Our attachment to the liberal principle of separation of powers, and our liberal hostility to coördination of authority and a permanent governing class, necessarily make for irresponsibility in the use of power—political or economic. It is only in the fields of specific offenses against the State, the person, and property, or fields chiefly covered by the criminal law and the laws of torts, that personal responsibility can, as a practical matter, be enforced to any significant extent. As for the responsibility which is supposed to be implicit in our electoral system, it is farcical, due to the way the system necessarily operates.

For example, a governor of a state may direct the militia and police, and the powers of his office, in ways to prevent labor from making an effective use of economic weapons like the strike and the picket, thus materially contributing to the imposition on thousands of mine or factory workers of an economic status more unfavorable than that which they might win if allowed by the governor a freer use of certain economic weapons at their command. He may also appoint members to a state public service regulation commission, a factory inspection service, or a bank superintendent, who will give the utilities, the manufacturers, and the bankers, regulation pretty much as they like it. This governor of the Tweedledum Party is finally beaten at the polls by the gubernatorial candidate of the Tweedledee Party, who, in the campaign, exploits the partiality of his rival the Tweedledum governor to the mine owners, factory owners, and employers generally.

Does this electoral result mean that any significant measure of political responsibility has been established thereby? Not in the least. The outgoing governor of the Tweedledum Party is not sent off to shiver in a petty governmental function in Alaska, or to sweat in a similar function in Panama or the Philippines. Oh, no; he goes back to the practice of law, to cash in on the policies for which he has been punished by defeat. His punishment takes the form of increased professional income, all legitimately and honorably supplied him by the interests he so faithfully served while in office. And the incoming governor of the Tweedledee Party continues the same partiality to the same interests, for he, too, is a lawyer who has to think of making an honest living when, sooner or later, he has to go back to private life. He, therefore, uses his term in office to build up good will and friendships among those who can be his best paying clients when he leaves office.

It is no meaningless coincidence that about seventy per cent of the men in Congress are lawyers. It is the calling which makes the political pay-off easiest to give and to take with perfect legality and decorum. The law, however, is not the only calling in which the pay-off is easy.

It is not strange that there are so few cases of technical graft in political office judicially established. It is strange that there are so many, when the payment of graft in legal and conventionally proper ways is so easy. What makes it easy, primarily, is the simple fact that almost every official in office is constantly thinking of business or professional opportunities when he leaves office. Often, the official in office has interests which can be legally and properly helped while he is still in office. If one undertook to compile the concrete examples of what is being said somewhat generally in these paragraphs, one would be writing the case histories of tens of thousands of American political careers, including those of Presidents and chief justices of the Supreme Court, where the on-again, off-again, make-a-million-in-the-interval tradition has been duly established.

In making these obvious observations about our political customs, it is only fair to remark that nothing said here should be taken as expressing a personal censure of American Presidents, Supreme Court justices, and public officials of all ranks, who have followed our good traditions. In England and other liberal countries, of course, it is a tradition that a judge may not return to the private practice of law. In those countries, civil service and public service traditions much closer to those of fascism or an authoritarian state have been developed. We, however, have been more faithful to the authentic liberal prepossessions against a governing class. We have carried liberalism in this respect to its logical extreme or a practical absurdity. But no one is to blame for doing what is both legal and good form.

Political responsibility of any significant sort is possible only under a system in which political officials, at least of the executive and judicial branches, with few exceptions, have only a public career open to them once they have put their hand to the plough. It is not punishment or censure to be beaten for a ten- or twenty-thousand-dollar-a-year public office, the expenses of which are much greater, to take up a hundred-thousand-dollar-a-year law practice or position as an official in a corporation, working for the interests one has favored while in office. And it is not to be expected that the average office-holder, while in office, can fail to be influenced in his official acts by consideration of what will be good for his future personal livelihood.

In this connection, it is also to be remarked that public opinion in this country tends to rank a man in his profession or business according to the amount of money he makes and leaves behind him. Under liberal capitalism, it may be said that for the vast majority of cases, the only real sense of responsibility which operates strongly on official conduct is that of behaving so that a good law practice, job, or money making proposition, will be waiting for the official—within the law and good usages—when he has to leave public office, as our traditions demand that he must do—with a few exceptions in the cases of judgeships for life.

Not only is irresponsibility a result of non-professional government, or rather government by men whose profession is making money at the law or something else, but corruption and incompetence are also inevitable concomitants of such a system. The bitter truth is that the majority of the American people feel definitely that government is a graft or a racket for most office holders, and rather admire the successful for getting away with as much as they can without getting caught. The system, by making certain types of corruption of public officials legal and proper, makes the corruption of mass standards of honesty inevitable.

The other result is that of an incompetence which is also inevitable if few public officials are allowed to acquire the experience and expertness which only a lifetime devotion to one profession can give. It is a deplorable blindness, and one of the products of liberal indoctrination, that the people believe that public interest can best be maintained by ever so often giving a new gang of ambitious lawyers a chance through public office to get experience, contacts, and good will, to enable them to get ahead later on.

The point, of course, of this lengthy and digressive discussion of a peculiar phase of American liberal government is that power over the destinies of the people is exercised under our system by individuals quite as much as under any so-called authoritarian system of national planning, but that the operation of our present system tends to make all exercises of power, whether economic or political, largely irresponsible.

Fascist planning does not involve the introduction of force as a new principle, and quantitative measurements of coercion and freedom are impossible. Any new scheme of planning has to be pursued with the power of the state. It is essential to have these general principles clearly understood, both by way of answering the liberal or conservative attack on fascism as a phenomenon of coercion, in contradistinction from liberal capitalism, a system of freedom, and by way of meeting the counter proposals of innumerable schools of socialists and liberal reformers who would solve our social problems without involving themselves with the problems of government and coercion.

When planning enters the realm of reality, it enters the realm of force and coercion. And this is seen in the cases of millions who are forced to suffer privation and humiliation under liberal capitalism, as well as in the cases of millions under the authoritarian systems who are forced to accept various impositions of the state plan. The idea that one social plan gives freedom while another imposes coercion is like the idea that the difference between a horse and a cow is that the one has a head while the other has a tail.

CHAPTER XI

STATE ABSOLUTISM

THE State, through the instrumentalities of government, has to express and enforce the social plan which, for one country, has to be unique. We have already seen why the social plan for any one country has to be unique. This plan the State has to express and enforce through the instrumentalities of government. The methods by which the State does this may follow the liberal formula of the policeman State or the fascist formula of the executive State. In any event, the political power of the State has to be exercised in many matters without limitation if any type of social order is to be maintained. The point is that the power exercised by the totalitarian State in economic and social planning is no greater than the power of the State exercised in other ways under any other political system, or more simply still, that the social plan always requires exercises of the absolute power of the State.

The popular type of denunciation of fascism on the ground that it stands for State absolutism, or a State of unlimited powers, as contrasted with the liberal State of limited powers, is based on misrepresentation of the true nature of the liberal State. The issue between liberalism and fascism is not one of an absolute State versus a State of limited powers. The fact is that the powers of every State are in pure theory unlimited, except by physical impossibilities and by engagements the State chooses to respect in deference to the demands of certain class interests. The powers of the fascist State are unlimited as to doing certain things, while the powers of the liberal State are equally unlimited as to doing certain other things. The important differences between fascism and liberalism in this respect lie between those certain things which each State, respectively, does without limitation, or those fields of State action in which the State is inhibited by no limiting constitutional or legal engagement not to do certain things.

Let us for a moment talk in terms of concrete examples to clarify this obvious point that State absolutism is not the issue but rather the specific applications to be made of the absolute power of the State or rather the specific interests to be favored in the unlimited uses of State power. Let us suppose that, under our liberal system, a United States marine in 1927 had applied to one of our courts praying some kind of court order restraining the President of the United States, as commander-in-chief of the armed forces of the United States, from sending this marine to kill Nicaraguans in order to carry out the pact which Mr. Stimson, personal representative of the President, made with General Moncada, a revolutionary leader at the head of an army in the field in June, 1927. This marine might have argued, with entire correctness as to fact, that the President's representative, Mr. Stimson, had no constitutional authority to make a pledge to General Moncada that the United States Government would disarm all the armed forces in Nicaragua and supervise the elections to be held over a year later in November, 1928. The marine might also have pointed out that the President of the United States is nowhere in the Constitution given power to use the armed forces of the United States to supervise elections in a foreign country, to disarm all its armed forces, and to kill all nationals of that country who might oppose with arms the presence of American troops on their territory, all without a formal declaration of war by the United States. Had the marine made any such petition to one of our liberal law courts, what would he have learned?

For one thing, he would have learned that our courts have no power to enjoin the President of the United States from sending the armed forces of the United States anywhere in the world, or from ordering them to kill other people, or to commit any other act, however arbitrary or unreasonable it might seem to be.

Let us suppose, again, that the wife, mother or other dependent of a marine killed in battle in Nicaragua had attempted to prove a claim against the United States in the Court of Claims. This is not a far-fetched supposition, as over a hundred and twenty marines were killed in battle during our war on General Sandino. What would she have been told? She would have been told that the United States Court of Claims had no jurisdiction to hear such a claim. The United States Government is wholly without legal responsibility to its own citizens for losses of life and damage to their property which any military adventure of the President with American troops may occasion abroad.

The power of the liberal State to cause its citizens to be killed either in official or unofficial warfare abroad, through exercises of the discretionary power of the President over our armed forces, is absolutely unlimited by law or the courts. But it is a bulwark of liberal liberty that the President's power to regulate commerce, or to do any one of a thousand executive acts in the public interest, must be inhibited by the Constitution or subject to judicial review for its reasonableness. The President has virtually no limitations on his power to get us into war, through the conduct of foreign relations or the command of the armed forces, except such checks as legislative action might impose through impeachment or a failure to vote necessary funds.

The features of the liberal system we are now discussing are fundamental. It is constantly forgotten that the quintessence of liberalism and liberal liberties under a constitution is the maintenance of a régime of special or exceptionally favorable considerations for private property. Briefly, private property cannot be taken for public purposes, not even in war time, without an obligation to pay just compensation, while human life may be so taken without an obligation to pay any compensation. The liberal doctrine giving property a measure of protection and bargaining power against the State denied to human life may be said to have fully emerged as a political principle of good liberalism when Cromwell sent King Charles the First of England to the block and established the rule that the King, or the executive branch of the government, cannot take the money of the rich by means of direct levies but must first have the money for the King's wars voted by Parliament, which, as a practical matter, has meant financing wars by loans instead of capital levies. This doctrine, of course, goes under a different name from that of special privilege for property. Its most popular identifying formula is "No taxation without representation." Of course, few people ever pause to inquire "Representation of whom and of what?"

The right of private property to be treated by the State with greater consideration than human life in the matter of conscription for public purposes is the essence of liberalism. This right, once established, becomes not only incompatible with the demands of humanity but also with the requisites of strong nationalism. An interesting sidelight, showing the power of this doctrine as a political principle, is the fact that good liberals before 1914 constantly speculated about the possibility of financing the next big war. But no liberal ever imagined that a war would be impossible because the State would be unable to mobilize the necessary man-power. A human life has no right to deny itself to its country, or to bargain with the State for a fair price, or have appeal to a neutral judiciary to fix for it a fair bargain with the State, according to the same theories of equity which are so extremely partial to property.

Before Cromwell's Revolution, the executive branch of the government represented by the Crown used to conduct foreign relations and make war much as it does today in all States. But the Crown, under the Stuarts, tried to collect money levies from the rich tradesmen with the same arbitrariness that it took the lives of the people for war. The 17th century English shopkeepers did not like that way of financing wars. They did not mind how many wars the Crown fought. On the contrary, they were usually favorable to, or eager for, the Crown's wars, on which they made so much money. Nor did the rich merchants at all mind putting up all the money required for the wars of the Crown on the condition that they got government obligations in return for their war contributions.

The proof that the foregoing statements about democratic

government and war are substantially true is found in the facts
that neither the British nor the American national legislature
has ever refused to vote a declaration of war on the recommen-
dation of the chief executive, to vote all the money the chief
executive has asked for, to vote compulsory levies of all the
men the executive has demanded, or to support the executive
in the continuance of the war as long as the executive saw fit
to wage it. But not once, in the long history of British and
American liberal capitalism or democracy, has a national legislature voted a levy on capital, though it has repeatedly voted
the conscription of men of fighting age.

Several counter arguments to what has just been said about
the partiality of liberalism to property may be advanced. For
one thing, it may be said that the liberties shown to be taken
by the executive branch of the government with the lives of
citizens are taken only as measures deemed necessary for national defense in an emergency like war. For another thing,
it may be said that the liberal State is not constitutionally
inhibited from taking property by taxation. (Taking property
by right of eminent domain does not furnish any rebuttal to
the point of this chapter, for property so taken must be paid
for.) And then it may be said that the property and labor of
the poorest citizen enjoys the same protection from taking
without due compensation.

It would seem almost enough to demolish these arguments to
point out that the liberal democracies have not drafted wealth
when they have drafted man power; that the poor have no
money worth mentioning to enjoy the protection of liberal
law; and that the bargaining power of labor is by no means
comparable with the bargaining power of capital under the
liberal régime. It is one of the sharpest tricks of liberal dialectics
to exploit the fact that legally a measure of protection is
enjoyed equally by the rich and the poor, or by capital and
labor. The fact, of course, always is that for large numbers of
cases equal protection of the law for property can only mean
equal justice for all the people where property is fairly evenly
distributed. Liberal equality before the law means, as a prac-

tical matter, that any two fortunes of a million dollars are approximately equal before the law.

The immunity of property from taking without just compensation is, of course, enjoyed in a legal sense quite as much by the man who has no money the State could take as by the man who has a million the State could take. Obviously, the protection of this immunity avails only to those who have enough money to be taken by the State, and whose money, as a practical matter, is taken, but in exchange for government bonds instead of the sort of compensation a conscript receives. Stripped of liberal verbiage of the law, and stated in terms of larger social results, the immunity liberalism gives to property but not to human life from taking by the State without just compensation, means that long wars result in a greater concentration of ownership of wealth, as a result of war financing by borrowing from the rich, whereas long wars would result in a drastic equalization of wealth if the funds needed were taken by levy from the only sources from which they can be taken.

It is one of the great propaganda and indoctrination achievements of the London shopkeepers and the Manchester mill owners, as well as of their American cousins, that it has been possible over a couple centuries of Anglo-Saxon liberal democracy to generalize the belief that the liberties of the people depend on the maintenance of liberal principles which operate to exempt wealth from sharing with personal service the burdens of the liberal state. It is amusing to see how poor devils who will never own anything that the State would find it worth while commandeering except their ability to serve as cannon-fodder will support a Constitution which protects capital from mobilization and social direction by the State except under conditions of profiteering by the capitalists. These poor devils do not realize that there is no clause in the Constitution which they, in their troubles, can ever invoke to check government impingement on their lives or to obtain government relief. When they turn to the Government, it is for a charity hand-out for which they can invoke no right granted them by the Constitution. Under the Constitution and under liberalism, there is a right not to have one's property taken without just compensation—i.e., compensation the courts approve of—but there is no such right for one's life, nor is there a right not to starve for want of work and lack of the instruments or facilities of production.

Indeed, what the Constitution protects is not the right of the hungry to eat but the right of the rich to keep what they have and to eat while the poor starve. Nothing augurs so impressively the end of liberalism today as the changing temper of those on relief who are coming more and more to feel and assert a vested right to be cared for by the State. To the extent the State is being forced by the demands of public order to grant relief—still on the theory of an emergency—it is creating a vested interest or a de facto right which the Constitution does not recognize and a right which a new social order must recognize.

Never was the social theory of liberalism more clearly or instructively clarified than in the Louisville Federal Housing Project decision, in which the Court held that the Federal Government is without constitutional authority to condemn private property by the right of eminent domain for slum clearance, low cost housing, or work-making projects, for such purposes are, in the opinion of the Court—i.e., the Constitution of the United States—"not public purposes."

Ours is supposedly a government of delegated powers. The Federal Constitution nowhere delegates to the Federal Government the power to take property through condemnation proceedings in exercise of the right of eminent domain. But, in the opinion of the court—i.e., the Constitution of the United States—the Federal Government, by virtue of the fact that it is a national government, must have such power. The Federal Government may exercise this power inherent in government only in accordance with the social theory of the Court—i.e., the Constitution. In the social theory of the Court, government can properly take property through condemnation proceedings for an arsenal—but not for slum clearance or low cost housing.

In the theory of the Court—i.e., the Constitution—the one is a public purpose and the other is not.

It is the same bias of 17th, 18th and 19th century liberalism, namely, that of seeking to limit the unlimited powers of the State in ways suitable to certain supposed property interests, and of making the courts the exponents of those peculiar limitations on political sovereignty. In so far as these limitations on political sovereignty have significance or effectiveness, whether in the Dred Scott decision, the Income Tax Decision, the leading child labor decisions, or a long line of decisions abridging the power of the State to modify property rights in the national interest, they almost always show the same bias.

The time has come when the limitations imposed by liberal theory on the sovereignty of the national State in respect of property rights, wealth, and economic activities generally, are no longer to be considered by a hard-thinking man of property as calculated to protect his interests in the long run. The day has come when property must no longer assert any immunity from government taking and government commanding which a poor man cannot assert for his life or labor in war time when drafted for national defense. Fascism insists that property or capital and private economic enterprise must be called to the colors as well as conscripts in time of war. And fascism insists that the term of service for both capital and labor is not for an emergency but a new and permanent scheme of social organization and operation. Fascism insists that the new social adventure cannot be conducted on the good liberal principle of having the State always buy the coöperation of the owners and managers of property, as well as of the workers, by paying the price which any economic factor is able to hold out for, in a bargain in which there is great inequality of bargaining power as between different individuals and groups.

The argument of this chapter has been that what is commonly thought of as more power over private property for the State does not mean any greater State absolutism than we have already, or, indeed, any new power over private property. It means new techniques, theories and methods in the application of State power and, also, the application of State power for the service of different interests and for the pursuit of different social objectives. In pure theory, or in concrete fact, fascism or any other political system, cannot be said to create new powers for the State or to give it powers it did not already possess. Fascism merely means that the State announces and adheres to the purpose of using the powers inherent in national sovereignty, or in the monopoly of force held by all government, to meet new needs and desires in new ways.

CHAPTER XII

THE DICTATORSHIP OF ECONOMIC NECESSITY

Fascist emphasis on a clear and realistic notion of the force factors in government, social control, or planning—three synonyms when used in this connection—is the only workable premise for humane as well as efficient undertakings in these fields. It is a favorite and basic axiom of liberalism that might does not make right. It is a self-evident fact that under the liberal, as under every other, régime, might does make right and always has made right. In this respect, a distinctive peculiarity of liberal ideologies and liberal régimes in action has been to create and lend plausibility to the fiction that force or coercion is lacking, or is operative only to a comparatively insignificant extent—chiefly in the cases of criminals and lunatics. This fiction as to right being above or independent of might has depended for much of its plausibility on that other great fiction of liberalism—freedom of contract or the free market. We shall have occasion, in passing, to mention briefly some of the more important explanations why and how these peculiar rationalizations of the liberal régime have gained such wide acceptance. But our main essay in this chapter is to show that rationalizing or explaining out of existence the real coercions or force pressures experienced in daily life under every liberal régime does not serve any good or humane purpose. Rather, it encourages unworkable and abusive policies and ways, until the latter find their inevitable correctives in the most disastrous examples of resort to force and violence which has been so scrupulously eliminated by the liberal rationalizers through the pleasant and easy processes of definition and assumption.

If the eliminators of force by definition and assumption since Versailles, could only have eliminated the depression, the class war of communism, the challenges of triumphant fascisms, and the mockery of the League of Nations, by the facts of increased armaments and the inevitable sequels of such increased armaments, their case would merit respect. As matters stand, their theses have about as much validity or relevance to current events and problems as a thesis of perpetual motion. The liberal leaders of thought and action have been talking about a world of dreams which they have done nothing effective to make come true, and which probably will never come true. They have not been talking about the world in which men have lived since the beginning of recorded history, or the world in which we, in 1935, have to live.

Much of the falseness of liberal premises, whether in ethics, politics, jurisprudence, or economics, rests on a deliberate and persistent refusal to take cognizance of force in economic necessity, or to perceive the coercion implicit in the more or less impersonally and anonymously applied pressures of given situations, whether of individuals, groups, or nations. Broadly stated, a basic premise of the liberal thesis has been, and still is, that anything done or got away with within the law does not involve a resort to force. This premise or assumption, obviously, is purely a matter of arbitrary definition to suit the purposes of propaganda. It is palpably absurd and contrary to experienced or observed fact, either as a premise for discussion or as a definition of force. The simplest explanation of why the premise is absurd and contrary to fact, is to point out that law may, and always does, provide for contests of sheer force or might. It specifically makes possible and easy ways in which the strong can use force to crush and oppress the weak. The simplest illustration of this truism of course, is that furnished by war, which it has always been lawful to declare and wage.

Now it may be granted, for sake of argument, that human welfare is better served if contests of force to determine men's fate are conducted as they are under liberal capitalism, than if they are conducted as they were in medieval Europe when private warfare was the rule and banditry of the road the prevailing custom. It may also be granted that we are better off to have fewer and bigger wars than to have more numerous and smaller wars. But, as for the propositions that the reign of liberal law has secured a type of justice (whether among individuals or nations) which insures against resort to the violence of revolution and war, or that the reign of liberal law rests any less on force than any other scheme of public order, they are palpably absurd both in the light of theoretical analysis or simple observation of what today is going on in the world. All talk about our having progressed from the reign of force and violence to the reign of law is pure moonshine. We have increased the degree of the monopoly of force and violence exercised by the national State in ways to make it one of the results that the application of force and violence by the strong against the weak takes the more complex, impersonal, and anonymous forms of the assertion of the rights of national conquest and dominion over subject peoples and lands, and of private property rights (private dominion) over the tools of production.

To define force or coercion merely as that which happens outside the law, then, serves no useful purpose, and specifically begs the questions of revolutions which succeed, and international wars. Wars and successful revolutions have surely been too frequent in the past, and are surely too probable in the near future, to make any such question-begging premise admissible in discussion. If a highwayman takes my purse at the point of a gun, everyone agrees that an act of force and violence has been committed. The significant fact about this act, of course, is that it is contrary to law.

If a rich and powerful individual or corporation uses vast economic and legal resources to levy on my daily product a heavy toll, all within the law, there is, according to liberalism, no resort to force involved. I have paid my toll through the mechanism of the "free market," or in freely made contracts. The facts that in millions of contracts under liberal capitalism one party is coerced by hunger and the other by no immediate personal necessity, or that international relationships rest mainly on rights acquired by force and violence in war, are entirely ignored by liberal theory in its definition of force and violence. If two men fight or shoot out a difference of opinion or a clash of interests or wishes, every one will agree that this constitutes a resort to force. But if two competing economic interests wage, within the law, a destructive economic competition in which one finally triumphs and the other is crushed, liberal theory recognizes no resort to force or use of violence and coercion. In fact, of course, there are for every individual winner in the economic struggle scores if not hundreds of losers.

International war is the one big fact which liberalism has had to admit some difficulty in rationalizing. The rationalizers have met this difficulty with the fiction that war is an exceptional, unusual, irregular, and abnormal state of affairs. Obviously, war is no more exceptional or abnormal than peace, either in the 20th century, A.D., or the 20th century, B.C. War and peace have always been, and still remain, the two phases of the continuing political relationships between states. When these relationships are not in the one phase, they are in the other. When these relationships are in the one phase, nations are preparing or fighting for the other phase. One can say that war is an interval between periods of peace, or that periods of peace are intervals between wars. To assume that war is exceptional is as silly as to assume that rainstorms, old age, or death, are exceptional.

Fascism finds no good purpose served by the liberal definitions of force or the liberal fictions about its character and its functions. The reasoning and facts which support this finding are fairly simple. For one thing, there is the consideration that no operating scheme can long run on assumptions which experience continually contradicts. The assumption that right, independent of might, can ever be anything but a figment of the imagination, or that might does not make right, or that a given norm of right can prevail except by might, is invariably refuted by the conflict which always follows an attempt to assert a right without might or against a superior might. Indeed, the falsity of such assumptions may be said to be proved by every standing army, every police force, every governmental act of coercion, and every war or successful revolution.

To proclaim that the decision of a judge is right because the law says so, rather than to say that it is right because the armed force of government will, if necessary, carry it out, and because the still mightier potential force of violent action by the people will sustain and not overthrow the government in such enforcement, serves no good purpose. So to falsify the true relation of force or might to right merely leads to mistakes like the American Civil War, prohibition, the Treaty of Versailles, and such disregard of inevitable reactions of strong men to frustration as so usually leads to civil war or revolution.

Once ruling classes, kings, statesmen, judges or influential leaders of opinion, begin seriously to believe that right is not might—but rather what they think, or what some written document says or is understood by them to say, or what some system of ideas and logic leads men to say, they are invariably by way of sowing the seeds of revolution and war. The theologians of the medieval Christian Church reasoned thus, and the result was the Reformation, a series of nationalistic wars and the rise of a new cultural order. Democracy is valid only in so far as it postulates and expresses in effective action the might of the people.

It is useful to think of might or force as the only ultimate or conclusive control for propositions of right and wrong, or for arguments affecting men's lives and provoking responses of men's wills. What is the sense of "X" building up a system of concepts of right or ethics to prove that "a" equals "b," if "Y" has interests or volitions which make it impossible for him to accept the premises and moral equations of that system? So far as those ethical propositions or moral values and the persons "X" and "Y" are concerned, there is but one determining factor—force. Can "X" force "Y" to accept his ethical propositions or moral values? If "X" thinks of his ethical or moral values in these terms, the results are likely to be more humane than if he thinks of his moral values as absolutes which must prevail because they are right. For if "X" thinks of his values in terms of force required to assert them, he is likely to relinquish or modify many values which will not seem worth the costs of attempting their maintenance by force. If "X" eliminates force factors from consideration on the assumption that right is above and independent of might, he is likely to assert all sorts of values or rights which will require him ultimately to fight battles and pay prices he had not envisaged.

If an attempt is made to erect a working system of duties and obligations on any other foundation than might, it not only fails, but its failure entails needless suffering and disorder. As a matter of fact, of course, liberal capitalism, no less than the medieval Christian Church, has seldom hesitated to use force to assert or realize its values. The mischief begins usually when the rationalizers of a social system, the theologians, lawyers, economists, and other learned clerks, begin exerting an influence, the net result of which is to encourage attitudes, decisions, and policies, which must lead to war or revolution on the assumption that, inasmuch as the attitudes, decisions, and policies, are right, no contrary might can prevail against them. The crime of these learned clerks is not that of committing a people to attitudes and policies which must mean war or revolution, for there will doubtless always be decisions and policies deemed by those in power, and by a majority of the people, as worth fighting and dying for. No, the crime of these learned clerks is that of deception as to the consequences of certain policies and decisions. This deception is implicit in any assumption that one's own theory of right is above might. Of course, any one who denies that might makes right never thinks or speaks of his theory of right. Instead, he merely talks of right. If the other fellow has a different notion of right, the other fellow is merely assumed to be wrong and to have no right.

As history so often shows, the trouble is that after those who reject the control of might have involved others in the assertion of a right or absolute value, these pious rationalizers of the wishes, interests, and purposes of their group as the unique right fail either to prevent the counter-assertion of an opposing might, or to lead or assist the resistance to that opposing might. These rationalizers, of course, are excellent propagandists, and something may be said for their logical position as a means of strengthening the convictions of those who already have these same convictions. But, as propagandists of the right, they are always miserable failures at proving their case to those who have conflicting interests and desires, and, hence, opposite norms of right. Once propaganda undertakes the conversion of those of opposite interests, propaganda needs nothing so much as force and coercion.

To cite a recent case in point, it may be said that at least ninety per cent of the exponents in the Allied countries of liberal ethics, law, economics, and social sciences generally, proved conclusively to themselves, and to ninety per cent of the inhabitants of the Allied countries, that the Treaty of Versailles was right and executable. But they did not prove it to the Germans. Hence all their argumentation or invocation of moral absolutes was futile, if not silly. It would have been better for humanity if, instead of following the procedure of the liberal leaders at Versailles, the greatest galaxy of liberals ever assembled, other delegates of the people had proceeded somewhat as follows: They might have outlined the same set of material objectives embodied in the Treaties. They would then not have applied to professors of law, economics and history for rationalizations of these demands. But they would have asked a council of Allied generals for a plan of ways and means to enforce the fulfillment of the desired objectives. The generals, being realists accustomed to achieving the objectives of their masters against opposition, instead of rationalizing the objectives of their masters for the approval of their masters, would have outlined a program of military intervention and occupation, the implications of which would most likely have caused a swift popular reaction among the peoples of the Allied countries.

But, assuming, as it is quite plausible to assume, that no such common-sensed reaction had immediately followed the announcement of the new war of treaty enforcement, and that the passions engendered by the war had demanded a continuance of the war, it seems evident that a few years of such a mad undertaking would have sufficed to bring the Allied peoples and governments to their senses and to renounce most of their war aims and claims. The administrative, mechanical, and economic difficulties of a military occupation of Germany, and its utter unproductiveness of economic advantage to the occupiers, would have taught far more than the Treaty revisionists were able to teach.

Within two or three years after the Armistice, given an Allied occupation of all Germany, it is probable that the Allies would have been seeking a German government to release them on German terms from their mad venture. In this connection, it is to be borne in mind that the facilitating functions of finance could not have served to prolong the folly of a military occupation and intervention as they served to prolong the political and economic folly of the Treaty of Versailles. German bonds issued by a military government occupying and terrorizing Germany could not have been sold as were German bonds issued by a German republican government, the puppet of the international bankers.

What was it that contributed most to making allied statesmen, leaders of opinion, and the masses in the Allied countries believe that Germany could be made to pay and perform according to the stipulations of the Treaty and agreements made pursuant thereto? Fundamentally, it was the essentially liberal refusal to recognize that, in the last analysis, only might can make right. It was this refusal to see human relationships in their true light, this liberal ideology of freedom of contract, which led Allied statesmen and peoples to assume so stupidly that if German statesmen under the pressure of the Allied blockade and the starvation of the German people could be made to sign a given document, the definition of right therein embodied would constitute a right, above physical force and might, by which the German people would for generations remain bound. This premise of liberalism as to freedom of contract, the premise of freedom of a political economy in which millions are jobless and on relief, is undoubtedly leading millions of conservative and ordinarily sensible people in this country to support a system which the frustrated and beaten seem most unlikely to tolerate forever.

Nothing impairs and distorts the thinking of otherwise sensible people, whose lot is still either tolerable or downright agreeable to them, so much as the premises that the existing order is right and that right is above might. And nothing could be more futile in the way of discussion than the attempt of a man who is satisfied with things as they are to prove to a man who is not so satisfied that the existing scheme of things is right. A state of things in which ten millions are unemployed is wrong and not right. It is wrong fundamentally for the reason that the potential might of ten million unemployed men and of an indeterminate number of the élite who, though not in acute distress, are increasingly irked by the conditions in which they find themselves, is too great to make the present status quo maintainable with peace.

To summarize the argument, it may be said that the operating plan is always an expression of the might of the people, that it derives its moral validity and its practicability from the might which makes it effective, and prevents contrary might from making it ineffective, and that it is desirable for human welfare to have social policies shaped with a clear recognition that only might can make right right or effective. If one is advancing a new policy or norm of right, one will recognize that its triumph or realization requires a necessary amount of might. If one is defending against attack an old policy or norm of right, one will recognize equally that the only final issue is that of the might of the defenders to prevail against the attackers. One will then appraise one's values or norms of right in terms of the probable costs of attempting to uphold them. This is a somewhat different process of reasoning than that of proving to one's self that the founding fathers, a hundred and fifty years ago, intended things to be run in a certain way. The dead will surely not rise to defend any given application of their social theories. And the living, after all, have never been known to lack the means or will to challenge what does not suit them.

CHAPTER XIII

THE NATIONAL PLAN: AN EXPRESSION OF THE POPULAR WILL

AFTER reading what has been said in the preceding chapters about the national plan being an expression of the might of the people, most exponents of the liberal philosophy will doubtless be inclined to advance many of the old arguments about a written Constitution and written laws, duly interpreted by the Courts, being the expression, and the only satisfactory form of expression, of the will and might of the people.

Fascism holds that the national plan or social scheme is always an expression of the might of the people, and that this expression must be made explicit and effective through interpretation and administration by those in power. Fascism finds absurd and untrue the liberal thesis that the will of the people is expressed in the written word of a Constitution or body of laws. In so far as a written document is instrumental in expressing the will of the people, it is through interpretation and enforcement of such a document. In other words, they who interpret and enforce a law and not the written law, give the expression of the will of the people.

It is a beguiling myth of liberalism that people can be governed by laws and not by men. It is a charming illusion that we can provide a machinery of government which is free of the faults of human personality and which is the very embodiment of moral absolutes and social wisdom. This illusion relies chiefly on the further illusion that, whereas the members of legislative and administrative councils, and particularly chief executives, are persons affected with all the weaknesses which persons are heirs to, judges are not persons, but the court, in reference to their official acts. Obviously, a judge is as much a person as anyone else. A person can never function except as a person.

The trouble with any theory of impersonal government, or government by laws and principles rather than by men, is that it attributes to written documents, or statements of principle and purpose, qualities which the written word can never possess and with which only human beings can be endowed. A man, or a group of men who are in agreement with each other, in response to any question as to what is the will of the people, can easily give at any time an answer that is explicit and intelligible. They may also give an answer which they are in a position to enforce. Whether such answer always expresses the true will of the people, or is a wise or good answer, are open questions to be decided according to the facts of the case and the point of view from which judged. But there can be no question that an ordinarily well endowed individual executive or executive group can say intelligibly what he or they hold to be the will of the people on any given problem. The written word, on the other hand, can never possess this quality, which is obviously peculiar to human personality. The written word can never be made to fit all possible cases which will arise, and the written word always requires interpretation and application to the given case by a person.

Disregarding for the moment the whole question of interpretation and application, and assuming agreement by all parties as to the meaning of a document, one may say that a written constitution or law can never express the will of the people beyond an extremely limited field of reference. The limitations on the field of reference are those of time, place, and situation. With changes in time and conditions, laws very soon need rewriting. It is absurd to suppose that when the makers of the Constitution drafted that document they meant to say that it was the will of the American people that the Public Service Commission, of the State of Maryland, or Arkansas, might not fix a rate for a public utility which allowed less than a seven per cent return, or that one theory of rate-making instead of another was just and non-confiscatory. The makers of the Constitution had no knowledge of the present field of application of the principles they sought to express. Indeed, on careful thought, it must seem sheer nonsense to say that the makers of the American Constitution willed any one of hundreds of constitutional interpretations rendered by the courts as expressions of the sovereign will of the people.

It is not possible for any group of men either to express the will of the people living at the time in respect of problems arising a hundred years later, or to express the will of the people living a hundred years later as to the problems of that later period. The law can express only the will of the people with regard to current problems which are the subjects of contemporary thought and feeling. And whenever a question or uncertainty arises as to the will of the people as expressed in any law, only the responsible executive or legislative authority holding the mandate of the people can reasonably be assumed to have competence to say what the people now will. Certain it is that the present will of the people in respect to the application of an existing law to a current problem cannot, except by luck, be arrived at through the processes of legal ratiocination.

The processes of legal logic expressly disclaim, and methodically eschew, any undertaking to render a constitutional or legal interpretation to express the present opinion or will of the people, though, as Mr. Dooley remarked, the Supreme Court may sometimes, departing from the legal rules of interpretation, follow the election returns. The processes of legal interpretation specifically undertake to render an interpretation or application of the Constitution or the law in accord with some theory held by the judges as to what the men who wrote the Constitution or the law would have meant in respect of the issue submitted had they had cognizance of that issue. The courts do not attempt to express the present will of the people, for they admit that they have no means of knowing it, but they try rather to express their theory of the will of dead people in respect of a present living issue. They, of course, assume that their theory of the will of dead people in respect to a current problem submitted is also the will of the living people. It was the hope of many, if not of most, of the framers of the American Constitution, and of the subsequent builders of the American constitutional system during the first half of the 19th century, that separation of powers and the judicial veto would effectively curb expression of the popular will in ways disagreeable to the propertied classes.

It is the fact that the written word can have meaning only through interpretation and application, which establishes most conclusively the point that the popular will, or the ruling social purposes of the people in respect of the national plan, must be expressed from day to day to meet changes both in the popular will and in the conditions about which it has to make decisions. The oath to uphold the Constitution really amounts to nothing more or less than an oath to uphold what the courts may pronounce the Constitution to be. A rational oath of allegiance or of office must be an engagement to uphold the sovereign will or might of the people as made explicit by a duly authorized leader or representative of the people. A person can intelligently swear to obey and uphold the commands of a king or a supreme council or leader. But one cannot intelligently pledge one's self to uphold a document which one is incompetent to interpret, a Court interpretation of which one cannot obtain to settle a given doubt, and all the thousands of court interpretations of which no finite mind—not even that of a Philadelphia lawyer—can possibly encompass.

Let us consider briefly the nature of the absurdity of an oath to uphold the Constitution. As a practical matter, what does the oath mean? In the case of the executive officials, other than governors of states and the President of the United States, it merely means that the office-holder will obey the orders of his superior and abide by any court orders which may be addressed to him. If the office-holder is a judge, the oath means that he will try to follow the constitutional interpretations of the higher courts where they seem applicable and, where no such precedents are available, that he will guess at the correct interpretation of the Constitution as best he can, his guess being subject to subsequent revision by a higher judge. If the office holder is a legislator, the oath to uphold the Constitution means that he ought not to vote for a measure he considers unconstitutional, but that he has no means of knowing whether a measure he is asked to vote on is constitutional or not unless and until the measure has been enacted and challenged before the courts.

The essential fallacy of the constitutional oath, or any system which makes judicial interpretation of the Constitution the supreme definition of the popular will, is that although every one, including particularly government officials charged with law enforcement, is supposed to know the law, no one can know what the Constitution means with regard to a specific act until the courts have passed on that act. The constitutional oath is a pledge to uphold a court's interpretation of the Constitution before the interpretation has been given, and before any one can possibly know what the interpretation will be.

Now the favorite argument of liberal jurists is that a system of constitutional law and judicial interpretation of the law affords a degree of certainty which is not enjoyable under any system of what these jurists like to call personal government. The very reverse, of course, is the case. Certainty as to the law or the will of the people in reference to every problem of great moment is obviously desirable. But the liberal constitutional system is the worst imaginable way of giving certainty as to what is the will of the people. The argument of certainty is knocked into a cocked hat by the fact that whenever there is a constitutional or legal question of great importance before the courts, the best lawyers are usually as divided as to the tenor of the final decision as the laymen, or as are the players at a roulette wheel as to whether the next number will be red or black, or as are the bettors on the result of a prize fight. Whenever the case is sufficiently uncertain to cause large sums of money to be spent on both sides, the most scientific and economic way in which to select the final decision as to whether a given law or governmental act is constitutional or not is to flip a coin.

Trial by battle is one of the most essential features of the theory of Anglo-Saxon and liberal jurisprudence. The underlying assumptions are that there is such a thing as an absolute right and wrong to everything, and that if both parties to any dispute select a champion to wage a battle, the champion of that side which is right will win the encounter. The champion used to be a knight in arms. Now he is a lawyer. The pursuit of this will-o'-the-wisp of absolute justice or right is made into a sporting event exactly like a prize fight.

Now it is of the very nature of sporting events that one can never get scientific advice as to their outcome when, as is ordinarily the case in such events, the opponents are fairly evenly matched. One can get scientific advice as to whether a given structure or machine will stand certain strains, meet certain tests, or perform in certain ways. Rarely is that advice proved wrong by experience. Skyscrapers don't fall down. John W. Davis, ranking constitutional lawyer in private practice, in ten years has won seventeen and lost fifteen decisions challenging the constitutionality of a law. James M. Beck, another eminent, self-constituted exponent and guardian of the Constitution, lost eight out of ten constitutionality bouts. It would be lèse-majesté to give Chief Justice Hughes' record in private practice before the tribunal from which he took a ten year leave of absence. The N.I.R.A. episode is the latest example of certainty under liberal constitutional law.

One can hire a prize fighter or a lawyer to wage a battle for one, and one can be quite certain that the professional will put up a better fight than the amateur, and that the more skillful the professional fighter, the better the fight he will put up and the better will be his chances of winning. But one cannot possibly derive any certainty either as to the result of any given legal bout, or as to the realization of any given absolute norm of justice, assuming that the definition of such a norm could be the subject of general agreement. The chief certainty of the liberal system of law is that the popular will will be expressed with a greater bias to private property and things as they are than to national interests and social change.

The theory of pursuing absolutes like justice, fair competition, equality, and so on, by means of trial by battle is obviously incompatible with any rational theory of national planning. Whatever methods rational planning may employ, it is fairly certain that it cannot find much use for a sporting event as a means of selecting social policies or decisions expressive of the public will. The sporting theory of administering justice is simply unscientific. It is not a means to any rational end of social action. Its vogue under liberalism probably is due mainly to two considerations: First, making right superior to, and independent of, might as a theoretical premise, and then conducting a legal battle to settle any arguments as to what is right, though logically most contradictory, will serve admirably the purpose of easing Christian consciences as to the predatory features of the economic struggle under liberal capitalism. The successful in the acquisitive struggle can exculpate themselves of all wrongdoing or abusive uses of force and violence if they can say that they have kept within the law. Moreover, they can make the State, through the exercise of the police powers, do most of their fighting for them. The legal rules can be made to allow, and even instrument, the pressures which the economically mighty wish to use, and to bar the pressures which the economically mighty cannot advantageously use.

The second important consideration which explains the vogue of the liberal premise that right is above might, and the liberal practice of trial by legal battle to settle disputes as to the definition of right, is the professional interest of the lawyers in having a social system operated on these principles. It means highly remunerative work, prestige, and power for thousands of men.

The liberal ideology as to right is the most important single factor for making more business for lawyers. Let two persons have a clash of interests or purposes which can be brought before the courts. How will they reason? They will think in terms of their rights and the possibilities of asserting them in a trial by legal battle. Nine-tenths of all civil suits could be settled by conference, compromise, and agreement, without litigation, and with a law clerk or lawyer needed only to draw up the final agreement, if all parties would think of the judicial process as a costly sporting event, the results of which are uncertain and costly—certain only to be unfortunate for one party and likely in most cases to be more costly for the winner than a generous compromise.

But liberal juristic ideology inhibits almost every one having an interest which can be made the subject of a legal battle from thinking in common sense terms. Often, of course, especially where large amounts are involved, clashes of interests are settled out of court by compromise arranged by counsel for both sides. In these cases, counsel will take anywhere from ten per cent to all of the amount affected by the compromise, or legal costs which often run into millions of dollars, when the same or a better agreement for the parties in interest could be reached through simple, non-technical negotiation as to real interests conducted by honest representatives, such agreement to be embodied in documentary form at small cost by lawyers, accountants and other experts acting as technical aids and not as vultures. In the Paramount-Publix Corporation receivership and reorganization, a typical example of banker-lawyer racketeering, or trying to get something for nothing, Federal Judge Coxe slashed the fees demanded by the lawyers and bankers $2,213,117, allowing only $1,026,711 of the $3,239,-828 asked. One of the largest and most reputable New York law firms asked $700,000 and was allowed only $200,000. Another Wall Street law firm, Cravath, de Gersdorff, Swaine and Wood, asked $150,000 and was allowed nothing. The second ranking private bankers of the country, Kuhn, Loeb & Co., asked $114,287 and were allowed nothing.

Written law, courts of law and judicial process have a place in every social scheme. But their function must be that of an instrument of the popular will, not that of making original expressions or creative interpretations of the popular will, and not that of making economic relationships a racket for lawyers and bankers. The function of law must be that of shop or institutional rules and regulations. It is obviously impossible for the highest mandatory of the people to administer the will of the people in thousands of civil and criminal cases which necessarily arise. For this purpose courts are necessary, and laws are obviously indicated merely as a guide for the courts, and a means of averting the necessity for continual reference to the highest authority expressing the public will. When the judge makes a ruling or gives a sentence pursuant to law under any system he is interpreting or expressing what has to be assumed to be the will of the people, and in ninety per cent of the cases his ruling will be acceptable. But if a case arises in which there is an ambiguity as to the correct application of the law, let the court always apply to a combined executive and legislative council of the representatives of the people, or to their delegate for an interpretation.

It must not be supposed that such a theory of administration need bar appeal or the thorough ventilation of conflicting points of view as to a given law or governmental act. This theory merely directs the contest along other lines of procedure. For instance, suppose under a fascist State a legislative or executive measure of an economic character were deemed unwise, unjust, or undesirable by a party to whom it was applied. He would be allowed quite as much opportunity to contest the measure, if the points of contest had not been finally adjudicated, as he has under the present system. But the principles on which the contest could be waged would be different. The property owner or corporate management which contested a new law or government measure would not be allowed to advance any arguments asserting a private right as superior to the right of the State. On the contrary, the paramount right of the State, or of the public interest, or of the might of the people, would always be established beyond challenge. The contesting private party would try to show that the measure or act in question was not calculated to serve the purposes of the public interest as they had been authoritatively defined by the representative of the people. In other words, the measure or act was a mistake. The argument on these grounds could be as involved, and the issues as difficult, as in any legal contest under the present system, but the standards or rules would be different.

The contest or reëxamination of the law or measure would be settled finally by the decision of the government, which could the more easily reverse or modify a law or administrative act because the instrumental fitness of the measure, and not the authority of government or the State, had been contested. It is a favorite and thoroughly absurd argument of liberal jurisprudence and politics that the State should not be the judge of its own cause, or in a conflict between itself and a private person.

The argument is absurd on analysis for a number of reasons. The judge is supposed to be on the side of the rule or principle which expresses the will of the people. The officer or department of government representing the State in the legal action is also supposed to be on the side of the people. Suppose the judge disagrees with the executive branch of the government as to what is the will of the people, as often occurs, the case really presents the farce or absurdity of two parties asserting representation of the will of the people. In other words, the State, through the voice of the judge, tells the State, represented by another officer of government, that the State represented by the latter is wrong, and that the State represented by the former is right as to the will of the people. One voice of the State discredits another voice of the State. But how many voices or personalities should the State have? If the judge is the voice or personality which is always right in the State, why not have him decide all questions in the first instance so that there shall be no contests? What public advantage is gained by having a sporting event to decide a conflict of views between two persons, both supposedly representing the State? The argument that the private citizen does not have his case against the government judged by the government is rendered absurd by the one fact that the person, the judge, giving the final decision is the State or the government. The whole procedure of having one officer of the State pronounce another wrong, on the basis of metaphysical arguments as to the rights of individuals versus the rights of the State, serves mainly the purpose of providing professional income for lawyers.

The end of avoiding mistakes of administration in ultimate policies can only be served by scientific examination of the rationality of given means to given ends. Challenging the rationality of given means to given ends requires no challenging of the authority or powers of the State or government. Cases of alleged excesses or abuses of authority by an official should provide the subject of no legal battle but of a simple inquiry, stating the facts, and submitted to the highest public authority.

Challenging the authority of the State encourages a spirit of lawlessness and a disposition to thwart or circumvent a government which so often pronounces itself guilty, not of a mistake in the use of means, but guilty of a violation of law. How absurd are the daily spectacles afforded the populace by our liberal jurisprudence of a government haled into court by a plutocrat or large corporation and there found guilty of violating the law. Challenging the rationality of given governmental means to given public ends encourages no such lawlessness, and contributes to the understanding of current problems as a metaphysical argument about the powers of the State, or the authority of a given official in a given matter, cannot possibly do. There is no better reason why a billion-dollar corporation, which can spend a million dollars on one legal battle, should be allowed legally to oppose the considered ends of the State duly ratified by the legislature than there is why a gangster should illegally make such opposition.

In the regulation of private conduct, a fascist government will facilitate appeal, reexamination and discussion of government measures and policies. The appeal would be based on the same grounds on which an economic regulation or measure could be challenged. Any governmental interference with reli-

gious, cultural, or recreational activities of private citizens
would be open to contest on the argument that it did not serve
the announced and accepted ends of the State. A discussion
of a given measure in these terms would be useful. A discussion of any governmental measure in terms of an individual's
right to worship, cultivate his mind, or exercise his body as he
sees fit is absurd, for the simple reason that no liberal State
will tolerate religiously-practiced cannibalism, human sacrifices, or castration, or any one of innumerable ways of culti-
vating the mind or body.

The fascist State entirely repudiates the liberal idea of conflict of interests and rights as between the State and the individual, such conflict to be settled through the sporting event
of trial by legal battle under the umpiring of a neutral third
party supposedly represented by the judge. The major concern of the administration of justice under fascism is not the
protection of the individual against a State assumed to be
prone to abuse the individual. The chief purpose of any judicial
examination of public measures, whether such examination be
made by the courts or specially constituted tribunals, is the
protection of the State against its own mistakes. In this respect
the salient points of the conflicting assumptions of liberalism
and fascism are these: Liberalism assumes that individual welfare and protection is largely a matter of having active and
powerful judicial restraints on governmental interference with
the individual; Fascism assumes that individual welfare and
protection is mainly secured by the strength, efficiency, and
success of the State in the realization of the national plan.

It is easy to draw alarming pictures of a powerful State
against which the individual would have the resource of no
judicial veto on governmental acts. Conceivably, of course, a
State and government might fall into the hands of a few individuals whose every act would be an abuse. But such an even-
tuality seems most improbable in any modern State, least of
all in the United States.

On the other hand, it has to be recalled that the judicial
checks of liberalism on government rarely avail the poor man

in this or any other country where such checks are provided for, the reason being that judicial process, especially that required to overrule government, is expensive and outside the means of the poor man. So far as the abuses or mistakes, as you may choose to qualify them, of public administration are concerned, and so far as the welfare of the masses is affected thereby, any relief available through appeal and judicial review must be largely proportionate to the free facilities for such appeal and review which the State itself affords. The fascist State, through government-assisted unions of workers, government-regulated associations of employers, and special executive tribunals for hearing appeals and complaints, can afford far more redress and correction than the liberal State with its judicial process available only to the rich individual and the large corporation.

In considering the problem of providing redress and correction in the cases of mistakes and abuses of public administration, we must think in terms of the practicable, or of might rather than abstract concepts of right; in terms of the mechanics rather than the norms of government. There is no right, in any useful sense of the term, for a man who has not the economic might to assert a right, or who cannot, for whatever the reason may be, avail himself of the existing machinery for redress and correction. Once the problem is viewed from this angle it will become apparent that no machinery for affording relief and correction in numerous cases, promptly, cheaply, and easily can possibly operate within the framework of liberal political and juridical rules and practices. Judicial norms of liberalism obviate any such result. Liberal redress through judicial process is an expensive luxury for the rich. The State must provide and operate judicial machinery of relief and correction of the mistakes of public administration as a necessary part of the national plan. Once liberal principles like those of the State versus the citizen and separation of powers are abandoned, and the older and more rational concept of the State adopted, developing and operating machinery both to formulate the national plan and to examine scientifically complaints against alleged mistakes and abuses in its realization will be found a comparatively easy matter.

Thus a series of tribunals culminating in a tribunal of last resort, composed of the highest mandatories of the people, would be organized to function for the examination of complaints arising out of public administration, in much the same way that committees of a vast corporation function for similar purposes. Those in charge of government would have the most obvious self-interest in making these tribunals function efficiently. For, while those exercising a public mandate have an interest in upholding the power and authority of the State, they would not have an interest in upholding its mistakes which could be corrected. This is especially true where those in office feel secure of a permanent tenure of office and realize that they must ultimately bear in one way or another the consequences of all mistakes in public administration. The art of insuring a desired standard of performance by public officials is to be found in making it their professional pride and self-interest under the system created so to perform—not in creating a system of checks, restraints, and interferences, the principal results of which will be irresponsibility in administration, frustration of efficient government, and the fostering of rackets, rather than protection of the weak or curbing of the mighty.

CHAPTER XIV

WHY FASCISM INSTEAD OF COMMUNISM?

WE HAVE now given ultimate values and the force factor sufficient consideration to be warranted in assuming that the field is cleared of many of the most confusing and frequently advanced objections and supposed alternatives to national planning and what it necessarily involves. We are therefore ready to engage in some wishful formulation of values for fascist planning for the United States. We shall assume that an ideal fascism for America must provide for maximum economic production and consumption with a steady rise in living standards and a progressive expansion of productive plant, all without either a class or civil war or the expropriation of all private rights in the instruments of production. The alternatives of such a formula seem to be only those of making liberal capitalism work better or accepting communism, the emergence of a triumphant dictatorship of the proletariat from a bloody class war and expropriation of all private property rights in producers goods. It is appropriate at this point in the discussion to undertake some explanation why the fascist formula seems preferable to the communist formula. This explanation is particularly indicated in connection with a statement of the radical ends and means embraced in the fascist plan.

Now the ideals of order and planned abundance are not, as ideals, peculiar to fascism, liberal capitalism, or communism. Many readers will undoubtedly find fault with this book for not being a detailed outline of a fascist utopia and for having too much to say in the abstract about fundamentals, ends and means. The chief reason why so much is said about fascist social philosophy, and so little about an ideal or probable fascist handling of specific problems, is that it is mainly in the discussion of fascist philosophy that this book can be useful.

Most socialists and radical would-be reformers within the liberal framework naïvely assume that the ideals of social order and welfare are peculiar to their philosophy, and they spend a lot of time telling us in glowing detail exactly what they would like to see happen, without conceiving that most people would also like to see these ideals realized. The problem is how to realize these ideals, and that problem is one of social engineering rather than technology. And when you talk social engineering, you must talk social philosophy before you can draw blue prints. The solution involves radical social or political changes rather than technological rationalization. (We are now beginning to make use of the term rationalize in a different sense, in the sense in which industries are said to be rationalized when they are reorganized in the most rational way to make means serve ends.) Industry is highly integrated. It is organized for perfect centralized control. It has no fixed constitution or aversion to daily improvement and readjustment. Indeed, it furnishes for social organization a model of rationality or aptness of means to ends.

Both fascism and communism are, in the technical sense of the term, radical schemes for rationalizing the social machinery, just as the engineers have rationalized the machinery and technology of production. By rationalization we mean, in this connection, organizing and operating productive instruments in the most rational way for the productive ends which they are supposed to serve. Obviously there is no unique scheme of social rationalization. There can be as many schemes of social rationalization as there are schemes of objectives to be sought in the social order.

As for realizing the ideal of maximum production, and raising living standards, we have to guide us as to the technical possibilities a wealth of useful studies and persuasive propaganda. We are not dependent on Marxian communism either for rational exposition or popularization of the ideal of material abundance. To men like Stuart Chase, Veblen, John Dewey, and some of the more serious thinkers associated with movements like the late Senator Long's Share the Wealth

Movement, Father Coughlin's Social Justice Movement, the La Follette crusades, Technocracy, Major Douglas' Social Credit Plan, the Farmer Labor Party, the Utopians and the Epic Planners, is due more credit than to the Communists for the familiarization of the American public with the ideal of greater material abundance.

Even many of the orthodox and professional economists are beginning to recognize and proclaim, with due reserves and modesty, the rationality of the ideal of maximum output, as well as to intimate (most guardedly, to be sure) certain radical changes looking to that end. An interesting and important trilogy of current economic studies by the professional economists and statisticians of the Brookings Institution, on *America's Capacity to Produce, America's Capacity to Consume,* and *The Formation of Capital,* while making no such extravagant claims for our productive capacity as $20,000 a year for every family, such as was made by some of the more exuberant Technocrats, indicate that about twenty per cent of our 1929 potential productive capacity was unused. Had we used only this productive potential and distributed the product to the poorest families, we need not have had any family incomes below $2,000. As it was, in 1929 we had sixteen million families, or fifty-nine per cent of all the families, with incomes under $2,000, twelve million families, or forty-two per cent, with incomes of less than $1,500, and nearly six millions, or more than twenty-one per cent, with incomes of less than $1,000 a year.

There is reason to guess, on the basis of many estimates, that our productive plant could be made to furnish every family with an annual income of $5,000 within ten years of reasonable expansion and rationalization of industry. A minimum family income of $2,500 seems a comparatively easy objective for attainment within two or three years. A study, entitled *The Chart of Plenty,* by Harold Loeb and Associates, a national survey of potential productive capacity carried on under C.W.A. with responsibility to F.E.R.A. and the New York City Tenement House Department, and many other studies of a similar import, afford a fairly well documented basis for many generalizations which, for sake of brevity, will merely be mentioned here to indicate broadly the possibilities of increasing our total production and consumption.

Professional economists have, as a whole, always been agreed that there is no such thing as over-production. And the most orthodox of them will go further and say that just before the collapse of a business boom there is under-production to maintain the capital values then imputed to property. As for over-production, it can be said that, from a humane viewpoint, up to date there have been both under-production and under-consumption for a satisfactory standard of welfare.

A routine circular (No. 296 of November 1933) of the United States Department of Agriculture on *Diets for Four Levels of Nutritive Content, and Cost*, studied in combination with official figures of agricultural acreage and production, will establish the conclusion that, if the entire American people enjoyed a liberal diet, we should have to increase our acreage under cultivation by 40 million acres, instead of withdrawing 50 million acres from production, as Secretary Wallace concluded we should have to do unless tariff reduction enables us to dump abroad about twice as much of our cotton and wheat as present exports allow. If everyone were adequately equipped with clothing, our cotton production of 1929 would have to be increased to supply the domestic demand. In housing, the deficiencies are too apparent to the hurried glance of a traveller through our cities and towns to make any figures or elaborate details necessary to establish the point. In education, the capital outlay in 1934 was only twenty-seven per cent of what it was in 1930. In 1931-34, two thousand rural schools in twenty-four states failed to open, and over two million children missed schooling altogether.

Without piling fact on fact, or figure on figure, to support an obvious generalization, we may say that there can be no question either as to our need or capacity for increased production. The only real problem in this connection is that of mobilizing our productive factors and keeping them active. It is precisely at this point in the quest for planned abundance that fascism imposes itself as the only alternative to communism.

The choices we have are in the development of social machinery to make our material machinery give us the standard of living we desire. A fallacious assumption of all liberal reformism is that if the people can be induced to give, through a decisive majority vote, a mandate to their government to bring about some ideal measure of social justice and economic abundance, and if education and moral indoctrination inculcate the right attitudes, this mandate can be carried out within the framework of existing institutions and ways. To prove this assumption, they pile up irrelevant statistics and talk learnedly in the several jargons of the social and natural sciences. They quite simply do not take account of the fact that a better social order requires, in the field of social institutions, ways, attitudes, and mechanics, not only new objectives but a driving force, a guiding hand, and a coördinated system of control. Utopian wishes do not furnish a driving force. A series of majority votes arrived at by the parliamentary or Congressional methods of majority group pressures, lobbying, and the individual pursuit of reëlection by hundreds of office holders, do not constitute a guiding hand. And a political system of checks and balances is not coördinated control.

The driving force of any national undertaking may be called nationalism, patriotism, love of country, consciousness of kind, and loyalty to kind, or by any one of countless other terms or phrases. The reality which unites and animates a group in a feeling of solidarity, and in an enterprise of common interest, is too traditional, too universally felt and manifested, and too inevitable, to call for any attempt at exact definition. Communist Russia operates as a nation, and is driven by the dynamic force of national patriotism, or love of country and loyalty to kind, quite as much as any fascist country, or any liberal country in time of war. Little need be said by way of attempt to explain why and how this force will animate an American fascism. The generative sources of this force are inherent in every nation. It is necessary only to tap them and provide an orderly system through which they can flow. We do not need communism to get the forces of nationalism, and communism cannot provide a substitute for those forces.

Now communism professes to derive its driving force from the will of the workers to overthrow the rule of the owners of property, and substitute that rule with the dictatorship of the proletariat. As a matter of fact, of course, communism in operation has been a series of phenomena whose driving force has been derived from two main sources: First, the personal motivations, too complex always for brief analysis, of the initiating leaders—motivations springing from a sense of frustration under the existing order, feeling that this order was evil, and the love of power common to so many strong men; and, second, Russian patriotism, which was captured and mobilized by these initiating leaders of communism, exactly as French patriotism was captured and mobilized by a Corsican second lieutenant of artillery and soldier of fortune.

The class war, the classical myth of communism, like every other war, has been the war of one crowd against another. There is nothing much to starting or keeping up a war any more than there is to starting and keeping up a fire. It needs only the first spark and then plenty of fuel. The Communist ins, in Russia, have fought, and continue to fight, the outs. The ins of Russia would incite the outs of other countries to espouse the faith of the communist international and fight the ins of their respective countries. All this is simple. But nowhere is there apparent any significant manifestation of the driving force of a proletarian will to fight as proletarians, whether in Russia or anywhere else. Russia presents the spectacle of a national government on the defensive, just as do Britain, Germany, Japan and Italy, not the spectacle of a proletariat on the warpath against the capitalists of the world.

The choice between fascism and communism, then, turns largely around the questions of the inevitability and desirability from some assumed standpoint of the class war myth as a rationalization of what is just a war between two crowds, and, of course, of this war as an event. Here it may be said that the best way to start a revolution or civil war in the United States is not to use the Marxian class war myth. But more important still it may be said that it is not necessary to have a civil war in order to effect a social revolution. These two considerations seem rather effectively to eliminate communism as a desirable choice for any one who has not already been "converted" to communism.

Those who have not been converted to communism will do well to ask themselves these questions: Is such a war a necessary means to the end of a social order which will afford the people as a whole a better average life? Is such a war a necessary means to a good end for me as an individual?

The answer to the second question, of course, depends largely on who I am, or whether I should be among the liquidators or the liquidated. To answer the first question affirmatively, it must be assumed that a proletarian party will have the will to start such a war, the might to win it, and the competence, after they have won it, to run things more efficiently than the leaders or managers of the class they have liquidated could run things.

It is the last of these assumptions which is most open to challenge. The assumptions that a proletarian communist party can mobilize enough proletarian wills to fight the Marxian battle on the inspiration of the class war myth, and develop enough might to win the battle in the advanced industrial countries, can plausibly be ridiculed in the light of present indications. But no impregnable argument can be founded on such ridicule, for the wills of the masses can conceivably be changed quickly and galvanized into action for the pursuit of the maddest objectives—witness the Crusades.

It is the assumption that a proletarian party triumph in the classical Marxian battle could leave enough competent technicians unliquidated to run things in a way to maintain as high a living standard as could be maintained if these managing classes were allowed to function, which is open to the most effective challenge. And on that challenge much of the case for fascism rests.

In this connection it must be remembered that while the Russian communist revolution has liquidated several millions, it did not have to liquidate the same percentage or total number of middle class technicians found in the United States. Moreover, Russian economy was not as dependent on these middle class elements as are our economy and standard of living. And during the Russian communist experiment it has been found necessary to import foreign experts. In the field in which the class war in Russia has effected the most drastic or significant liquidation of people—agriculture—the output is lowest and still below pre-War levels.

Obviously, from the point of view of the interests of the owning and managing classes, there can be no question as to the undesirability of the communist civil war, which will necessarily mean for them liquidation—a euphemism for such experiences as being stood up against a wall and shot. It is from the point of view of the workers in the Marxian definition, or those whose income is not derived mainly from owning and managing productive property for a profit, that, for the sake of any possible argument, it has to be shown that the triumphant Marxian dictatorship will not yield advantages. It is most seductive to some workers to be told that they have a chance under communism to oust the present bosses and themselves become the bosses. Obviously this promise is a lie. For under communism the workers would merely have a different set of bosses. There is no way of running industry without bosses, and there is no way of making every man his own boss. The only question of real interest to the masses is whether they would be better off to liquidate in communist fashion all the present bosses and proceed thereafter with new bosses developed under communism, or to try some social formula which would take advantage of the skills of the present bosses. Once the question is considered in this light, the answer is fairly obvious in countries like the United States, where a communist class war liquidation would deprive the country of some twenty millions of its workers out of a total of fifty million, these twenty millions including some six million farmers, all of whom are on the wrong side of the communist fence.

At this point a word should be said to refute a commonly made communist argument that most of the middle-class executives, experts, white collar workers, farmers and small enterprisers would go over to communism in the course of the class war and thus escape liquidation. This argument runs counter to any expectancy based on experience. When a fight starts, the lines between friend and foe are tightly drawn, and it rarely happens during a war that any significant number of those on one side of the line go over to the other. It is not in the nature of most people, especially most members of the middle classes, to prove turncoats in a fight. The longer and harder the Marxian class war, the greater would be the solidarity of the enemies of the communists. There is, of course, no doubt in any mind which thinks straight on this subject that a large percentage of the non-owning, non-managing, and non-enterprising workers would, in the United States, side in the Marxian war with the owners, managers, and enterprisers from the very start. Most of the American workers would side with the managers and enterprisers because of the force of tradition or attitudes formed by education and long habit and, also, because of the prestige or moral authority which the managing and owning classes deservedly enjoy in the United States where their competence is demonstrably superior to that of the élite of the Czarist régime of Russia.

We may conclude then that, because of the unavoidable liquidation of so many competent experts through a communist victory in the Marxian class struggle, the results would not be as favorable for the people as a whole, or even for the non-owning and non-managing workers, as a régime which required fewer human sacrifices to get started. But the driving force of a consciousness of group solidarity and common group objectives is needed to run the social machinery of any planned economy. If it is not the Marxian class war spirit, it must be some other martial spirit. This force fascism develops by intensifying the national, spirit and putting it behind the enterprises of public welfare and social control.

Here fascism is not introducing a new force but merely intensifying a force inherent in every nation and putting this old force behind new public enterprises.

The unifying principle of national fellowship already exists. Unlike working class or proletarian class consciousness, it is not something which exists only by virtue of a logical classification of men into owners and workers. This Marxian classification is entirely valid for purposes of logic and definition. But it is a classification which no more creates two separate class consciousnesses or class identities for purposes of common thought and action than the division of all mankind into red heads and non-red heads.

Obviously, the more inclusive the unifying principle, the more conflict is avoided and the greater coöperation is achieved. Nationalism would be more inclusive in the United States than any formula of unity based on race, religion, profession or tastes. As Americans, we are all of one nationality, though not of one race, religion, profession or set of cultural tastes. Of course, a perfect internationalism would be still more unifying and inclusive. This consideration leads many humane minds to aspire to a social formula or unifying principle which would include all mankind or transcend national limitations. Here the inevitability of some limitation to the inclusiveness of a formula of social organization and operation is largely a matter of traditional imponderables and problems of sheer administration. If the world were to go one hundred per cent Communist or one hundred per cent Roman Catholic, any attempt at international unity would necessarily founder on the rocks of group traditions and in the complexities of administration, for which neither an international Communism nor an international Christianity would prove a solvent.

It is idle to hazard a speculation as to the possibility of ever effecting a workable formula of international unity in a distant future. It is worse than idle for any one nation to attempt to force on an unwilling world any ideal of international unity.

If an international formula by universal assent is ever workable, it will not be necessary for any one nation to force any part of it on any other nation. And surely no one is interested in an international formula imposed and maintained by the might of one nation. Communism, of course, masquerades as an international formula to be made effective by the universal assent of the workers (thus eliminating international war) once the capitalists have been eliminated by the Marxian class war. But communism in action has developed no reasons for supposing that workers are any less Americans, Russians and Englishmen than capitalists.

In regard to the guiding hand and the mechanisms of social control necessary to a planned society, we may dispose at once of a great deal of confusion by saying that fascism and communism equally require centralized control. In the larger essentials of social control, so far as problems of technique, mechanism, and means are concerned, fascism and communism have many similarities. It is under this heading of the imperative principles and mechanisms of social control that it seems eminently fitting to compare fascism and communism in respect to private property rights, private initiative in production, profits, and the free market. It is understood, of course, that fascism stands for the maintenance of all these institutions. Here there is a real problem of choice. Fascism regards private property rights, private initiative, and the free market, subject to a proper régime of public interest, as useful institutions— useful means to public ends. The difference between fascism and liberalism, in this respect, is that fascism considers these institutions as means to national ends, whereas liberalism makes the nation and national government a means to the ends of private property and the free market.

The instrumental merits of private property and the free market can best be appreciated by analyzing any attempt to dispense entirely with them, such as is being made by communist Russia. Now, communism or socialism sanctions property rights in consumers goods but not producers goods. But, in a large field of property, such as farms and small enterprises, it is impossible to draw a line between producers and consumers goods. One must either accept some measure of private ownership of the instruments of production, or soon one is driven to the extreme of a régime in which everyone will be in the position of unpaid soldiers or pensioners of an institution who have certain things deemed necessary and found available supplied to them, with no money for purchasing, or means of producing, anything else. Russian communism shows definite trends in that direction. As a matter of fact, of course, no professional army today is conducted on the extreme principle of complete rationing of everything. All soldiers are given some small pay with which to make optional purchases of things selected by themselves to suit their tastes.

A socialism which gives the individual a property right only in the clothes on his back and a few simple articles of personal use is fraught with administrative difficulties which can hardly be exaggerated. For such a socialism imposes on government a formidable amount of details or administrative minutiae in matters of directing all production, determining distribution and rewards, and taking care of one hundred per cent of those incapable of earning a living. To whatever extent private ownership and small savings exist, just so many more aged and dependents, as well as persons of difficult social adjustment, are provided with incomes and occupations without engaging State responsibility for the details of taking care of them. Institutional care is indicated for many people, and government ownership is indicated for efficient production in many fields. But ownership of small homes, farms, and productive enterprises are also indicated for many more people and many other types of production.

There is a large field of productive activity in which small enterprise is unquestionably more efficient and satisfactory in every way than large enterprise. Farming, of course, is the best example. Soviet Russia has yet to demonstrate that public administration can operate farms as efficiently or economically through collectivized units as private enterprise. It is doubtful whether government feeding stations will ever equal the culinary achievements of small private kitchens. Small-scale private production is not only more efficient in many fields but it is also fairly safe or free of significant monopoly power and abuse.

Socially significant monopoly does not arise either in agriculture, or in the production of special goods and services of a unique character, where the total volume produced is relatively small and where the article can easily be substituted by another. The monopoly of a unique voice, or talent, or resource may bring a high reward without conferring any power to commit a social abuse. And neither the farmers nor the small enterprisers are ever likely to challenge the public authority or interfere with public administration in the ways that large corporations and financial institutions have frequently done. It is, of course, possible for small owners and enterprisers to constitute a pressure agency through special association, but the State has ample means for dealing with large associations. Besides, an association representing and controlled by a large number of small property owners is not likely to prove the pressure force that a large corporation controlled by a few insiders can exert.

Private ownership of savings, as well as small ownership and management units of productive enterprise, can be socially controlled. The social abuses connected with savings are encountered mainly in the mechanics of investment and financial management by the large banks, savings institutions, and insurance companies which handle savings. It is a relatively easy matter for the State to preserve the present de facto rights and interests of small savers while completely nationalizing the financial institutions which now administer their savings, or while imposing on a private management of such institutions any State dictates. It cannot be repeated too often that what prevents adequate public regulation is liberal norms of law or constitutional guarantees of private rights. There is no need to expropriate private ownership of either savings or small scale enterprise in order to maintain adequate social control. It is necessary only to nationalize large financial institutions and monopolistic industries, as well as all corporations whose services are indispensable but whose management has become completely divorced from ownership, and to discipline adequately all private enterprises.

Wherever ownership and management have become separated, there is no good case to be made out for private ownership or private management. In these cases, ownership is held by an army of stockholders and bondholders, who cannot possibly have any say about the control and management exercised by self-perpetuating hierarchies of bankers, directors, and officials on the inside who are virtually irresponsible either to the owners or to the State for the results of their economic policies. Obviously, a governmental bureaucracy is preferable to a corporate bureaucracy, for the governmental bureaucracy can be made more responsible, more disciplined, and better integrated into a national plan. A corporate bureaucracy divorced from the control of owners is just a private army at the service of any pirate captain who may be made chief.

The fascist State can easily convert the great monopolies and bureaucratically-managed large corporations into State-controlled enterprises, the present owners and creditors of which will receive income bonds or shares in a government investment company and never know any practical difference between their present capitalistic relationship to the property and the relationship which a fascist State will define and maintain for them. The corporate bureaucracies, except for a few big shot men at the top, will never know the difference. For there is no real difference between being a yes-man official of a billion dollar bank and being an official of a State bureaucracy, except possibly as to compensation, and government owned or controlled corporations under fascism would allow generous compensation to efficient executives.

So far as considerations of efficiency are involved, almost any rational régime, either of complete government control or some modified government dictation of policies and management left in private managers' hands, would mean no greater or different administrative and practical difficulties than those already encountered under the bureaucratic management of self-perpetuating bank and corporate dictatorships. Actually, the management of all large corporations is wholly bureaucratic, subject only, as a practical matter, to the modifying dictation of big bankers and financial interests. Between the hierarchical bureaucracy of a political State and the hierarchical bureaucracy of a large corporation with its permanent dictator and his army of yes-men executives, there are no significant administrative or technical differences. In either case, all the advantages of owner-management are lacking and all the disadvantages of bureaucratic control are present.

The case for leaving owner-management to function where it can do so more efficiently than large scale enterprise (which is necessarily bureaucratic) and, with only two or three exceptions, enterprise where management is divorced from ownership, rests on sound considerations of public policy. In the fascist view, only through a combination of privately-owned and privately-managed small scale enterprise and State-owned or State-managed large scale enterprise can social control be maintained. It seems too obvious to need explanation that many types of production must be conducted on such a large scale that the advantages of owner management must be sacrificed for the greater advantages—in these cases, of mass production by highly integrated trusts. Such types of industry, just as the Panama Canal, are monopoly propositions which indicate public ownership or public administration.

In so far as property rights and private enterprise are concerned, however, the strongest argument for fascism instead of communism may be found in the regulatory functions of an open market. The strongest criticism of any socialism of complete expropriation is that it leaves no free market, no pricing mechanism and no valid basis for economic calculation. Pure socialism is collective ownership and unified central direction of all material instruments of production which, sooner or later, must leave little or no freedom of choice for the individual as to consumption or occupation. These criticisms may be found brought up to date and made relevant to communism in operation in Russia in the symposium of Professors Hayek, Pierson, Barone, Halm and von Mises entitled *Collectivist Economic Planning*, and the work of Professor Boris Brutzkus entitled *Economic Planning in Soviet Russia.*

Under a pure communism, the products of all enterprises are poured into a common pot, and all the enterprises are given out of this pot the means for further production. With no market indications to guide them, how can the supreme managers of national socialist production receive directives as to further production, or measure the intensity of social needs? Without a free market there can be no determination of economic values. The labor theory of value breaks down completely as a means of determining rewards for labor or for the use of labor and machinery in production. Marx, of course, recognized that an hour of every man's labor was not equal owing to differences in skills. But how is the inequality in worth to be measured if not by market demand? Is it to be measured according to the cost of creating a given skill? But many labor skills are natural gifts acquired without any training and with very little effort. Is the value of labor to be measured by the physical output? But what about exactly similar labor expended in working an easy and a difficult mine, or lands which produce unequal quantities of the same material? How would rewards of skilled German and unskilled Russian labor be determined in international communist trade?

At the beginning of 1931 there was a union conference of industrial managers at Moscow. Ordzonikidze, President of Workers and Peasants Inspection, said at that conference: "With us, the State bank pays for everything and the undertaking is materially responsible for nothing at all. Wages are paid without referring to you (the industrial managers). Goods are paid for regardless of quality. People take your products away and distribute them." "That's grand," said the audience. In the publication *Za industrializaciu*, the organ of the Supreme Economic Council, in its leading article of December 19, 1930, it is said, "Among industrial managers there is a popular notion that however great the financial deficits, the State will always make them good, for finance is not to impose any limits on the expansion of production and the extension of capital construction." The result of having the State pay all deficits in industrial production is a steady depreciation in the value of the Russian ruble, not that this difficulty alone need prove fatal to communism, for, conceivably, the currency could be inflated to the vanishing point of value for each unit ever so often, and a new currency started after each debacle. The real difficulty is that under such an economic régime the most efficient use of labor and material resources, or the use most satisfactory to the people, cannot possibly be made, for the simple reason that there is no means of measuring value or output in terms of the quantity of satisfaction afforded to consumers.

It is, of course, easy to keep everybody at work and to produce a great deal (much of which, like the output of many Russian factories, may be useless) without any regard for the indications of market value. And this is exactly what communist Russia has been doing. But the results are a great waste of productive effort and the necessity for taking inferior consumers goods with little choice. In a symposium on planning, Miss Van Kleeck argues that a plan requires measurement, that money is an unsafe guide, and that a planned economy "does not make money but makes and distributes goods," adding that "Obviously the basic common unit of measurement is the man hour." The trouble with making goods without the controlling indications of market demand and profits for successful producers is that there is no way of knowing the right quantities to make, the right proportions of labor and machinery to use in production, or other right combinations in the productive processes.

The extreme liberal capitalist position that only effective demands made in a free market should be satisfied is equally untenable. There is a large field of economic goods in which production can be conducted by arbitrary assumption and dictation. Police protection, sanitation, public education, are goods which are already bought and paid for without any reference to market demand. Light and power, transportation, and basic foods and textiles in given but limited quantities, can be assumed necessary at an arbitrarily fixed price, and State intervention can insure the production of an adequate supply of these goods within an arbitrarily fixed price range for the common good. If there is a deficit it can be met by taxation—provided it is not too large. It is well to remember that it will never be possible for the State to have provided as much of everything as may be desired. Hence, there must be selection and rationing where arbitrarily determined production and prices are enforced. For the selection of goods to be produced at given costs, for sale at given prices, and in given quantities, and for the selection and combination of productive factors in producing these goods, the State must have the guidance of prices or values determined by a comparatively free market. It is impossible within the limits of a brief discussion to elaborate the reasons and examples showing why the controls of freely made prices and competitively made profits are essential as guides, whether for State directives or private enterprise directives of production.

Fascism does not accept the liberal dogmas as to the sovereignty of the consumer or trader in the free market. It does not admit that the market ever can or should be entirely free. Least of all does it consider that market freedom, and the opportunity to make competitive profits, are rights of the individual. Some measure of market freedom, competition, private enterprise, and profits and losses for private enterprise, in the view of fascism, must be deemed essential as guides to any measure of social control.

Under fascism, private property, private enterprise, and private choice in the market, have no rights as ends in themselves. They have different measures of social usefulness subject to proper public control. If these institutions and ways are to have social utility to the State, the liberal régime must be ended, the great monopolies nationalized, and all the economic processes subjected to the discipline of a national plan. The ultimate objective is welfare through a strong national State, and neither the dictatorship of the proletarian nor the supremacy of private rights under any given set of rules.

CHAPTER XV

ENLARGING THE MARKET: A FINANCIAL PROBLEM

PERHAPS the simplest and briefest way of stating the basic objectives of national economic planning today is to say that the market must be enlarged and social control achieved. Just as the more logical and hard-minded communists like Lenin predicted, liberal capitalism is slowly going to pieces on the failure of the market to continue to absorb adequately the increasing supply of goods which must be produced and sold if the system is to work, and, also, if the unemployed are ever to work again. We have already, in another connection, disposed of the classical argument of capitalism that the production of goods and services inevitably though tardily provides the necessary market for the total output. The fact and old custom of hoarding, now in revival, is knocking that argument into a cocked hat.

Increasing the domestic market presents difficulties mainly in the field of finance. No sensible person questions that there are desires and needs for a larger output or that there is ample capacity for its production. The only serious objection raised is, "But where is the money to come from?" The answer, obviously, is, "From the same sources which have furnished all our money for wars and industrial expansion in the past."

If the objection takes the form of the question, "But how is this additional production and consumption to be paid for?" the answer is, "With more production." Things have ultimately to be paid for (if they are really paid for) with other things, money symbols being only the counters. The making of the money, whether by a turn of the government printing press or a stroke of a banker's pen, is always an extremely simple and easy matter. As the act of paying out money, whether for consumption or producers goods, initiates the necessary production, it is with a use of money that the economic process seems always to begin.

So strategic is the rôle of money that it seems to many people the only thing that matters in the economic process. This seems especially plausible, due to the fact that, from the point of view of the individual, with money he can buy or command almost any good or service, and without money he can do or obtain practically nothing. The trouble here, of course, is that the individual cannot make money with a stroke of a banker's pen or a turn of the government printing press. The individual cannot make money—he can only obtain it from those who have it. And this he can only do if they will give him money for something he can produce or lend him money. Hence, if he cannot sell his product or labor for money, or borrow money, the question "Where is the money coming from?" completely floors him. As long as most individuals, under liberal capitalism, could readily sell their labor or products of their labor, skill, land, and tools, there was no economic or monetary problem. A prospective sale only can make a sound loan under private capitalism. No sale in prospect, no bank loan requiring such sale for repayment. This explains why bank loans to business are shrinking and why the banks in 1935 are buying 91% of the new government bonds, the banks now holding 53% of the total federal debt.

Now, however, the problem of getting more money spent demands solution, and the solution requires the intervention of an initiating agent who is not embarrassed by the inability to make or get money except by the sale of something in an open market. In the present situation, that agent can only be the State or the person who has the right to make money and the power to get it back without having to rely on a sale in the free market to obtain it.

People hear with horror any mention of government-made money. They have been trained to believe that only money made by a stroke of a banker's pen in creating a loan and a corresponding deposit credit is good money. No amount of bank losses and failures seems to shake his faith. An old fashioned liberal professor of economics or finance would try to explain the creation of bank money or bank deposit credit as constituting not creation of something that did not exist already, but merely as the mobilization of money or credit which existed already but which only a bank could mobilize. The bad faith of this explanation lay in the fact that if it were invoked to justify a government creation of money it was indignantly rejected by those who used it to rationalize a banker's creation of money.

Obviously, all creations of paper, token, or bank deposit money, whether by the government, a central bank, a public, or a private bank, are creations of fiat money and are fraught with the same dangers. Every depression is a series of proofs of the unsoundness of a large volume of bank-made money or credit. Only commodity money, like gold and silver, which, as a commodity, is worth its face value, is not fiat money. All our economic prosperity and achievements have been financed by fiat money, and all our economic blunders or misfortunes can be attributed to fiat money, facts which should indicate the pointlessness of using terms like fiat money to disapprove of any given expenditure or investment, public or private.

Every effort should be made to avoid the evils of inflation, or a depreciating currency and collapsing credit structure. But these evils can never be avoided through the use of definition. It is not certain that these evils, as a practical matter, can ever be entirely avoided. But, certainly, every reasonable undertaking should be made to avoid them. The only way to avoid or minimize these evils is to keep the volume and velocity of circulation of all money, paper and bank deposit money, in a fairly stable relation to the volume of production.

If the total sum of money payments made in a given period increases markedly faster than the total volume of goods and services produced for sale in that period, there will ordinarily be inflation, rise in prices, and a fall in the value of money. Incidentally, it is to be remarked that communist Russia has been steadily inflating its currency and depreciating the purchasing power of the currency in the execution of its construction and five-year programs. And, as every one knows, no capitalist or fascist country since the War has enjoyed prosperity except when, and in measure as, it was indulging in inflation.

It remains to be shown, therefore, that the evils of inflation are entirely avoidable. Anyone who claims he has a sovereign remedy against the evils of inflation is sure to be a charlatan, for if there be such a remedy, it has not been demonstrated and, until the demonstration has been made, no one has a right to assert that he knows that he has a remedy. But the fact that no one knows a sovereign preventive of the evils and mistakes of inflation is no reason why money should not be created and spent by government to end unemployment, increase the supply of goods, enlarge productive capital and, presumably, thereby to increase the sum of human happiness. After all it must be remembered that capitalist America, communist Russia, and fascist Germany, enjoy great additions to their productive capital and current income as a result of inflationary spending and capital goods construction. And, after all, these benefits undoubtedly outweigh the real evils which have attended or followed inflation.

Obviously, every attempt must be made to keep physical production and the quantity-times-circulation velocity of money in the right relation—quantity of goods to quantity of money—and thereby to avoid or minimize the evils of inflation. This problem, however, cannot be solved by legal definitions or prohibitory law. The only prohibitory law which would be adequate and relevant to the prevention of the evils of inflation under liberal capitalism would be absurd, for such a law would have simply to prohibit depressions. If depressions can be prevented or minimized it will not be by prohibition or legal definitions. It will be by executive management. This is one of the reasons why the fascist formula must supplant the liberal formula which, in the economic sphere, really allows the State little more than the remedies of judicially defined and applied prohibition and punishment after the act.

Among the rules for avoiding inflation, the simplest to state can be worded briefly somewhat as follows: (1) Create new money, bank deposit money, or paper money, only for the retirement of debts and payment for the production of new physical goods and services. (2) Create and offer no more money for goods and services than is required to obtain the maximum attainable output from the existing plant. When more goods are demanded with money than the available supply and means of production can satisfy, prices go up, money goes down—and inflation is on. Creation and use of additional money for speculation and for attempts to force production beyond physical limits must be avoided if inflation is to be averted.

If it is easy to state these simple rules, it is by no means easy to know how and when to apply them. What is even more important at present is the fact that, within the framework of liberal capitalism, it is out of the question even to make any serious attempt to enforce observance of these rules. Among the chief reasons why no serious attempt can ever be made under liberal capitalism to apply the first rule are the following: Banks create money for loans in proportion to the interest they can obtain on loans with safety as to repayment. Speculators pay the highest interest rates, and often are able to give excellent security. So banks prefer loans to speculators if, as is usually the case, there are satisfactory guarantees of repayment of loans to finance speculations. Call loans on Stock Exchange securities as collateral are perfect examples of good loans for bankers and bad loans for economic order. The guarantees of these socially bad loans inhere, not in the economic soundness of the loan, but in special market machinery, special legal contracts, and the fact that there is always a buyer (usually a sucker who buys on a falling market) for bad and overpriced bank collateral to take it off the hands of the bank before that institution gets stuck.

Banks, we see, then, do not ordinarily, and could not effectively if they would, control the uses made of money they create and lend so as to check inflation and speculation. A borrower may say he wants a loan for a given purpose, like building himself a home, or a corporation may say it wants a loan for some stated business use or investment. The borrowing individual may build the home, and the corporation may make the stated business use or investment of so much money. At the same time, however, the individual home builder, or the corporation, may make a speculative use of a similar amount of money which would not have been made had the loan not been obtained for the other alleged purpose. The point, of course, is that, as a rule, borrowers (certainly the rich individual and the large company) usually have lots of money at the time they borrow a given sum in addition to that sum. Consequently, in most cases, a given loan merely swells the cash holdings of the borrower. It is, therefore, absurd to say of a given loan to a borrower, through whose hands several times as much money flows every week or every year, that that particular loan went to a given purpose. Such a statement is exactly like saying that a small rivulet which runs into one of many streams which feed many reservoirs which supply New York city with water is the rivulet which furnishes the water for the City Hall or the Union League Club.

In brief, whatever they may advertise to the contrary, banks have to be guided in making loans mainly, if not exclusively, by two rules: (1) Get the highest return possible on the loan. (2) Get the loan repaid. Loans which meet these rules have to be made, whatever harmful social effects they may produce. And loans which do not meet these rules have to be avoided, whatever beneficial social fruits they might bear. This being true, private banks must necessarily pour oil on the fires of speculation when they start burning, and they must fail to prime recovery in a crisis like that of the present, when good loans in sufficient quantity cannot be found. To prevent the creation of new bank money by banks to enable speculators to pay higher prices for Florida real estate or Stock Exchange securities, it is necessary to take the power to create new money for loans from private bankers, who must always use such power in a way to feed the fires of speculation, because loans to speculators on price changes are usually the most profitable to banks.

But even if the State has the monopoly of banking, as in Communist Russia, the State may, as Communist Russia is doing, create the evils of inflation by creating and spending money to pay for more physical production than the productive plant of the nation is capable of furnishing. To avoid the evils of inflation, it is necessary among other things, to have no creation of money to finance speculators in bidding up prices of goods already produced, and also to have no creation of money to finance a greater demand for new production than the available productive resources can supply.

Now, as I have said, no one can claim for any formula that it will insure adequate observance of these two rules and any others for avoiding inflationary evils. Furthermore, we cannot be sure that a State following and enforcing these rules might not still run into inflation through the operation of factors beyond its control producing scarcity. All that can fairly be claimed for fascism, in this respect, is that it offers the best political and administrative formula for keeping money and production in the right relation to insure stability and to avert inflation. Keeping production up to capacity, and not trying to force it too much, may be said to constitute problems in scientific measurement of a sort which presents no real difficulties, value selection problems which are exercises in imagination and power, and administrative problems, the like of which have to be met in all large human undertakings.

The ends of successful executive attack on this problem will not be helped by the usual arguments and concepts employed in discussion of monetary and economic questions. Nor will the standards of sound or successful finance for private banks and individuals furnish much useful guidance for the government undertaking to spend or invest enough money every year to take up the slack in private spending and investing. The rules for sound private or commercial banking can be found in hundreds of text-books. These rules amount to saying "Don't make a bad loan." When times are good it is hard to make a bad loan, if ordinary precautions are taken against embezzlers and frauds. When times turn bad, the formerly good loans go sour and it proves impossible to find enough good loans (that is, loans that will be repaid) for one's idle funds.

All of this merely proves that most of the rules for sound banking, beyond those aimed at frauds, are largely superfluous. The maker of a private or bank loan has chiefly to rely for repayment on a set of conditions and events over which he cannot possibly exercise any control. As the elder Mr. Morgan once testified, in 1913, before a Senate Committee, character is about the only useful standard for making loans. Borrowers may be selected according to character. The rest, to a large extent, lies outside the control of borrower and lender. Assuming character factors and general conditions are favorable, the private or bank lender relies mainly on the open market to provide the borrower with funds to repay the loan.

Government creations of credit to finance spending and investing, however, cannot rely on the character of borrowers, favorable business conditions, and a market which will put the borrowers in funds for the repayment of the government loan. If this happy combination of conditions were present, there would be no need for government intervention in the economic process. If government could find good borrowers, such borrowers could find ample accommodations from the banks. If ample borrowing demands of the right sort met ample supplies of loan funds, there would be no depression.

No; government creations of credit to finance social expenditure and investment must rely on entirely different mechanisms and principles to keep credit and money sound, or to keep production and money in the right relation one to the other. For one thing, government expenditures on social services cannot be recovered by the sale of such services in the open market. If the parents of the children who attend the public schools had to pay the cost of the instruction of their children, most of the children now in school would not be there, much to their joy and the joy of the taxpayers who are constantly denouncing high taxes. For another thing, government investments in slum clearance, grade crossing elimination, and highway and public works projects of all sorts, cannot possibly earn their capital costs, through charges collected, in a free market. If they could, private initiative and private funds would finance and execute most of these projects for the rents, tolls, or charges, obtainable from them. The chief reasons, of course, why capital charges on so many desirable building projects are more than rentals would cover are high interest rates and inflated land values.

From the foregoing considerations, it follows naturally that if government is to make large social expenditures and investments, government must exercise two important public powers in this connection. First, it must levy the appropriate tolls or taxes to get back into the public treasury each year as much money as it puts out on such expenditures and investments. Second, largely for reasons of administrative convenience and facility, government must exercise the monoply of bank credit creation, which government can do only through nationalization of the banks. Government, of course, might allow the private ownership and management of banking to continue and obtain whatever it wanted of them by forceful taking or commanding. But there are difficulties about such a course of procedure too obvious to need mention. It is possible, as is happening in many European countries, for government to to get much of what it wants from privately owned banks through a system of procedure which combines in varying degrees government coercion and voluntary banker coöperation.

Nationalization of the banks is the simplest method, but the simplest method is not always the easiest to initiate. In this country it is little realized how powerful government can be, or how meek and coöperative bankers and big business men can learn to be once they have to deal with a strong government, to defy which they cannot every minute run into the courts with an expensive legal action.

The power to get the requisite amount of money for spending, in the first instance, by recourse to the device of bank credit, and the power to get the money back through taxation for re-spending, however, are not the only requisites for safely spending our way out of a depression. In exercising these powers, there are many problems of a highly technical character to be solved fairly scientifically if ultimate inflationary disaster is to be avoided. This is but another reason why these powers cannot be safely exercised by government under the liberal formula of divided powers and responsibilities.

Take the creation of credit, for one thing: This act, and the spending of the fiat money so created, imposes on the entire community a corresponding amount of forced saving. Under the liberal system, the bankers get the interest or profit on forced saving thus taken from the whole people and invested to produce wealth. Waiving the question of the moral right of the bankers to levy a profit on the enforced savings of the community, there is this to be said for a system of credit creation only by private bankers: it formerly had the control of some degree of banker responsibility. When banks were strictly private affairs, managed by men who had their entire fortune in the bank, and on terms which made the banker's entire fortune responsible for the bank's liabilities, this control was significant and fairly effective to check excessive inflation. Now that the biggest New York banks have come to be dominated by high pressure executives who hide their personal fortune under the ownership of their wives, or of dummy companies which the bank executives control but do not own, the control incidental to the responsibilities or liabilities of ownership does not operate. The dominating executive can wreck a bank while enriching himself, and when the wrecking is completed and he is ousted, he can find himself still a rich man by reason of the money he has salted away in his wife's name.

All of this merely amounts to saying that the controls of private ownership no longer apply to large banks managed by men whose only stake in the bank is their yearly salary and bonus, and whose ruling principle of management can be to make hay for themselves while the sun shines. But a control on the creation of new credit is necessary, and it remains for any government using the power to create credit for social expenditure and investment to perfect satisfactory controls.

The only way to develop such a control is to follow the principles of honest accounting. By allowing a large field of private initiative in which private enterprise will make a bid for private and voluntary savings, the State will have the guidance of a capital return rate to indicate just how much people must be paid, as a practical matter, to induce them voluntarily to save the full amount required for business uses. When the government asks the people, or rather forces them through the credit financing of a five- or ten-year building program, to make a given amount of saving (which is, of course, returned to them or kept for them in the public assets created and the services so rendered), the government will be able to tell exactly by simple accounting methods how much, corresponding to an interest rate, it has levied on the people in this way.

It may be argued that government should always pay an interest on its borrowings in order to be governed more effectively by some control. Such borrowing is practiced on a large scale internally by communist Russia. Where there are no private banks, it is free of many of the evils of government borrowing from private banks, for then it is always direct borrowing of genuine private savings.

In a communist State, where there is no private business bidding for private savings, such borrowing has much to commend it as a guide or control to indicate the state of the personal or psychological factors in respect of saving. In a fascist State, such borrowing would be unnecessary for that reason, since some private enterprise would serve the same purpose of control by bidding capital return for private savings. Moreover, such public borrowing under these circumstances would be harmful, for the reason that it would tend to divert voluntary savings from private enterprise. It would make the government a harmful competitor of private enterprise in the free capital market. This evil would be most vicious in the area of large investment funds and private fortunes. They are naturally apt to seek maximum safety and accept minimum return. It is socially desirable that large fortunes be forced to take average safety, run current business risks, and take their full share of current business losses. If large fortunes or funds are not thus kept pruned down, but are allowed to grow in geometrical progression at compound interest, without risk or managerial responsibilities, by the simple expedient of being invested in secure government obligations, it will be necessary to have such fortunes kept down by drastic direct government taxation or by terrific economic collapses and currency devaluations. The simplest way to keep private fortunes small is to force them to run all the risks of private enterprise. A few fortunes may thus grow large under the skillful or lucky management of one or two men for one or two generations, but in time most large fortunes will get broken up in this way. Besides, as long as a large fortune is kept intact by personal and successful management of production, it is entitled to plead some of the defenses of private capitalism which are now absurdly invoked for fortunes, the owners and managers of which render no socially useful services.

Taxation still remains the most important instrumentality for averting or minimizing the evils of inflation and subsequent currency devaluation naturally inherent in any large government program of social expenditure and investment with the aid of credit money. Taxation, as most people understand in a vague sort of way, is also an extremely complicated technical problem which should be given the most scientific solution possible. This is no place for the most summary discussion of tax theory and practice. Suffice it only to state a few obvious generalizations.

In the first place, fascism, by exalting the ideals of nationalism, must tend to change popular attitudes toward the payment of taxes. It is not good form in any reputable association, a good club, a sporting party or an army, to be trying all the time to welsh out of some obligation to the group. Paying one's full tax, and paying a heavy tax, should be as much a matter of personal pride as paying for a round of drinks in any social group.

In the second place, the altogether rational idea that taxes are merely payments for services rendered must be indoctrinated in the people. The larger the tax, the larger the service received. It does not really matter whether the service is rendered by the State or by the barber around the corner. What matters is whether the service is desired, and whether it has been efficiently and economically furnished. If the rich paid heavy taxes to eliminate the slums and beautify our cities, they would, given the cultivation of the right attitude, receive quite as much aesthetic satisfaction from the change in the environment which they are forced to live in or near as they derive from a few weeks or months a year spent on a private yacht or a country estate, or in the possession and contemplation of an expensive work of art. After all, the richest citizens in New York have to live within a stone's throw of the slums, and as they drive to and from their country estates they have to suffer the sights and smells of the slums. Since, by reason of the ease of locomotion and the universal mania for movement, all of us are tending more and more to live in the entire country, money spent to make the country, as a whole, more pleasant to live in must be a service to all of us.

In the third place, the idea that some arbitrary equalization of fortunes and incomes by taxation is desirable must be popularized, even among the rich. As has been explained again and again in technical expositions of the principles of the capital levy, equalization by taxation does not need to involve any interference whatever with the organization and operation of large productive or service enterprises.

No sane tax or capital levy would put the Ford plant up for sale or force a change of management. Any amount of taxation or capital levy could be laid on that plant, or any other industry owned by a single family or individual, in a way to leave management unchanged and to provide for the payment of the tax or levy out of income. The Government could become a ten, fifty or seventy-five per cent shareholder of any productive plant without disrupting thereby the successful management of such a plant. The owners of the remaining shares of that plant would have just as much interest in maintaining efficient and profitable operation if the government owned fifty per cent of the income as if it owned ten per cent.

The notion that the intensity and attentiveness of a man's efforts in a business are proportionate to the extent of his proprietorship rights is as silly as it is to suppose that a man owning a ten million dollar business is ten times as efficient and attentive as a man owning a million dollar business. It is not the size of the share, but the fact of having a share both in the profits and losses, which counts. After all, the executive owner of a very large enterprise is far more the slave of that job than the common laborer who can turn to a hundred different jobs, any one of which he can do equally well. The bigger the executive, the fewer the opportunities for his peculiar talents.

And in the fourth and last place, the idea that taxation must be cut to meet the operation requirements of successful business must yield to the idea that business must be conducted in a way to meet the requirements of successful government taxation. It is perfectly true that business on the liberal capitalist formula can stand only limited taxation, for taxation is a cost which reduces profits, and liberal capitalist business needs large profits to flourish and offset large losses. But this merely proves that liberal capitalism is doomed, not necessarily private ownership and management. For the latter can flourish without either a high rate of profit or a steady compounding of surplus. To run private ownership and management on the theory of a small profit and a stable income is a feasible and fascist ideal, but not an ideal of liberal capitalism.

The basic problems of a large program of government spending and investing to take up the slack in private spending and investing are those of honest and scientific cost accounting, taxation, measurement, value judgments, and sheer administration. These problems cannot be attacked within the framework of the liberal, parliamentary systems. Desirable results cannot be realized by legal enactment, prohibition or definition.

They must be achieved only by successful management. This means the inevitability of the organization of an executive State and of the person of an adequate leader.

It is the custom to deride the ineptitudes and inadequacies of government officials. In connection with the proposal of a strong executive State and an adequate social program for that State, such derision is absurd. It is not true that government officials are notoriously incompetent or that the techniques of economic measurement, cost accounting, budget making and budget balancing, and scientific taxation, are not thoroughly understood by enough men to insure the success of an executive State which had our situation to meet.

Under the existing system, government officials have no chance of applying the science and skills which they have, or could have, simply because of the inhibitions of liberal social norms. It is a significant fact that business men and scientists rarely criticize army and navy officers, who are government officials, for failing to use science and technology in killing people. There is little doubt that every army and navy is using the latest and fullest resources of science and technology to the best of their ability or as well as possible with the appropriations and personnel available. So far as financial technique is concerned, we are quite as competent as we are in the arts of war. And the financial techniques can perform quite as well to facilitate a State undertaking in peace as in war. The goods can be produced, the means of payment can be provided, and the rhythm of payments and collections kept in proper relation to the rhythm of production and exchange, with such errors and failures as characterize all human undertakings, provided only there is the will to achieve these results.

CHAPTER XVI

CONTROL: THE PROBLEM OF POLITICAL ORGANIZATION

AFTER requisite enlargement of the market, economic control is the next largest problem for an American fascism. Control, management, or government (as one may prefer to term it) of the right sort, or thoroughly adequate to the demands of social order, may be thought of in two broad divisions: First, there is political organization, or the mechanics of control through the use of the coercion of public authority; second, there is indoctrination or the inculcation of right social attitudes to make the social order work.

Under political organization, the two major functions can be called those of administration and representation. Administration is government. It includes the making, interpreting and enforcing of laws, regulations and public policies. No useful distinction can be drawn between making, interpreting, and enforcing law, or the national plan. Administration is getting the national plan realized and preventing its defeat or frustration. Representation is the process through which government is kept apprised of the popular will and through which government makes the popular will understand and will the means and ends of public administration.

The term democracy will not be made the subject of any essay at definition, but the point may here be interjected that, if democracy means the rule of the people, it must mean that rule under some efficient formula of political organization. The people do not rule by legal definition but by efficient political machinery. The efficiency of public administration in controlling the conditions of life in a country is the measure of popular rule.

It is a distorted sense of reality which calls the rule of impersonal necessity under extreme laissez-faire the rule of the people. The people rule to the extent that they are disciplined and cannot individually do as they please, and not the extent that every man can do as he pleases. The people rule to the extent that the nation can do as it pleases. Anarchy is not the rule of the people or any individual. It is the rule of disorder or nobody. There is no one model form of popular rule. Most of the rules of liberalism which are most touted as safeguarding popular rule merely insure the rule of the rich, powerful, irresponsible, and selfish who, under liberalism, can produce expressions of popular will and opinion to suit their selfish interests at the rate of so many dollars a given unit of expression of popular opinion or will.

The scheme of political organization should make the most rational provision for efficient administration and useful representation of group interests in the determination of public policies. At present it may be said of the American political scheme of organization that tradition is its ruling principle, while in every other American scheme of organization rationality, or fitness of means to ends, is the ruling principle. Fascism would make the American scheme of political organization conform to the standards of fitness of means to ends which govern in all our other important schemes of organization. In other words, fascism would rationalize our scheme of political organization. Fascism holds that we must be administered as a nation, not as a confederacy of sovereign states, and represented according to group interests which have the greatest importance and which are prepared to accept responsibility for full coöperation with government, not according to regional residence.

Integration of governmental agencies and coördination of authority may be called the keystone principles of fascist administration. Applied in the United States, these principles would mean the end of our federal system, of state's rights and of the fictions of a functional separation of powers as between the legislative, executive, and judicial branches of government. And, needless to add, these principles would mean the replace-

ment of the existing organizational pattern of public administration by that of a highly centralized government which
would exercise the powers of a truly national State, and which
would be manned by a personnel responsible to a political
party holding a mandate from the people. This party would be
the fascist party of the United States—undoubtedly called,
however, by another name.

The ruling principle would be instrumental rationality, or
fitness of means to ends. As every one who has a nodding
acquaintance with American history should know, the rationale of the federal system, with its forty-eight states and one
federal State, is not that of fitness to any logical scheme of
present day ends of administration and popular representation,
or to any real or strong present day feeling of the people. The
rationale of the federal system is that of a compromise made
among representatives of regional group interests after the
American Revolution.

Most of the people in these regional groups of the American
colonies, whether the influential or the poorest classes, had no
national citizenship other than that of the mother country.
After the American Revolution, most of them did not have
even that. They had come to America in flight from distaste-
ful religious, social, or economic conditions in the mother
country. America, for them, was not a new nation but merely
a place of escape and an opportunity to work out a new scheme
of life with as little government, and as much laissez-faire, as
had ever been known in a civilized community. Few of the
American colonists in 1776 or 1789 wanted an American or any
other kind of nation. At first they wanted simply to be English
colonies almost wholly free from English control and taxation.
When the stupidity of George III and his advisers denied the
American colonists the boon of a large measure of laissez-faire,
they had no choice about relinquishing British nationality.

It was only by dint of vigorous argument and hard trading
that the nationally-minded few among the triumphant American colonists succeeded in making the American Constitution,
and the federal system based thereon, as national as it emerged

in 1789. And it was only after the triumph of American nationalism in the Mexican and Civil Wars that we could be said to have passed the stage of loosely confederated colonies which had thrown off allegiance to a foreign nation but which still had not created a nation of their own.

Without laboring further these obvious historical facts, we may say that the American system, in so far as it is expressed in a literal interpretation of the Constitution, was never intended to meet the requirements of any adequate scheme of national aims, but merely to hold together as well as possible thirteen colonies which wanted neither to be separate nations nor yet to be welded into a new nation. We may say further that the trend of Constitutional interpretations, as well as of institutional developments in American politics, has been definitely and overwhelmingly in the direction of making the United States a nation with a strong central government.

Those who talk in favor of a stricter interpretation of state's rights and against an enlargement of the powers of the federal government are, therefore, in harmony with the dominant thought, feeling, and purposes of the American colonists who created the federal system, but against the trend of developments in the system ever since. This being true, we may ask which is the more American, the thought, feelings and purposes of a majority of the founding fathers, or the trend in the thought, feeling and purposes of the dominant majority of their descendants? Surely the only good Americans are not dead Americans—and those longest dead.

After all, there is nothing un-American about centralization. No country has carried national integration, coördination of authority, centralization of power, standardization, and rationalization further, outside of the governmental structure, than the United States. In the economic sphere, the great trust, or the billion dollar corporation, or the holding company, as well as myriad legal devices for centralizing control, are tremendously important cases in point. In the field of cultural and recreational associations, no country has more national associations, economic, fraternal, cultural, and recreational. And in no country is there found more homogeneity in such organizations.

In matters of taste and distinctive habits, no country a third as large as ours is as standardized as to dress, styles, architecture, customs, speech, daily reading, and recreations as we are. Travel a hundred miles in England, Germany, France or Russia, and distinctive regional difference assail the eye, the ear and the palate. Travel three thousand miles in the United States and remain on the same economic level, and you will scarcely notice a difference—unless it be in climate or natural scenery. The scenery of a hotel lobby, the main street, any store, church, or railroad station interior, will not enlighten you as to whether you are in Maine or California. No country has been better prepared for political and social standardization, whether under fascism or communism, than the United States. Our national corporations and social organizations have unified and nationalized us into the most standardized people on earth, mostly during the past thirty years.

The early American colonists were not American nationalists but British colonials. In their peculiar and favored situation of that period they wanted none of their original or ancestral European nationalisms and felt no need of an American nationalism. Ever since, we have been steadily perceiving our need of being a nation, and we have been modifying accordingly the original work of the founding fathers. Today we find ourselves faced with the need of completing the rationalization of our social order by becoming a rationally organized nation. Has this trend of adaptation of political means and institutions to changing needs and problems been un-American? If American is defined to mean 18th century English colonial with a dash of insubordination to the mother country, and a lack of necessity, nerve, and cultural homogeneity to create a new nation on this side of the water, then an American fascism can rightly be called un-American.

The fact is, as a few of the founding fathers were far-seeing enough to foresee, since the American Revolution we have had either to become a nation through the unifying experiences of several wars and the steady expansion of our territory, or else finally to regularize our colonial status by reunion with the mother country or some other European country that was a nation and acted like one. A people blessed with our resources cannot, in a world of competing nations, enjoy the advantages of group culture and solidarity without becoming a nation and acting as a nation. Had we chosen not to act as a nation, we should have received the same treatment China and Ethiopia are receiving today. And today the extent to which we must complete or rationalize our nationalism is being largely dictated by world conditions over which we have no control. We are too large and significant to play the rôle of a Switzerland or a small Scandinavian country which is protected from foreign intervention by reason of being in a strategic position near great powers, whose peaceful relations, being maintained in a delicate balance of power, will not allow the absorption of these little and comparatively defenceless States. But such circumstances will not protect a large country like China or the United States against a predatory great nation.

So we may say that it matters little how American jurists, historians, political scientists, or states-rights men, profess authoritatively to define the American nation and delimit the powers of its metaphysical forty-nine separate sovereignties. What they have to say is important mainly to themselves. The only definition of the American national leviathan which has validity must be written by the necessities of group self-preservation and assertion of group values in a world situation which no one nation can control. In the face of prolonged foreign menace or aggression this would mean, concretely, that the national government would be forced to choose between scrapping the Constitution and scrapping the country. It would be an easier and more satisfactory transition to a purely national state and a centralized executive formula of government if it were worked out more leisurely in peace time under the immediate pressures of only domestic order imperatives.

Were there space for it, a lengthy and well documented case could easily be submitted to show that purely domestic prob-

lems indicate only slightly less urgently than foreign challenges to our security the inadequacy of our federal formula to
the demands of order. In matters as different in character as
waging war on desperate and nationally organized criminals,
the policing of every sort of business activity, domestic relations and divorce, industrial regulations for social protection,
or simple relief for the army of the unemployed and destitute,
it is easy to show that satisfactory results can only be obtained
by the national government.

The time has come to ask, Why the States? and to reject
answers which amount merely to saying, "Because, while the
American nation was still unborn and only a series of colonies,
the fathers of the Constitution and colonial confederation
found it necessary to make compromises with ideas, feelings
and purposes which were then widely and tenaciously held and
which are no longer held." It is time to recognize that not one
American in ten really thinks any of those 18th century American colonial thoughts, feels any of those feelings, or cherishes
any of those purposes in deference to which our system was
originally devised. Many more than one citizen in ten, possibly,
will be found to profess all sorts of faith in and attachment to
state's rights, out of respect for past tradition, and current
opinion as to what is the correct attitude in respect to such
tradition. Abundant proofs of the insincerity of these professions
of attachment to state's rights can usually be remarked even on
superficial notice. Thus, a man who professes great attachment
to his state, will often be found maintaining outside of his state
a legal domicile or business headquarters to lessen his tax bill,
or going outside his state for cheaper labor or materials, or
sending his children to school outside the state, or invariably
spending his vacation outside the state, or using great ingenuity
and pains to get the better of the state in a dozen different
ways.

In most cases of particularly vigorous champions of state's
rights, one can go through the man's history with a fine tooth-
comb in vain to find one instance of his ever having made a
sacrifice for, or a voluntary gift to, his state, or any other

person, merely on the ground of a state tie. People feel some special ties to fellow members of all sorts of associations, religious, fraternal, professional, and commercial. But one seldom finds instances of people showing real evidence of feeling a stronger bond with a fellow Pennsylvanian or Californian solely because of state origin.

It is nothing for any one to deplore or apologize for that he or someone else never gives evidence of a genuine and disinterested partiality to his own state or of a feeling of peculiar solidarity with a fellow Kansan or Rhode Islander. Associational groups, to merit any respect or admiration from outsiders, or to deserve the loyalty of insiders, must have some logical reason for their existence, or must serve some purpose useful to insiders and outsiders. Today it is difficult to find a logical reason for the existence or functions of state governments as provided for in the Constitution. The state boundaries, generally speaking, correspond no longer, if ever they did, to economic or useful administrative divisions of territory. The states are just survivals, the explanation or rationalization of which has to be made exclusively in terms of the 18th or 19th century conditions, feelings and purposes, most of which have long since ceased to be operative.

To say that an American fascism can find no use for the present federal set-up is not to say that fascism would have no use for regional subdivisions for political and economic administration. It is only to say that political subdivisions must correspond to some rational and useful purpose to which the states cannot be said to correspond. Nor is the rejection of the federal system as prescribed in the Constitution tantamount to a rejection of local self-government or a denial of representation to any significant group interests. The forty-eight American states are not divisions of territory, people, or interests which are any longer significant or relevant to useful purposes. State boundaries in many instances arbitrarily separate areas which are united by a series of community interests and which could constitute political and administrative units. Thus, the metropolitan area of New York, a useful geographical unit for administration and representation, is divided by state boundaries. For purposes of political administration or representation of significant regional interests, the metropolitan areas ought to be separate units.

So far as regional divisions are concerned, it would seem today that they should be drawn from time to time solely with reference to the needs of efficient administration. While as for regional representation, it would seem most doubtful that any good can come of attempts to provide for political representation according to geography. If there must be minority group representation, and it would seem that there must be, it should be representation only for groups having interests that are peculiar to the group and common to all or most of the members of the group. Now, it cannot by any stretch of the imagination be supposed that the people living in any one of the states, Pennsylvania, New York, or Illinois, have interests in common as inhabitants of those states, except as such community of interest is artificially created by the state form of government. The residents of the metropolitan cities of New York, Chicago, and Philadelphia, have more interests in common and of a nature peculiar to residence in a big city than the residents of New York City have with the farmers of upstate New York. The ends neither of rational administration nor rational representation are well served by the state organizations of the federal union. If this proposition be reasonably true, is it good Americanism to be irrational and bad Americanism to be rational?

So far as political organization for representation is concerned, it must correspond to the rationale of power politics and workability. If, as is the case under our present system, the attempt is made to give representation to groups like the inhabitants within an area artificially delimited to correspond to no present day significant cultural or economic boundaries, one gets, among other things, an unofficial and irresponsible representation through improper and often illegal ways of real group interests such as bankers, the utility companies, the manufacturers, the farmers, trade unions, the American veterans, certain religious associations, and so on. Liberals and eminent elder statesmen are constantly deploring the behavior of pressure groups in relation to government. And they insist on telling us that such behavior is not according to the rules of the game and should be stopped. With this naïve thought they are constantly investigating, exposing, and legislatively forbidding, the improprieties of minority group representations. They forget that these minority groups constitute real communities of interest, real force potentials, and thoroughly human factors and, also, that they have no legal and proper means of adequate political representation. Reform cannot remove or curb these force potentials, but fascism can create for them socially-disciplined instrumentalities of expression and representation.

The moral for the would-be reformer is that representation for unreal or economically and socially powerless minority groups like the inhabitants of regional subdivisions called states must be scrapped, and legal representation for real and powerful minority groups must be provided for in an adequate manner. Representation will always be proportionate to might, regardless of law or contrary ethical standards. The citizens of a state, as such, have practically speaking no political or economic might. These same citizens as members of a public utility committee, a manufacturers' association or a labor union, have, as a practical matter, a very real might. It is for this reason that the laws and administration of state governments, as well as of the federal government, conform to pressures of minority groups rather than to the pressures of the citizens of states as such.

It may be said that we have got along fairly well under this system. It is true that we have got on fairly well in spite of this system. The fact is that administration and representation will go on in spite of almost any institutional absurdities. The evils of the combination of a formal, legal, proper, and visible government by unreal group organisms called states, with an informal, illegal, improper, and invisible government by real group organisms are too obvious to need argument. These evils can be epitomized in one word—irresponsibility. Doubtless it is fair to say that no people deserve a better government than the one they get, or that the government can never be better than the people. A fascist government will be no better than the people and the leaders in power, but it will exemplify administrative functioning and group representation, which are responsible. That is to say, there will be government persons to take full responsibility for acts of administration, and minority group leaders to take responsibility for acts in representation of minority group interests.

In this connection it is apropos to remark, in passing, that the well-known hostility of the labor union leaders formed under liberal capitalism to the theory and practice of fascism is chiefly due to their innate aversion to an assumption of social or political responsibility. The labor union higher-ups are doubtless, for the greater part, fairly loyal to the interests of their clients, provided the permanent jobs and high incomes of the upper bureaucracy are secure. But they wish to play an individualist game for the smaller social group constituted by their members so far as the entire social group is concerned. Labor union leaders have, therefore, opposed laws forcing on the unions incorporation and publication of financial statements. They like to be able to play with the millions of dollars which flow in dues into their war chest, without any one outside of a charmed circle of three or four high officials knowing where the money goes. In this respect, the executive committee of an American labor union likes to work with the same secrecy and social irresponsibility with which executive committees of great corporations so often operate. Indeed, the best apology for the secrecy and irresponsibility of high executive action by labor leaders or corporate executive committees is to say that it is the universal way of exercising power under liberal capitalism. Fascism believes in, and provides for, labor representation, but with full responsibility of group organizations for organizational decisions.

Perhaps the greatest single vice of the liberal system is that of the anti-social or socially irresponsible behavior of powerful minority group interests in determining the decisions and policies of public administration. The right to behave in these ways is usually the right which minority group representatives complain that fascism violates. The logic of the fascist answer to these complaints is the logic of a discipline necessary for the welfare of the total group. Any discipline to meet the order and welfare imperatives of the total group must force minority groups to accept representation of their interests, and coöperation with the scheme of the total group, in ways to make the totalitarian group scheme work. The logic of this discipline is that the members of the minority groups will not long prosper if the larger or total group does not prosper. Concretely, this would mean that the rate a power company might charge in a given community, or the wage a small group of special workers might obtain, would not be whatever could be had by the use of the monopoly power in the one case or the blackmail power of the strike in the other case.

On careful analysis, it will usually be found that the rights of the minority group alleged to be denied or curtailed by fascism are rights to use a pressure in a given situation, really against society as a whole, for all it may be worth at that moment to that group. Obviously, if minority groups exercise their powers within the latitude allowed by liberal or libertarian principles, the results will be anarchic, as they so often are, certain groups getting the best of it and the majority of the people getting the worst of it. One of the functions of government is to impose a national discipline on minority groups rather than to furnish a playground with umpires and constables for the free play of minority group pressures.

The specific problems of mechanisms to effectuate national administration and rational representation cannot be advantageously opened up in anything but a highly technical treatise. No useful purpose would be served by a brief description of fascist mechanisms abroad, for such description would have to be too brief to be adequately informing and, however adequate it might be, it would be largely irrelevant to our peculiar needs and problems. No one need worry about the technical capacity for rationalizing governmental administration and group representation to be found in a country which has our record in the rationalizing of industry and the development of great trusts. We have working models in the modern corporation for organization for centralized control and management. In a great variety of trade, professional, and fraternal associations we have the models, techniques, and experience for solving all problems of representation. The State has all these resources at its command. And, in the United States, these resources are more abundant than in any European country.

The fascist issue is not how to rationalize public administration in the technological sense of the term, that is, in the sense of making means suit ends. The only real issue raised by fascism in this respect is that of whether we shall rationalize our political system. This issue will doubtless be resolved not by the pressure of arguments such as those advanced in this book, but by the pressure of necessity in the face of challenges to our national security, the most dynamic and creative of such challenges probably arising first in foreign war, or threat of war, rather than in domestic difficulties.

This rationalization of our political system in the direction of fascism is in progress. It has been going on, at different rates of speed, since the days of John Marshall. President Franklin D. Roosevelt is forcing the issue, or being driven to force the issue, more than any of his predecessors. The use of the modern trust and the present-day uses of the modern corporation began during the last two decades of the 19th century. These institutions and ways have done more to make fascism inevitable than any European precedents. Economic conditions and events in the world today, the subjects of early analysis in this book, are providing the pressures which are driving this country and President Roosevelt towards fascism. And, as we have already amply stated, these conditions and events have to be met with measures of social adjustment for survival, not with attempts to disprove the actual, or with moral denunciations of what is wholly unaffected by the pronouncement of a moral judgment.

In any secular or long term trend of this sort—from one social system to another—it is idle to speculate about, or attach too great importance to, the exact moment when the greatest or more or less final change will take place. It seems too obvious to need saying that there is little likelihood that, within the next four or five years, the United States will be transformed into a fully rationalized national State, which, in this book, is called fascist for purposes of identification with certain familiar characteristics of now operating systems also labelled fascist.

The purpose and usefulness of this discussion may be considered as the preparation of enlightened opinion and effective leadership for the inevitable trend of social change and readjustment. The greatest single merit of the founding fathers of the American system in the late 18th century was their grasp of the political theory of their times. The greatest single demerit of our leaders today is a grasp of that same theory to the exclusion of any other. Times have changed, and a political theory to suit the changed times is required.

CHAPTER XVII

CONTROL: MAKING GOOD CITIZENS

In this chapter, continuing the discussion of social control, we shall be concerned with the processes of education, indoctrination, and inculcation of right attitudes. We may, then, divide all human institutions into those in which education is purposive, or done with certain purposes pursued by those in charge of the institution, and those institutions in which education is non-purposive and purely, or chiefly, incidental. The school is one institution which most people will readily admit has this purpose and educates with definite purposes. Accordingly, I am including in this chapter a reprint of an article I contributed to a symposium on "Indoctrination, The Task Before the American School," published in *The Social Frontier, A Journal of Educational Criticism and Reconstruction,* January, 1935, for permission to reprint which I make acknowledgment to the publishers of that magazine. This article expresses the fascist philosophy with regard to education and indoctrination done by that institution, the school, which every one recognizes to be engaged in purposive education.

Before entering upon a brief discussion of education by the school as one of the important agencies of social control or government, let us run over one or two considerations which link up certain other institutions with the school as educators with social purposes. The church, the press, the theatre, the moving picture, and the radio undoubtedly do more educating than the school, if for no other reason than that they educate people throughout their entire lifetimes. These institutions also educate with definite social purposes. Sometimes these purposes harmonize with the larger purposes of the social plan, and sometimes they certainly do not. In the fascist view of things, all institutional formation of character, mind, social attitudes, and opinions with a social purpose, must harmonize with, and not be antagonistic to, the larger purposes of the national plan. This means that fascism holds that no institution forming people's minds, characters, and attitudes should have among its purposes or effects the unfitting of people for good citizenship as the State defines good citizenship.

It is obviously impossible to list all the offenses which purposive education, whether by the church, school, or radio, can commit against the national interest. It is only possible, in a brief space, to outline certain guiding principles in reference to purposive education by powerful social institutions. The first consideration in order of logical approach, perhaps, is the one most ignored, or openly denied, by liberalism. It is the consideration that institutions like the church, the radio, or the press, to mention only three examples, do form people's minds and social attitudes with definite social purposes which are determined by the persons in charge of the institution, or, more particularly, by the persons in charge of the particular unit of the institution in question. No one can work on a farm or in a bakery without getting a good deal of education from the experience, but the social attitudes acquired while undergoing these experiences may vary greatly. Few persons, however, can read the Hearst papers daily, or tune in daily on certain radio programs, or attend weekly certain churches, without having their social attitudes and opinions markedly determined by these experiences. In the cases of a majority of those constantly exposed to one of these institutional educators with a purpose, it may be said that most of their opinions and attitudes will be derived almost entirely from two or three of these.

From the consideration just stated follows a second one, that given units of some of these important institutional educators or opinion- and attitude-formers are largely—at times, wholly—controlled by powerful persons or economic interests for private ends which are not always consistent with public ends. These rich persons who can own a newspaper, buy time over national hook-ups, and command the resources of expensive publicity experts, or these powerful interests which, because of their economic power as advertisers and contributors to persons and institutions, can dictate largely the policies of churches, newspapers, moving pictures, and radio, or of cultural leaders, can and do, through the sheer might of money, use these educational institutions or leaders to make people think and feel as it suits their interests. The facts are matters of such common knowledge, and have been exposed so many times and in so many connections, that it seems superfluous to support the foregoing generalizations with detailed examples. The consideration, then, that people by the million are being made to think, feel, and vote as powerful economic interests desire, through the use of the character-, mind-, and attitude-forming techniques of important institutions, constitutes one of the best refutations of liberal premises and one of the strongest arguments for fascism.

Liberalism talks freedom of the press, the pulpit, the radio and, in fact, all the institutions which educate people and form social attitudes. But liberalism cannot make such freedom a reality in a world of present-day complexities of economic organization and of present-day inequalities of economic power. Fascism does not talk in preposterous terms of a freedom which is non-existent and impossible to maintain, but rather in terms of a social discipline which it is possible for the State to impose in the name of a given ideal of national interest. So far as freedom is concerned (if that term in the abstract and by itself can ever have much meaning) it may be said that the people as a whole have most freedom where they have most opportunities to do what they like, and where they most like to do the things they have opportunities to do. Liberal freedom in practice today means, among other things, freedom for powerful economic interests to manipulate public opinion, and the social attitudes of the masses, to suit selfish private or corporate ends. It cannot be shown that a large measure of freedom for such manipulation gives the people as a whole more freedom than a drastic State discipline of it in the public interest would afford.

Stated somewhat differently, the question really is: Who shall

manipulate the opinions, feelings, and attitudes of the masses?
—for manipulated they must and will be in a civilization as
complex and highly organized as ours. Is it preferable to have
mass opinions, feelings, and social attitudes manipulated by
powerful private interests for personal or minority group ends,
or to have mass opinions guided by a national State in the
pursuit of some idealized plan of social well-being and order?
In this connection, the case against the manipulation of mass
opinions and social attitudes by private or corporate interests
pursuing personal or minority group ends, is that these manip-
ulators have no concern with, or responsibility for, public order.
They ask freedom to use economic power to manipulate mass
opinions and emotions, but decline all responsibility for the
social consequences. The State, or those in charge of government, can never act with such irresponsibility, for, after all, it
is those in charge of government—not those in charge of count-
inghouses—who, in a crisis, must deal with the hungry and
unemployed mob and must ensure that the trains run and the
banks reopen.

Liberal theory may be said to regard the great social institutions through which the characters, minds, and attitudes of the
people are formed somewhat as one might have regarded the
village well in a 17th century English hamlet. The well was
free for every one, who could take from it as much water as
he wanted. It was run by no one, and had no social purpose.
It was a social institution which was just used by every one as
he saw fit, and which was never, as a practical matter, subject
to serious misuse or abuse by any one. For one thing, water in
England was abundant. For another, people in 17th century
England used comparatively little water, and had no reason to
misuse the well. Any selfish person who might have thought of
establishing a monopoly over the well would have been dealt
with adequately by the town constables—if not by a few strong-
armed villagers.

Up to about the middle of the 19th century the press and the
platform, like the village well, were, more or less, institutions
available for the free and equal use of those competent to use

them. When rich men patronized the arts and letters, their demands and impositions were of socially slight significance. Once the monopoly of the State religion was broken sufficiently to allow substantial tolerance of other forms of worship (from about the beginning of the 18th century in England) different social ideas then current competed in a fairly free market and on terms of a considerable degree of equality.

The radical British liberals, utopians, socialists, and idealists of the late 18th and early 19th centuries had practically as much access to the public mind as the extreme conservatives. For the small élite of literate persons to whom such ideas were accessible, there was considerable freedom both in presenting and accepting ideas. Capitalists had not yet begun to use mass propaganda. In England, they controlled Parliament through the rotten boroughs, in which a handful of personal employees or friends of the lord of the manor would elect him or his designate. With the reform of the rotten boroughs in England toward the middle of the 19th century, with the enlargement of the franchise, and with the growth of population of the United States from the time of Andrew Jackson on, the powerful economic interests began to find it necessary to buy political control more and more through the instrumentalities of those institutions now under discussion, namely, those which educate with definite social purposes.

Up to the middle of the 19th century the masses had not acquired enough economic importance or buying power to make it worth while for capitalists to buy up control of the colleges, newspapers, and intellectual leaders as instruments of mass control, business promotion, and property protection. Up to the beginning of the era of nearly universal literacy and suffrage, the consumers of intellectual products were a critical, discriminating, and strongly opinionated élite. They were persons of high personal cultivation and well-grounded tastes. On the intellectual élite of the 17th and 18th centuries the arts of modern advertising and propaganda would have been largely wasted. The 18th century Americans who read the heavy political literature of that period, such as was produced by the

Adams, Jefferson, Monroe, Hamilton, and Franklin, would have furnished no market for the arts of the contributors to the popular publications of our day.

Those Americans of the élite were doubtless wrong in their opinions as often, or as much, as the Americans of today, but they were able to expound and defend their opinions. Whereas the masses who get their opinions from subsidized institutions at the present time can only repeat them parrot-like in the terms in which advertising and propagandizing technique have planted such ideas in their minds. Most of the liberal assumptions about freedom of speech and the press presuppose that the written and spoken word is addressed mainly to an élite which maintains high standards of critical judgment.

Modern democracy and mass purchasing power, really, are most to be blamed for the creation of a selfish interest in the control and use of the institutions which can be made to educate with any desired purposes. The modern lobby is the creature of liberal democracy. It pays to advertise. It pays to educate the public to your purposes. Because it pays to educate the public to suit anti-social purposes, the liberal assumptions are fallacious and in this respect the fascist principles are inevitable. The more money you can make, the more you can control public education. Fascism does not seek to end the control of might, but it does aim at ending the control of irresponsible might such as is so often exercised under liberal capitalism.

Under a desirable form of fascism for Americans, national interest should not require the same drastic measures of suppression and assimilation of institutions as have been taken in Germany in connection with the church, the press, the theatre, the moving picture and the radio. Adequate observance of the essential principle for public order simply means in this connection that all institutions which educate with a social purpose must be careful to avoid educating people to be bad citizens and must coöperate with the State in its attempts to fit people for good citizenship. There are a great many differences of opinion, taste, and personal behavior consistent with satisfactory observance of the principle just stated. Different people can have different ways to suit their different types of personality and different personal aptitudes. Different people can also be educated to be good citizens in different ways, or through playing different rôles.

It is not a difficult matter to pick out a hundred lessons in bad citizenship which are being given currently by our educative press, movies, radio, or schools. What is needed in this respect is less talk about an abstract freedom, which is essentially anarchy if really applied, and more effort to develop a rational technique of control through purposive education, with a view to making such education serve the ends of social welfare and order. Such effort must not be restricted to the field of child training but must be exercised in the entire field of purposive education of adults. Every social institution which is used to educate people with definite social purposes must be made to coöperate with the national plan. There must be no anti-social formation of character, mind, or group attitudes by any institution if it can be prevented. The rest of this chapter is devoted to a discussion of the problem of educational control, with reference especially to the school, which is a recognized educator with a social purpose. Most of what is said here in connection with the school (the reprinted article referred to above) will be found to apply equally to all institutions which are used to educate with definite social purposes.

"To say that the school should be used to influence positively attitudes favoring one or another type of social living seems to me merely the making of the trite observation that the school ought to do what it has always done and what it cannot help doing. The school cannot help imparting knowledge of social facts or ideas. That, of course, is its special business. But it is also one of the daily performances of every human institution. It is not the peculiar feature of the school that it educates. Its most distinctive peculiarity is that it educates with consciously conceived and willed purposes. Those purposes are mainly to serve the supposed interests of the prevailing social order, or, really, certain interests conceived and willed by the dominant classes. It is one of the peculiar delusions that the school is the chief educator of the community. All human institutions are educators. The school, however, unlike the market place, for instance, educates with avowed purposes.

"An academically popular superstition about the school is the notion that social facts or ideas are objects which the school can dispense like cigarettes wrapped in cellophane. Facts and ideas are not objects. They are personal experiences. Social facts or ideas are not things existing outside and independently of the knowing, understanding, or judging person. To whatever extent the school teaches social facts, the school causes persons to undergo certain peculiarly personal experiences which involve the processes of the reason and the emotions, or processes which take place in the torso as well as the skull. Ideas about patriotism, religion, sex, and art are apprehended mainly in the sub-cranial areas. One of the conditions precedent to the occurrence of the learning, knowing, thinking, or judging experiences is the continuous maintenance of a set of attitudes towards the prevailing type of social living and towards any other social scheme actually operative somewhere in the world or merely imagined, should such other scheme or schemes condition the given experience of the person.

"To suppose a person knowing a social fact independently of an attitude towards the social scheme in which he lives, and towards other social schemes which may affect his thinking and feeling, is as senseless as it would be to talk of weighing an object which was assumed to be floating through space an infinite and, hence, unknown distance from any planet. What gives sense to a personal experience (call it intellectual or emotional as you will) with a social fact or idea, is the relation or attitude of the person to his own and other social planets. We must reckon with the attraction or pull and also the repulsion of the social system operating on the individual in order to teach him a social fact.

"In the processes of education or knowledge and thought we can do things only with persons equipped with attitudes towards the social scheme. Every educational experience affects such attitudes and is affected by them, just as the movement of every object on this planet affects the earth's gravity and is affected by it. A person not equipped with and using, every moment of his conscious life, and particularly in respect to every intellectual experience, a set of attitudes towards the social scheme, is a hopeless idiot. He is not the mythical student with the objective mind.

"The school is expressly charged with the function of contributing to the formation of attitudes as a part of the processes of causing persons to undergo the experiences of learning, thinking, and judging. As the school specialist is normally the hired man and an instrument of government of those who exercise a directive influence over government in the broadest sense of the term, the school normally aims to create right attitudes towards the prevailing social order.

"Right, of course, is always a relative. A right attitude is an attitude which suits the purposes of the conceptual scheme of some person or the purpose of causing some given course of events to happen. There are, naturally, as many right attitudes or as many rights as there are conceptual schemes or courses of events, the realization of which would constitute a purpose to be served. Where such purposes conflict, whatever serves the realization of one's own preferred scheme is one's own standard of right. Civilization or social order is a matter of having a large group of people accept the same scheme or right. As a practical matter, any realizable scheme of interests or purposes of an individual, however selfish or reprehensible the person or the purposes may be considered, has to be a scheme which integrates the person in a social pattern.

"Therefore, all rational or realizable personal schemes are social or collectivistic. They cannot have the qualities of a specious individualism which are found in the contrary-to-fact hypotheses of certain confused minds. The isolated-man-on-a-desert-isle situation is never a reality. Most of the talk about individualism versus collectivism going the rounds today is a sheer confusion of terms, ideas, and issues. A working capitalism, for instance, is *ex-hypothesi* and according to Adam

Smith, a collectivism of freedom of contract. If it breaks down, it breaks down because its collectivistic characteristics fail, or, specifically, because the motives and mechanisms of the free market in their operation no longer secure the collectivistic result of an efficient and social coöperation of the factors of production.

"Why these motives and mechanisms so fail, or why capitalism fails in its collectivism, is another story. For the explanation you can try Marx, J. A. Hobson, Spengler, or Freud. The first purpose of any social scheme is to work. Whatever makes it work is right for it. If it works well as a system, it must involve the coöperation of a lot of people, for whom it must work well enough to secure their coöperation. People may coöperate with the social scheme by fleecing or being fleeced, by sending their first born to Groton or throwing him into the Ganges.

"The right attitudes which the school is supposed to inculcate are those which suit the purposes of the system, or make it work. If the social order is destroying itself, or, to be more accurate, if it is being destroyed by agencies and forces which are integral parts of its organic life, it will naturally follow that the well run school will serve those purposes.

"It may be objected that suicide cannot be a rational purpose of anyone or anything. But why not? In the life cycle of a human being, processes innate in his being begin destroying him as soon as he reaches maturity and achieve their work forty to a hundred years later. These processes are constantly killing Platos and Edisons, and breeding Jukes and Dillingers. It just is not one of the purposes of the course of events we may call life to make one person or one civilization live forever. The school will be as instrumental in the processes of culture degeneration as in the processes of culture generation. The idea that the right sort of education will preserve a civilization from decay is as absurd as the notion that the right sort of medicine or science will keep people from ever dying.

"In a dying civilization the school will naturally be the tool of the decadent élite until the vigorous barbarians of the new order, also of the élite (the outs over any length of time are always barbarians), capture the state and the government.

"If a realist feels moved to change his civilization he may seek spiritual leadership or political power, or both. In the one case, he may go into the wilderness and eat locusts and wild honey; in the other case, he may pick the crown of France out of the gutter with the point of his sword. In neither case will the drama of his passion for power over men be played in the rôle of an instrument of the order he abhors or despises.

"In government or politics, ultimately you either buy or shoot your way, or both. The cross, the crescent, the hammer and sickle, and the swastika, alike, have shot their way to power. The social revolutionist usually cannot buy his way; often he or his disciple can shoot his way. The school man can do neither. He follows those who can and do buy or shoot their way.

"There have been civilizations in which men at times cumulated successfully the functions of school teaching, political command, and spiritual leadership. Medieval Christendom, with its all-embracing spiritual synthesis, furnishes an example. Modern capitalism, by carrying to absurd extremes the principles of division of labor or specialization, separation instead of coördination of powers, and atomic fractionalization instead of purposive synthesis of social factors, has rendered this cumulation of the governing functions of the priest, the teacher, the soldier, and the administrator quite impossible. Hence, political government tends to be the work of specialists whose type pattern is the Tammany politician; economic government tends to be the work of specialists whose type pattern is a man of the Mitchell or Insull sort; while teaching tends to be the work of specialists whose type pattern is a frustrated old maid.

"It is, of course, possible for the superman to pass from the school to the White House, just as a Persian in the present century passed from stable boy to king. The point, however, is that the school, under modern capitalism, cannot be integrated with the highest mechanisms or personalities of government and social control. Exceptionally, a prophet or spiritual leader at war with the existing order, instead of serving as its docile instrument of mass conditioning for three square meals a day, will cumulate the functions of minor prophecy and petty pedagogy. If he continues to do so, it is because his influence is too negligible to warrant his dismissal. Ultimately, the *amour propre*, even of a very minor prophet, will require some substantial tribute to his effectiveness, such as a sensational dismissal can afford. Major prophets must either be crucified or crowned (king of kings and lord of lords) or both, for only such supreme tributes can satisfy the ego of a man big enough to impose his ideal on his fellow men.

"The social ideal of the prevailing system should be made explicit by the school. A contrary ideal should not be given a chance of success with any significant number of students. The educational theory that a scale of views and situations should be presented to the student in the hope that attitudes requisite for orderly social living under the given scheme will develop by the processes of individual selection is wholly fallacious. Either the theory is a misrepresentation of what is actually undertaken and accomplished in the educational enterprise, or else the theory is a statement of what has never been practised and what, if tried out, would result immediately in social anarchy. It is hard enough to preserve sanity in the machine age. The difficulties ought not to be aggravated by gratuitous misrepresentations of the educational process.

"Keeping sane requires that we recognize as the chief end of social agencies, including the school, the maintenance and enrichment of the social order, not the production of individuals as isolated entities, or disembodied personalities endowed with the faculty of living in or out of the social scheme as they may choose. The chief function of purposive education has to do with catching human beings in their formative years and integrating them into the social scheme as far as that can be done in youth. The end of this integration is a social order, not the formation of a lot of personal entities supposedly free either to fit themselves into society or not, mainly as the preference of each may incline him. As Hobbes taught, life is the war of all against all. One of the ends of any civilization is to mitigate the evils of this anarchy by resolving considerable groups of people into workable schemes of social organization which permit of social coöperation and the consequent enjoyment of some degree of order and peace in the world during lengthy periods of time.

"Now, few persons in the first twenty or thirty years of their lives, even if given access to the world's fund of social knowledge and Socrates for a tutor, could evolve a workable conceptual scheme of society of their own into which to fit themselves. And, if a number of people worked out such schemes, the schemes would all differ, whereas only one scheme of society could be operative for a large group. The problem of civilization is to make one social scheme operative for a given people, and this means, among other requisites, that it must be made explicit. The problem of the school is to help fit people into that scheme. Any opposite philosophy of civilization and education is absurd, impractical, and vicious. It is absurd, because no social order that has order can allow its schools to train people in ways deliberately calculated to make large numbers of them enemies of the social order. It is absurd because the premise of an individual in awful isolation from his group, is untenable for any useful hypothesis of social organization. Such an individual cannot exist.

"The theory of educating individuals rather than citizens is impractical for the same reasons. And it is vicious because it involves an educational technique of false rationalizations and deceit which contributes to mental and emotional unbalance, and because it creates a large number of enemies of the social order who do not become creative revolutionists but frustrated escapists, futilely flitting between a real world where they are unfulfilled and a fantasy world of wishful thinking where nothing is ever fulfilled except insanity.

"The escapists produced by an educational technique combining the worst of Bentham and Marx with the best of neither become split personalities. Part of the time they are trying to adjust themselves to a bread and butter job, and the other part of the time they are trying to adjust social reality to personal fantasy by impotent manifestations of hate and bitterness. Because we admire Socrates and Jesus is no reason why we should suppose that the purpose of the school, necessarily conducted by a host of salaried mediocrities, is to create social rebels. The social rebels will happen just as surely as civilizations rise and fall, or as men are born and die. They will happen in spite of the school, not because of it.

"The school must be one of the instruments of government of the group culture. The group culture should be the expression of the will of the dominant element of the élite, whose values are validated by the power to enforce them. This method of validating values is the only one by which an argument can ever be ended and coöperative activity made possible. You can have social order only to the extent that you can settle arguments or end conflicts, even if only temporarily. The boundaries of the dominant élite and the rebellious élite mark the only significant class cleavage. The masses divide naturally among the warring groups of the élite. As the élite are the leaders, the directives lie with them. Directions of social trends are determined by them. Education does not make or unmake the élite. It equips them and increases their social distance from the masses. It raises their potentialities as instruments of creation, destruction, and combat, processes which make up the mysterious drama of life.

"Purposive education and the technique of mass guidance are purely instrumental in the many enterprises of the leaders. These instrumentalities neither select nor validate ultimate values. Nor do they materially determine ultimate results of conflicts. No single instrumentality won the War. A preponderance of force factors determined it. Both sides used the same factors—machine guns, schools, tanks, press, etc. There can be no conflict except between classes or groups which have approximately the same instruments or force factors. (God and Justice are with all the belligerents.) This is a fact that Marxists disregard. There is no important conflict today between the hungry and well-fed in America, because command and possession of the force factors is with the well-fed. Foxes and rabbits don't fight. Today fighting has to be done by soldiers. Decisive conflict is between those who can command soldiers —not mere voters or trade union members.

"A kind, humane civilization should realize the following two conditions. First, it must suit my purposes as a person, or it must give me a suitable function as an individual. Every individual must be the center of his ethical or social scheme. For an individual there can be no validity to a social scheme in which he has no place. Whether the scheme suits him and whether he suits the scheme depends mainly on who he is and what social conditioning has made him. Let not this placing of the individual at the center of his own ethical system be called individualism. It is the purest collectivism. Any collectivism must successfully integrate a considerable number of individuals, for each of whom the collectivism centers around himself and his rôle. This merely means that the social scheme fits the individual and the individual fits the scheme. The point is that if the scheme works, those in charge of the social scheme will purposively direct most of the fitting, and some of their most useful fitters will be the schoolman and the priest. God, right, truth, and beauty are personal experiences.

"To be successfully adjusted, an individual does not have to have two cars or even a full stomach. He merely needs to have a place, or, to belong. The social system may fit me and I may fit it, I being a barefooted, penitent pilgrim, a missionary to the lepers, or a plumed knight in shining armor. People don't mind suffering. On the contrary, some of them love to suffer all of the time, and all of them love to suffer some of the time. What people cannot endure is not belonging. The tragedy of capitalism—unemployment—does not inhere in the phenomena of want and privation, but in the spiritual disintegration of large numbers of people from the group culture. Hitler can feed millions of his people acorns, and, yet, if he integrates them in a spiritual union with their community, they will be happier than they were while receiving generous doles from a régime which gave them no such spiritual integration with the herd. In so far as the school is a force for spiritual integration it is mightier than the dole.

"A second set of requisites of a humane civilization is that the dominant élite should know what they want, that they should give the people what they think best for the people, and that they should make the people both like and fit the scheme. The élite always determine what the masses get. Nowhere is this more apparent than in present-day Communist Russia, which enjoys an oversimplified dictatorship of the proletariat (and of everybody else in Russia) by certain of the élite. The élite leaders are a permanent power-holding or power-seeking class. When one set of the élite kicks out another, it is merely the old story of "The King is dead! Long live the King!" The average man goes on doing as he is told. It makes little difference to him whether his surplus goes to building private yachts for capitalists or an air fleet for the Soviet Commissars. Whatever the élite impose on the people, they should use good educational technique to make the people like. Whatever the élite demand of the people, they should use good educational technique to enable the people to do. This is the work of purposive education. Conditioning a people to like what they have and to do their part is a simple exercise in educational technique. The real difficulty arises not out of the inadequacy of educational technique but out of the failure of the élite to have unity in emotional responses or intellectual clarity as to ultimate values and objectives. In these matters the instrumental or purposive education of the school is of minor importance. The struggle for existence must educate and unify men's hearts and clarify their minds in ways to produce a dominant or efficient group of the élite.

"In so far as the school does a good job for its masters, who are never the schoolmasters, the school population will be in the rear-guard of social revolution. The education of the struggle for existence, however, sometimes gets at the student population, as it has done in most European countries which have not so effectively insulated their youth against the currents of social ideas, as the country club atmosphere of our colleges, or the kindergarten atmosphere of our lower schools, have done for our youth. In America today, the important social education is going on in shanty town, the bread line, the code conferences, mortgage foreclosure sales, and the relief committees. The social teaching of the schools, particularly in economics, ethics, and law, is largely out of date, contrary to experience, irrelevant, and trivial. So are most of the teachers. The American schools have no teachers of the social importance of educators like the late Huey Long and Father Coughlin. The pupils of the latter will fight and die for what they are being taught; the school pupil may vicariously fight on the playing fields for dear old Siwash, but he won't fight for what Siwash professors are teaching. The founders of Siwash had a fighting faith; but the endowed pensioners of Siwash deem it bad form to have a conviction.

"There is an irony and a moral in the social insignificance of the American school in the present crisis. No school has ever been more popularized, praised, petted, or pampered with money. It has been the kept darling of the plutocracy and the idolized plaything of the masses. In the main, neither group has numbered many devotees of any scheme of civilized values. Serious interest in the school has centered around getting a technical preparation, or useful connections for money-making, or else around getting a job in the schools. For the masses, the school is a necessary process to enable them to read signs and advertisements. For the more favored the school has been a playground.

"The moral is obvious. The school realizes its highest possibilities only as the instrument of a dominant élite who not only have cultural values but who also are prepared to express them in the manifold enterprises of social control, which include fighting and governing as well as teaching.

"The American school will come into its own when it becomes alive with the spirit of men of strong convictions and iron wills to achieve. The school will be an instrument of a high culture when it recognizes fulfillment, achievement, and deeds to be the test of truth, right, and beauty, not normative verbalisms, the precise meaning and correct application of which men can and will go on disagreeing about to the end of time. In short, the school can only attain its highest dignity or fulfill its noblest destiny as an integrated part of the creative machinery of a civilization."

CHAPTER XVIII

THE INEVITABILITY OF THE LEADERSHIP OF
THE ÉLITE

EVERY social order is essentially a phenomenon of leadership, for leadership is one of the most important or significant things about it. As a scheme of purposes, a social order is mainly the expression of the composite will of a dominant class and, as a body of achievements, it is largely the result of the leadership, management, choices, social planning, and control exercised by members of a minority. It seems useful to give this minority of more than average influence and power a name. That name will be "the élite." This term or classification is not like that of the literate, for which every one can be submitted to a uniform test. It is, however, unimportant whether a few million doubtful cases are classified on one or the other side of the line dividing, for our purposes, the élite from the rest of the population.

The élite may be defined roughly and arbitrarily as including capitalists deriving most of their income from property, business enterprisers and farmers, the professional classes, and, generally, the employed whose salaries are considerably above the average, or, say, above $3000 a year for the entire country.

Of course, thousands within the classes just named are knaves and fools, or apparently without any real influence or power. But one cannot find a meter to measure the influence and power of every individual. And one cannot go far wrong in working on the assumption that all those in the above mentioned classes, or say roughly one-third of the gainfully employed, or over fifteen million persons (not counting their dependents) are properly classifiable as exercising individually, and in various group aggregates, vastly more power and influence than the rest of the population. Any advertising man or organizer of anything for almost any purpose will readily appreciate why he can accomplish more with a given number of persons drawn at random from this third of the population than with an equal number similarly drawn from the rest of the population.

The term élite as used in this connection does not express a value judgment on those so classed, but merely an attempt at factual classification. The term is applied equally to those who are potentially influential and powerful, and those who are actually influential and powerful. It is also applied equally to those who are influential and powerful in anti-social and illegal ways. It is the fact that persons are influential and powerful, not how they use their influence and power, that classes them with the élite. A Karl Marx, living in penury on a meager dole from the funds of relatives and friends, and spending his time reading in the British Museum Library, or writing books which to most people at the time would have seemed incomprehensible or foolish, is, obviously, a more powerful and influential figure than most statesmen in office or captains of industry. And a Jesse James or a Dillinger undoubtedly exercises a more powerful influence over the minds and behavior of hundreds of thousands of unfortunate youths than the average school teacher, whose influence touches far fewer youths and whose influence over those it touches is far less potent than the influence of the example of a Jesse James or a Dillinger over those susceptible to such influence.

It will doubtless shock some tender minds to have a worthy school teacher classed as less influential and powerful than a Jesse James and a Dillinger. But it is absolutely essential to useful social thinking to face facts, and to recognize power and influence wherever they are found to be exercised. A bad example which is made dramatic and notorious can be more powerful and influential than a good example which lacks the qualities that inspire emulation. And a man whose life is branded as a personal failure may, by his example or teaching, make a mighty contribution to the disintegration or destruction of the existing order. The term élite, as here used, does not refer, then, merely to the ins at the top, or only to the people judged good by any standards. It refers to the influential and powerful, and includes also the outs who are potentially, if not actually, as influential and powerful as the ins at the top.

The mischief of soft thinking about leadership and the élite of power is that it causes so many people to disregard the influence of the anti-social criminal of influence, such as the leader or the brains of a criminal gang, as well as the influence of malcontents and maladjusted persons who sow the seeds of social disintegration and revolution. The power of the maladjusted social revolutionary, of course, is more significant than that of the common law breaker, however thrilling the exploits of the latter. The exercise of this power by social revolutionaries is most effective when it takes the form of piling up in the hearts and minds of millions, often more in the sub-conscious than in the conscious minds, the combustibles of hate and fear to which, at some later date, a more celebrated personality may touch the spark setting off a revolutionary conflagration. Again, the power of the élite who are maladjusted and who are enemies of the existing order may take the form of spreading a corrosive doubt or cynicism as to the essential values of that order.

A wise social philosophy, such as that of fascism, strives to make a place for all the members of the élite. If they cannot be thus eliminated as instruments of destruction of the social order, then other methods for their elimination are followed. The objective of the humane and pragmatic State in its policies with respect to the enemies of the existing order is prevention and not primarily punishment, and it is understood that punishment is an inefficient means of prevention. Fascism, unlike liberalism, does not dramatize the punishment of crime with the sporting events of chasing, capturing and trying the culprit, on which a commercial press, legal profession and movies can make huge profits. Those who cannot be made safe for the community as coöperative members must be made harmless by effective methods which do not allow repetition of the offense or encourage imitation by others.

Criminals of the élite must not be made centers of sensational police and judicial dramas, the principal consequence of which is predisposing thousands of sub-normal or abnormal persons to crime. Their cases must be handled by a system combining many of the features of administrative law and practice with the criminal law. A large number of the criminal élite and the revolutionary élite can be made safe for society by the simple expedient of making proper places for them before they turn to crime or social revolution. Most of the criminals who are mentally or morally deficient could be made safe if detected by proper psychiatric examination in childhood as moral or mental deviates and thereafter institutionalized as long as necessary, which in many cases would be for life.

Liberalism will not recognize, as does fascism, that, if a large number of the élite do not find adjustment to the social order and if, in one way or another, they become enemies of the social order, it is mainly the fault of the social order. The social order has the responsibility to fit people to places, and places to people, just as far as such fitting can be done. A social order which allows hundreds of lucky morons to make and keep millions of dollars, and keeps men like Karl Marx or Lenin out of a useful function because in their youth they displayed some innate queerness of personality, has only itself to blame if some of the frustrated conspire successfully its ultimate doom. A social order which allows success and riches for members of the élite having certain skills or aptitudes at a peculiar type of competition found in money-making, and leaves too many other members of the élite, not gifted for this type of competition, largely out of it, will last only as long as the in-élite hold the advantages of numbers, nerve, and lucky breaks.

After all, the only good reason, ethical or pragmatic, why a social order can be run in a way to allow fortunes to be made as most of our great fortunes have been made, instead of being run in a way to allow robber barons and belted knights acting as bandits to operate as they have operated for centuries all over the world, is that the élite who have succeeded, or who hope to succeed, at the money-making game have outnumbered and been more lucky than the out-élite. The right and wrong of any social order, after all, is only a matter of how it suits the dominant section of the élite to have the game played. And who the dominant élite shall be can never be permanently determined by law, but must always be determined by force factors, the ultimate play of which, as in war, takes place outside the bounds of law.

The most humane social philosophy is that which recognizes that the rules of the game must, ultimately, allow enough of the élite to play successfully to keep the losers from changing the rules. In other words, to be quite blunt about it, all that will keep the world from going back to a pattern of banditry similar to that which prevailed all over Europe for hundreds of years, and which prevails today in large parts of Asia, will be such changes in the rules of the game as will keep enough of the now frustrated élite satisfied. The scheme of social organization can and should be changed from time to time in ways, never to be foreseen far in advance, to keep any considerable or dangerous number of the élite from being on the outside.

What is needed is a social philosophy of realism which recognizes that there can be no right for the élite of today based on legal theories agreeable to the dominant élite of yesterday but intolerable to too many of today's élite. The legal right of today is always the physical might of the élite of yesterday. The legal right of today as a practical matter, however, always requires the support or acquiescence of the might of the élite of today. The right of some of the élite to hold wealth and exercise power, while too many more of the equally élite are denied these boons, and while they see no chance of attaining them, is sure to be challenged sooner or later by the over-numerous members of the out-élite.

Aside from the final test of force in the eventual clash of interests in armed conflict, the standards are purely relative. Just how many are too many élite to remain frustrated with safety for the existing order, it is always impossible to say in advance of the final clash. One can never tell with what exact degree of strain a complex structure like a skyscraper or a great bridge will collapse. One can only fix arbitrarily a danger point beyond which one can say there are serious probabilities of collapse which will increase as the strain increases. The best danger index today is the growing number of the frustrated élite. It is this danger signal which should dictate to the in-élite the necessity of changes in the rules of the game. Unfortunately, however, many of the in-élite look to the Constitution and a body of liberal principles guaranteeing the rights of property as the absolute safeguards of their privileged situation whatever may befall the out-élite, and however numerous these latter may become.

To say that the élite rule, or are socially influential, when the term élite is defined to mean such persons is clearly a piece of tautology. But to say that it is always a small minority of power-wielding persons (who may be called the in-élite) which rules directly, or with the legal instruments of social control, and that it is a small minority of others, also the élite, who are profoundly influential on social affairs (though many or most of them may be in poverty or in difficulties with the law) lays the basis for a wholly different social philosophy from that of liberalism. Liberalism says, "Let the people rule," and defines such rule as there is as that of the majority, thus denying or disregarding many obvious and important facts by the simple process of definition and assumption.

Communism says, "Let the dictatorship of the proletariat rule," and asserts categorically that a dictatorship of a small élite of the higher-ups of the communist party is a dictatorship of the proletariat, an assertion which is just as false as the liberal assertion of rule by the people or the majority. Fascism says that the élite, or a small minority, call its members by any term you will, always rule under any system. And fascism proposes a formula of national interest and national discipline under which power is exercised with responsibility to the State for the social consequences of its exercise and with a view to realizing the national plan.

The central point is that it is useful to think of government and management as being the function of a minority, and that it is not useful to any good social purpose to proceed on the theory that the people or the majority rule. It seems idle to speculate as to the nature of a social order in which it would make sense to say that the people ruled. Such a scheme of things would probably have to approximate the conditions obtainable in the small Greek city State, in which there were slaves to do the drudgery, an extremely simple scheme of economic production, and a small group of citizens who could have the time, taste, and requisite personal cultivation, for the complexities of public administration. Such a scheme of social organization is clearly unattainable within the framework of most of the basic features of the present system—features like mass production and division of labor, for instance. The best proof that it is idle to discuss ideal conditions for liberal democracy is to be found in the fact that the trend of all that has been called progress under liberal capitalism during the past fifty years has been unfavorable to the working out of the theory of liberal democracy.

Discussing the questions of who run things, why and how they run things, and how they ought to run things, is almost wholly a matter of using concepts and terms. The same realities seem different as one reduces them to different concepts or defines them differently. The liberal theory can be made to seem reasonable and ethically beautiful by a few simple turns of supposition and definition. One has only to reason that, because the majority has the potential might to transfer, without violence, power from one minority to another, or as liberalism would put it, to delegate power to different representatives of the people, the majority rules. To reason thus, however, is merely to make the ruling class mean by definition that class which, if it is united about doing a given thing, can do that thing against any opposition. Obviously, an overwhelming majority always meets this condition, and any sort of a majority usually meets it.

But the definition, or the underlying concept, is not useful as an instrument of thought for many good reasons. The majority supposed to be agreed as to initiating any important social change is extremely rare, if ever it can be said to occur. And a majority rarely remains long agreed on any important enterprise except war. Social changes usually are wrought without majority knowledge or support of their initiation. But even when social changes seem to have majority support for their initiation, it is always a minority which is responsible for first turning majority support in that direction.

The majority is purely a thing of assumption or definition on the occasion of some event, like an election, a Saar plebiscite, a referendum vote on prohibition, or popular acclaim of a declaration of war. Minorities, on the other hand, are not just things of definition. They are active factors which, twenty-four hours of each day, are on the job of getting what they want. With minorities you can do things with majorities. Without minority initiatives you cannot get a majority act or expression. The minority is as real as an army in the field. The majority is real only as a definition of those who do some specific act, usually under minority pressure and direction.

Fortunately for the advancement of the fascist case for responsible rule by the élite according to some idealized scheme of national interest, less argument is required in 1935 than would have been necessary in 1914. We have not time to undertake the demolition, point by point, of the liberal case for majority rule. Current events make it seem superfluous. We can only allude briefly in this chapter to two important groups of facts and considerations which invalidate liberalism and indicate fascism so far as the question of who rules is concerned. The first of these groups of facts may be said to have to do with the limitations and inequalities inherent in human personalities. The second may be called matters of the sheer mechanics of administration and management of large numbers of people and the complex instruments of modern civilization.

Now, as for the limitations and inequalities inherent in human personalities, it may be said that the trend of conclusions based on scientific observation, experimentation, and measurement, in the fields of psychology, psychiatry, biology, and many other related areas of specialized study of human beings as physical organisms and behaving subjects, has been, and continues to be, in the direction of establishing important and irreducible inequalities in intellectual capacity, aptitudes, and character, of different members of any large group. Contrary to one of the major theses of 18th century rationalism and 19th century educational optimism, these inequalities are being increased rather than lessened as a result of more widely diffused educational advantages.

Thus, in the free public schools of great cities it has been found that the small percentage of gifted children among all those enjoying equal public school advantages remains more or less constant, and that over ninety per cent of the exceptionally gifted children come from the homes of the more privileged classes or the classes which we are calling the élite. Putting generations of children through the same educational mill does not change the distribution of gifted, average and sub-normal children among the privileged and underprivileged classes. Thus, one of the most cherished ideals of 18th century rationalism has failed of realization. Education accentuates rather than levels out inequalities of natural endowment. Intelligence tests made of the same persons before, during, and at the end, of either the four-year college course or a seven- or eight-year combined college and professional course, show that the inequalities between different persons increase rather than diminish after undergoing the same course of training.

There is great social significance in the fact that the élite of exceptional natural endowment, who, as a matter of course, become the élite of power and influence, actual or potential, are a fairly constant percentage of the total population. From this fact it follows that no social system can long survive, once it tends strongly to declass more and more of the élite. In other words, the élite are more vital or resistant to suppression as wielders of power and influence than any social system. Civilizations come and go, but the élite go on forever. This point will recur in another connection in the discussion of the next chapter.

There is nothing really depressing about these facts concerning the élite. Nor is there to be deduced from these facts any good argument against more and better education for everyone. These facts, however, do indicate a revision of liberal ideals in education and social policy. They indicate the social convenience of non-liberal values. From the purely humane point of view, it is indicated that the chief object of education, as well as one of the highest group values, should be that of making each person realize his full potentialities and prove a good citizen within the rôle for which he will be best suited by reason of natural endowment and with the aid of the best training. It is not to make all men equal, or to enable every one to follow a more highly remunerated calling than that of his father.

Liberal education may protest, but in vain, that its chief objective has always been to fit people for the kind of life and work for which they are naturally best fitted. The values exalted by liberal education, and the influence of the liberally and expensively educated, have caused the vast majority of people in the liberal countries to think of education as an instrument to qualify every one to make more money. Hence we find our institutions of higher learning so overrun with the unfit for such training that the fit do not receive the training they merit and require in the best interests of the community.

To effect a necessary revision of cultural values in this respect many drastic measures are indicated, adequate discussion of which would exceed the limits of this chapter. The conscientious performance of the most commonplace tasks must be exalted through all the agencies forming social attitudes. A cult must be made of simple labor and faithful performance of duty. Those admitted to the pursuit of higher studies must be made to do fairly long tours of service at elementary forms of labor in connection with their course of training. The rationale of the new values in this respect must be that only character ennobles a person, while rank is but a convenience of administration.

From the inescapable fact of the inequalities of human endowment, it also follows that any well-ordered society must train and condition its élite under an efficient and hard discipline of national interest. Fascist theory, by recognizing personal inequalities and their full social implications, can be much more humane than a liberalism which assumes that all men are born equal and which, in practice, affords to those born with superior endowment, or favored with better luck than the majority, virtually unlimited opportunities to acquire and use power with irresponsibility for social consequences and in ways further to increase social inequalities.

The other important group of facts which invalidate the liberal theory of rule by the people, or the majority, and which indicate fascism, are found in the sheer mechanics of administration or management, political and economic. If one thinks in terms of the mechanics of running things, and not merely in terms of the hypothesis that, if the people were angry enough against their government, they could change it, either legally or violently, one soon realizes that the machinery, political and economic, inevitably must be run by a minority of technicians whose functions are mainly those of managing and choosing. The orthodox liberal would admit that the people cannot manage, management being a function which must be delegated to specialists in management. But he would insist that the people can choose the objectives of management and that, therefore, in their exercise of choice, they may be said to rule or govern.

It is precisely in the matter of making choices or decisions, however, that the liberal theory is so untrue to the realities. For one thing, they who manage, also, by reason of the very mechanics of power and management, make most of the choices and decisions which liberalism, by definition, imputes to the majority of the people. A majority vote at the polls or in a legislative assembly is, in the largest number of cases, nothing more or less than the product of a minority interest managing things and wielding power.

Then, for another thing, there is the fact that the really important or crucial choices or decisions are seldom made by a majority vote, even formally, or by a majority of selections in the so-called free market. Wars and depressions, for instance, are really important events. In so far as the cumulative choices or decisions which hasten or precipitate either event are concerned, it cannot be said that they often express the wishes or will of a majority of the people. The American people could choose in 1916 between President Wilson and Judge Hughes, but, as events and the since-disclosed correspondence and secrets of Mr. Wilson abundantly reveal, the American people could not vote in the elections of 1916 to keep us out of war, although that, undoubtedly, was their wish.

There was no candidate in 1916 with a chance of getting a majority vote who was committed to, or, if elected, would have been capable of, carrying out an effective policy of American neutrality. Similarly, it may be said that, while the people undoubtedly wish to avert depressions, they have no means, under the liberal system, of giving a mandate to the political and economic powers to do the things which would help to prevent or minimize depressions.

The chief reason, perhaps, why the American people cannot give an effective mandate to their political and economic rulers to do what may be necessary to keep the nation out of war or to minimize depressions is that the system does not allow the needful power to the people's elected or provide the requisite mechanisms of control. It is as though a national legislature were to vote a declaration of war while the Constitution forbade the maintenance of military discipline, and while the courts exercised the right to enjoin and restrain the military authorities under circumstances in which they require large powers and wide discretion.

Briefly, in reality the people can choose or will only such results as their public agents are empowered and equipped to bring about. When the people choose Tweedledum instead of Tweedledee, or Woodrow Wilson instead of Charles Evans Hughes, they are not registering any significant choice as to important social results, like keeping the country out of war. The more power and the more efficient and adequate instrumentalities the people allow their public agents, the more nearly correct it is to say that the people rule through their agents.

A powerful State guided by a capable élite loyal to some scheme of national interest is far more expressive of the popular will than a weak liberal State, because the powerful State can do more than the weak State to shape social events of importance, and also chiefly because the powerful State can make the people genuinely like or assent to what it does. Under the weak State, all sorts of things (like our entry into the war) happen against everyone's original wish; many things which every one wishes, fail to happen; and the weak State succeeds in making the people enthusiastically endorse its administration only when at war.

A further explanation why a majority vote (expressing the desire of the people for some important given result, and issuing a mandate to that effect to those elected) is so often meaningless is that there is no satisfactory means of proving relations of cause and effect in political or economic administration. It is asserted here, as the sincere belief of the author, that President Wilson and the international bankers were chiefly responsible for the initiatives or decisions which contributed most to getting us into the World War. It is also asserted here that the leaders in government and big business were mainly responsible for the initiatives which contributed most to the inflationary boom of 1927-1929.

But neither of these assertions can be scientifically proved as certainties. It is just never possible to prove in politics or economics, where important policies and events are in question, that a plus b equals c. Liberal theory assumes that it can always be proved that a plus b equals c in governmental or business management, and that, accordingly, if a government or banking house does a plus b, with the result that c happens, the people will hold certain parties in government or the bank responsible for having done a plus b things. As everyone should know, the liberal statesmen and the bankers always have an alibi for every political and economic crime which is committed by them.

To sum up, then, it may be said that the élite do rule, as liberal theory does not recognize; that they, and not the majority of people, make most of the important choices; that their acts are not subject to rational control by a cause-effect process of reasoning; and that their acts are not subject to popular control by the ballot or the enforcement of the Constitution in the way liberal theory supposes possible. All this, however, does not amount to saying, by any means, that the élite are subject to no control by the people, or that the rule of the élite under any modern social order is wholly capricious and irresponsible. If, as so seldom happens, the majority is agreed that one set of the élite in power must give place to another, and if the majority is capably inspired and led by the out-élite, it is self-evident that the majority can replace one set of the élite in power by another. In this way the majority can be said to determine a change in rule.

It is, however, equally self-evident from history and clear thinking that one set of the élite which happens to be out of power can organize and lead a successful overturn in which they will replace the élite who are in power—all without having the majority of the people with them. This is precisely what happened in the communist seizure of power in Russia in 1917. In elections held under the most liberal government Russia has ever had, the communists polled less than one-third of the total number of votes cast just a few weeks before they seized power at the point of the bayonet. The out-élite, of course, try to enlist and use as many people as they can get, but they do not need a majority in order to seize power. After they have seized power, as we have already stated, the out-élite can quickly and easily secure the appropriate majority vote ratifying their régime—as Napoleons one and three, Lenin, Mussolini and Hitler, to cite a few well-known examples, fully illustrate. In parentheses, it may be added, also, that historians are now pretty generally agreed that the American Revolution was fought and won by a minority.

The problem of order and welfare, in the light of the fore-going considerations about the inevitability of the leadership of the élite or a minority, appears to be largely one of getting the right élite or minority in power, and having their administration shaped by the influence of certain fundamental ideas and by certain effective personal motivations. These basic ideas for good government by the élite can be expressed in writing in terms of general principles or social ideals.

But it will serve no good purpose to have this expression take the form of written law or constitution subject to judicial exposition and interpretation. Any written statements of principle, serving chiefly the purposes of popular education and propaganda, must be subject only to interpretation by the combined legislative and executive agents of the people. Such interpretation will then be in terms of current needs and current opinion, whereas interpretation in terms of juridical canons must soon become static and expressive mainly of a body of theory or a system of logic developed by a caste of learned clerks or technicians in a logical system, and a procedure of their own creation. These technicians of their own peculiar logical system, however, are not technicians in social management. Most important is the consideration that the ruling principles governing the élite must be made a part of their conditioned reflexes, or their habitual and almost involuntary reactions, rather than a part of a legal code. In the next chapter we shall examine the question of safeguards for the rule of the élite, and the bases of the fascist appeal to the ins and the outs of the élite and to the masses.

CHAPTER XIX

THE ÉLITE ASSUME RESPONSIBILITY

In the fascist view of the crisis of capitalism, the great initial problem of insuring order and welfare is that of getting the right élite in power under a right discipline and plan of national interest. Liberal theory, it will be remembered, considers the problem of order and welfare as largely one of getting the right set of rules and institutions and then letting the majority work out the good life through this system. The definition of the rules is supposed to be made by the courts, and the operation of the system is supposed just to happen as a result of the fortuitous concurrence of three separate branches of government and all the personal and impersonal factors of the national community, the whole acting autonomously and subject only to the rule of law which is, by definition, wholly impersonal. Consequently, liberalism is the most perfect social system ever conceived for allowing great power to be exercised by individuals and groups, chiefly through property rights legally enforced, with maximum irresponsibility of persons or groups for the social consequences of their acts.

The fundamental objectives of order and welfare are common to liberalism and communism as well as fascism. Fascism is distinctive from both, however, in that it recognizes and makes a cardinal point of the functions and responsibilities of the élite. The issues or choices are as to different sets of the élite who may rule, and of different systems of making their rule effective and responsible. There is no choice as to whether or not some group of the élite shall rule. The fallacy of the communist ideal of a classless society inheres in the fact that there must always be a ruling or managing class.

It is always, of course, the out-élite who put over a social revolution, whether they do so in the name of one group or another or of one set of principles or another. It is the contention of this book that fascism makes a stronger appeal than communism to the out-élite in America, though it is fully recognized that communism can have an appeal to certain members of the out-élite, as occurred in Russia. Fascism, or the out-élite making up fascist leadership, must make out a case for the rule of the fascist élite, not because the rule of the élite is a peculiarity of fascism, but simply because fascism—unlike liberalism and communism—frankly acknowledges, or rather boasts, that its élite rule.

It is one of the merits of fascism, and a part of its appeal, that its leaders do not dissimulate their rôle or try to place responsibility for their rule on a phantom of definition and assumption—such as, the majority or the proletariat. They do not stress a class war, though they naturally fight for their objectives as nearly every one else does. They do not stress a class war, because the formula of solidarity is a national union which includes all citizens. They do not demand a class monopoly of power, except in so far as the ends of order and administration require that the class of the most competent be entrusted with power necessary for efficient management.

The appeal of fascism to the out-élite is too obvious to need much persuasive statement. They have roughly the choices of fascism, communism, or slow degradation, as a necessary accompaniment to the present and unchecked decline of free capitalism. They must turn fascist in large numbers for reasons which make up the subject matter of most of this book. It is the appeal of fascism to the in-élite and the masses which calls for most explanation. One might as well recognize the divergence of interests at any given moment, as between the in-élite, the out-élite, and the masses who are not factually classifiable as being exceptionally influential or powerful as separate individuals or collectively as members of any group. The appeal of fascism to the masses has already been indicated somewhat briefly in the discussion of the question, "Why fascism instead of communism?"

The fundamental case is that the masses need the élite, and

that that social system promises most in the way of welfare for the masses which best uses and disciplines the élite. So far as the welfare of the masses is concerned, the problem might with good reason be called largely one of getting the best out of the élite. From the point of view of mass welfare, the best that can be said for liberal capitalism in the days of its success is that it was singularly effective in getting the best out of the élite. The worst that can be said against capitalism today is that it is not getting the best out of the in-élite, and that it is getting nothing constructive out of the out-élite, so many of whom are jobless and functionless. If communism can get more out of the élite as a whole than fascism or liberalism, then communism should be the choice of the masses. As we already have remarked in comparing communism and fascism, it is difficult to see how communism can be expected to get the best out of the élite when it involves the liquidation of so many of them.

The moving spirits of an emerging fascism are, obviously, the quintessence of the élite of influence and power, as we are using these terms. If they were not, there would be no emergence of fascism. They are also likely to be mainly recruited from the over-numerous ranks of the out-élite, except for such members of the in-élite as are wise enough to join them. Their bid for the support of the masses consists chiefly in a sincere and soundly-motivated undertaking to run things better or, expressed in economic terms, to increase the material output by more efficient management.

Fascism lays emphasis on the gains to be realized by more honest and efficient management, which would come largely from better coördination of authority and integration of control. Fascism does not stress the benefits for the underprivileged to be derived from simple transfer of wealth from the rich to the poor. The people are made to see that wealth is income or production, and that an equalization of ownership followed by a heavy drop in production would leave the masses poorer than before.

In other words, labor is better off with seventy per cent of an output of one hundred than with one hundred per cent of an output of sixty. It is not to be supposed, however, that considerable redistribution of ownership and percentage shares of the total income is not effected by fascism. But fascism proposes to raise the living standards of the masses chiefly by making a more efficient use of the available factors of production, such a formula alone being considered by the fascists as capable of securing the fullest or the essential measure of coöperation by the élite.

In this connection, it is pertinent to refer to the frequently exploited device of comparing economic statistics of the fascist countries with similar statistics of the more prosperous non-fascist countries, and drawing from such comparisons conclusions invidious to fascism. No attempt is made in this book to go into comparative economic statistics. There would be no space for doing so. If fair and adequate comparisons were to be attempted, the results would be unreadably technical, and the conclusions too doubtful, to justify the average reader's outlay of effort.

The tricks that can be played with statistics are amazingly deceptive. A few general explanations about statistical comparisons invidious to the fascist countries will be briefly offered. The first and most important set of facts to bear in mind about the economic sequels of fascism are that fascism, thus far, has always taken over control in a moment of extreme crisis. It has had to carry on with whatever resources it has found and against whatever obstacles it has encountered; and most definitely it has not inaugurated its régime under the auspices of a smiling fortune such as beamed on liberal capitalism in its infancy.

Fascism, everywhere, has been born of harsh necessity and not the lucky strikes of explorers and freebooters seeking new trade routes and lands for conquest. For instance, before the War, Italy received a yearly gift of over a hundred million dollars of unearned money from remittances by Italian immigrants to the near relatives and dependents in the mother country. Since the War, the virtual stoppage of Italian immigration by American law has necessarily resulted in a slow drying up of this stream of income. Rising tariffs everywhere have also operated since the War to the extreme economic disadvantage of Germany and Italy, which used to depend on the profits of foreign trade to help defray the costs of supplying many deficiencies in raw materials.

Fascism did not produce these external economic pressures, which have been developing for a long time and which have grown acute since the War. Fascism is the answer to these external pressures. If one says that one prefers in place of fascism the lush days of 19th century liberal capitalist infancy, with all its faults, one has said absolutely nothing logically relevant by way of a criticism of post-War fascism. Nations have to choose what is attainable. Wishes for the unattainable are not arguments against fascism or in favor of liberalism.

Another consideration of which the comparers of fascist and liberal economic statistics fail to take account is that countries like the United States, Great Britain, and France have much larger accumulations of surplus than the fascist countries, with which to carry the economic crisis for a time in good style. The privileged liberal nations are likely to go completely fascist when and as this surplus runs low. Germany lost its surplus through the War, had it replaced partially for a brief spell by foreign loans, and when they stopped the country soon went fascist. Italy never had much of a surplus, and after the War it faced a harder world market in which to compete.

America, England and France have a chance in 1935 to initiate the social plan of fascism under vastly more promising auspices than marked its inauguration in the fascist countries. The whole point as to living standards is that whatever fascism provides ultimately in welfare for the masses must be determined as much by the resources of the moment, and the exigencies of the situation, as by the mechanics of fascism or the wishes of fascists in power. The defense of fascism in Italy is not to say that it has given the Italian worker a higher standard of living than British workers, including those on the dole, have enjoyed during the same period. For it has not done so. The defense of Italian fascism is that it has done a better job of social management than the preceding régime was doing, or would have done, in the situation fascism has had to face.

Comparisons of living standards and real wages are further complicated or invalidated by the unpleasant facts that, while the three leading liberal countries, the United States, Great Britain and France, did most of their land-grabbing before 1914 and are now anxious to have the present status quo respected, the fascist countries, having yet to achieve their necessary territorial expansion, hold different views about the inviolability of existing territorial arrangements. The military burdens imposed by the obvious necessity of expansion for the successful maintenance of nationhood must inevitably limit in the fascist countries the living standard which any social management by the élite can afford the masses. The costs of military preparations for expansion naturally levy a heavier percentage of income per capita in the under-privileged than in the privileged nations.

The prevailing opinion of the liberal countries, of course, is that the fascist countries do not have to expand. This opinion can be rebutted by arguments too lengthy to develop here. But why waste time arguing that the present fascist countries need to expand when every one knows that they will try to expand or perish in the attempt? And if they perish as nations in the attempt, there is not likely to be much left of western civilization in the now liberal countries after the attempt. Propositions for which nations fight rather than argue cannot be met with argument but must be met with concession and compromise, or else war. There is, therefore, no sense to any liberal argument intended merely to talk the underprivileged nations out of a will to expand. Further discussion of the international aspects of this question is left for the chapter on the international implications of fascism.

Here it need only be said in résumé that the demands of an expansionist policy on an underprivileged nation must render pointless all comparison of its living standards with those of privileged nations on the defensive. And it must be repeated that fascism has not invented national expansion. The liberal countries founded their prosperity on expansion, and cannot now make a desire by the fascist countries for expansion the subject of a reproach. The underprivileged fascist countries will have to pay more dearly in individual sacrifices for their bid for expansion than the now liberal nations had to pay for grabbing South Africa from the Boers, or Texas and California from Mexico, just as the American settlers in the middle of the 17th century paid more dearly for the rocky shores of New England snatched from the Indians than the American expansionists of 1848 had to pay for the fertile lands of Texas and California taken from Mexico in a war which was little more than a summer picnic. What the people have to pay in living standards for national existence and expansion is not determined mainly by the scheme of social organization but by the limits of their resources and the nature of the obstacles to their expansion.

Perhaps the strongest point in the fascist appeal to the masses, so far as the rule of the élite is concerned, is one seldom considered by critics of fascism and not always fully appreciated by the rank and file of fascists. It is the consideration that the élite are more dangerous to mass welfare when rendered desperate than when well treated and well disciplined. Fascism believes in providing ample and satsifactory functions or careers and rewards for the élite. Communism disclaims any such belief but practices it with great thoroughness. Liberalism disdains haughtily, though insincerely, any solicitude for the élite, and affects an attitude of neutrality and laissez faire so far as the personal struggle for existence is concerned. Liberalism assumes that the élite will make jobs or careers for themselves, unaided by the State, a sufficiently good assumption until the élite start making careers for themselves in social revolution or banditry or international war.

The association of the élite with banditry may seem incongruous to many modern minds, which are accustomed to think of the élite as bespectacled intellectuals or bejewelled merchant princes. It should be sufficient to bring such minds to a sense of reality by pointing out to them that practically all the proudest noble houses of Europe, or those whose patents of nobility were won by gallant exploits and not bought with money since the French Revolution, were knightly bandits and warriors, who derived much of their income from periodically shaking down the money lenders and the common people. The masses are vastly better off under a nationally disciplined élite than by being at the mercy of an élite engaged in private, gentlemanly warfare and knightly banditry.

From the point of view of mass welfare, if one's perspective takes in the history of several centuries instead of merely several decades of capitalism in its youthful upsurge, and if one's perspective includes the trends of the hour, it should be fairly clear that the best protection for the masses is to have the élite provided for with useful functions, and driven neither to orderly international warfare nor the still more inhumane conditions of private warfare. Any accurate sense of the laws of life, of the struggle for existence, of the survival of the fittest to survive, must tell one that if the élite do not find useful functions provided for them by a booming capitalism in expansion, or by a benevolent, paternal State with unlimited powers, the élite will ultimately find functions for themselves, as did their ancestors, the robber barons of medieval Europe, the piratical buccaneers of Queen Bess, or, still farther back, the strongest savages.

It is a curious insensitiveness to the logic of history and the struggle for existence which allows many muddle-headed sympathizers with communism or radical socialism to deride or denounce fascism for taking care of the élite. The safety and welfare of the masses depend on nothing so much as taking proper care of the élite in exchange for their social contributions and disciplined service of public order. If the élite return to the ways of their ancestors of only a few brief centuries ago it will be bad for a large number of them, but it will be still worse for those who are not of the élite or whose fangs are not so long and whose cunning is not so great. Any notion that the élite of the genus homo will ever exterminate each other and leave the weak of the same species to inherit the earth contradicts any expectancy based on natural history.

The great contribution of fascism to mass welfare is that of providing a formula of national solidarity within the spiritual bonds and iron discipline of which the élite and the masses of any given nation, every one in the measure of his capacity, can coöperate for the common good. The achievement of conceiving and realizing such a formula is the alternative to a return to the types of the struggle for existence which prevailed up to the rise of modern capitalism.

If the so-called friends of peace, or the liberal leaders of the Allied powers at Versailles, in 1919, and their several followings, had had any sense of the realities of the struggle for existence and had possessed a genuine passion for peace, they would have given more thought to political and economic formulas to provide places for the élite of the defeated enemy nations and the underprivileged Allied nations. They would have reasoned that, as wars are desired, planned and provoked by the frustrated élite who see in war opportunities they do not perceive in peace, the chief problem in ensuring European peace was that of fitting as many as possible of these potential war-makers into a peaceful scheme of things. This would have made it apparent that the survival of liberal republican government in Germany depended on nothing so much as on tolerable solutions for the élite. Questions of territorial rearrangements, war indemnities, and colonies, would have been discussed with consideration for this major imperative of preserving the peace in Europe.

But, as I have had occasion to learn from scores of conversation with some of the most eminent and influential of the liberal preachers of peace, the liberal ideology makes it impossible for them to see any connection between realities like the frustration of the élite and international war. Liberal ideology forces them to see peace, like every other desirable social result, as being principally a matter of legal enactment, contract, and judicial procedure. Hence the silly mania for the League of Nations and the World Court as means of preventing war, while half the graduates of German universities each year found no jobs. A mind properly formed in liberal ideology finds the greatest difficulty in grasping the idea that normal or average men would rather fight, whatever the prospects, and even would rather go into a fight with the certainty of death (which no one has in going into a war), than face the certainty of life-long frustration, defeat, and humiliation, with a strong probability of slow death by malnutrition or some one of the concomitants of prolonged poverty and frustration.

From the point of view of the masses, there is to be considered the question of controlling the élite, as well as getting the best out of them and keeping them from plunging the world into war or the cruder forms of the struggle for existence. In the matter of controlling or disciplining the élite in power, fascist technique or theory marks a great advance over liberalism.

Fascism uses the science of propaganda, indoctrination, education, group conditioning, and a rational scheme of personal motivations, to make the élite behave according to a desired pattern. Liberalism, on the other hand, relies chiefly on law courts and policemen to make the élite behave, quite forgetting that the élite must make, interpret, and manipulate any law-enforcement machinery. If an ideal pattern of behavior by the élite is left to law enforcement, and if law enforcement is a game, the élite will play to beat the game. If an ideal pattern of behavior by the élite is made a matter of conditioned reflexes or habits scientifically formed by education and indoctrination, the élite will behave as desired in much the same way soldiers or other trained men behave. The trouble with liberal training of the professional élite, of course, is that they are not trained to be good citizens, as West Pointers are trained to be good soldiers. They are trained to make money.

On the score of conditioning the élite for social control, it has to be recognized first and foremost that there is no sure system of negatively controlling the élite. Education, indoctrination, and habit formation are the only scientific methods, and their effectiveness depends largely on the efficiency of the training. Communism certainly offers little to the masses in the way of control for the in-élite, as Trotzky and his fellow exiles, or millions of the slain by the Red forces, might testify. Fascism, as we have just observed, offers as its most promising instrument of control for the in-élite the motivations of self-interest and the logic of a scientific pragmatism. Fascism indulges in no such naïveté as attaching importance to constitutional or legal inhibitions on the élite, who, as long as they are powerful enough to be abusive, will be powerful enough to interpret or amend any constitution or law to suit their ends.

Under capitalism, as might be expected, the worst abuses of power are committed with the aid of the courts and law enforcement. Fascism attaches importance only to the guarantee afforded by a spirit of discipline by a consciousness of national solidarity, by a certain sense of noblesse oblige, and by the logic of self-interest under a given set-up for those who have power. These spiritual forces and fundamental motivations are the only measures of control for the élite, or the only effective safeguards against their neglect of duty or commission of errors and downright abuses.

Fascism, in other words, so far as the control of the élite in the national interest or the protection of the people is concerned, pins its faith on character, rather than on codes or on the training and spirit it gives the élite, rather than on the policeman it might put over them. Broadly speaking, the in-élite, as a whole, can be controlled or disciplined only by forces within themselves. External or institutional controls, like laws, courts, and police, are largely worthless for the in-élite, as a whole, for the simple reason that the in-élite themselves will operate such institutional controls. This is true equally under liberalism, fascism or communism.

While we are still on the subject of the fascist appeal to the masses, we should also stress the point that the élite, under fascism, are not an aristocracy of heredity except in so far as the qualities of the élite prove hereditary. Under fascism, every private carries a field marshal's baton in his knapsack. Fascism, to be true to its pragmatic principles and inner logic, must take care of the élite, and that means, of course, giving the élite, wherever found, the function and rewards appropriate to their possibilities of usefulness. The system is so organized that those in control have an interest in obtaining the best contribution of everyone, and consequently there is every incentive freely to admit to the functions of the élite all who are capable of exercising them. Fascism needs and uses all the élite it can command. Hence a fascist régime is likely to provide for the freest circulation of the classes or furnish the best facilities for persons of exceptional qualities to find their proper place in the scheme of things.

We have stated some of the more important elements of the fascist appeal to the masses. The welfare of the masses depends on the contributions of the élite, and on the élite being well enough cared for and disciplined under peace not to turn to war or the more primitive forms of the struggle for existence. It remains only to state a few important considerations which should make fascism appeal to the more intelligent of the élite who are still among the ins. At the outset, those whose one idea in the present crisis is to hold the fort until relief comes from another capitalistic revival, should be reminded that they are staking a great deal on an extremely uncertain event. About all that can be reasonably said for the happening of this happy event is that it has always happened before.

Then these stand-patters among the in-élite should be told that fascism is in no sense a fatal thing for them or their interests. We can well understand that they prefer liberal laissez faire to fascist discipline. But, after all, they should remember that fascist discipline may be self-administered, and that there will be no wholesale liquidation of the in-élite. It is also to be borne in mind that the sternest social or group discipline can be rendered agreeable to personal taste by the processes of scientific conditioning of the human personality. A scientist or a professional soldier who for years has been disciplined to certain habits will be made miserable, if not ill, by a life of complete idleness which so many persons crave. Disciplined service to the State or under State supervision, given the necessary conditioning, can afford to the élite the same degree of personal satisfaction found by so many of them at present in making money. The rewards of honor and power are equally gratifying and abundant under fascism or under liberalism.

And, most important of all, perhaps, are the considerations that, while revolutionary change is slow in getting started, it is extremely swift, once under way; that if the in-élite oppose fascism or fascist principles as long as possible, it may not be possible for them to jump on the band wagon of a swiftly emerging fascism at the last minute; and that, in the most happy circumstances of fascist success, the longer the in-élite stay out of the movement or oppose its principles, the less they will have to say about the formation of the new American fascism.

In 1935, a substantial number of the in-élite, adopting a clear-cut fascist ideology, could easily unite under a common political banner enough of the out-élite and the masses in a movement along orderly and non-violent lines of procedure to effect the most desirable sort of fascist revolution conceivable. The worse conditions become before fascism definitely emerges, the less the chances that its leadership, program, or methods will be agreeable to the in-élite.

Mr. Roosevelt, or the candidate of the Republican Party, or both, conceivably, could, by the middle of 1936, be offering to the American electorate what might be fascism in everything but name. It is not entirely improbable that Mr. Roosevelt may be pushed far in such a direction by the middle of 1936, especially under the pressure of world events. It is more improbable that a Republican candidate could be run in 1936 on anything but a platform of muddled liberalism. If capitalism cannot stage a full recovery, the in-élite will be far better off in the long run to join the ranks of a vigorous fascism at the start than to remain with a moribund liberalism until the ship sinks.

Whether the Democratic Party or the Republican Party, or both, turn towards fascism, and how far they move in that direction, will depend almost entirely on the in-élite, the consensus of whose opinions largely determines the platforms of both major parties. At present, the in-élite are combating fascism by name, and its ideology in all its phases, hardly less violently than they are attacking communism. Yet how infinitely better for the in-élite of the moment to have fascism come through one of the major parties of the moment than to have it fight its way to power as the program of the most embittered leaders of the out-élite. The old régime in France, at any time up to a few months before the outbreak of the French Revolution, could have averted that misfortune for themselves and their nation by merely initiating a régime comparable to that which eventually emerged.

From the point of view of the broadest consideration of all interests, and of the most humane interest, it seems clear that, if we are to have a social revolution, it is desirable to have its leadership representative of as many group interests as possible. By opposing fascism, the logical orientation for the out-élite, and communism, the program of peculiar though deceptive appeal to the masses, the in-élite are really condemning us to a dog-fight between the fascism of the out-élite and communism. What we need, of course, is a fascism of the nation, or a fascism which will embrace the largest possible number of the élite, which will have fewest enemies to liquidate, and which will attain most good will of the masses. Whether we get such a fascism or not at present depends mainly on the attitude of the in-élite.

CHAPTER XX

FASCISM AND WOMAN

FASCISM marks certain deviations from liberal trends in so far as woman is concerned, but such deviations are more in the nature of a return to tradition than revolutionary departures. These deviations are often more imaginary than real, or they are largely differences of definition of the same reality. The most important fact about these deviations, however, is that they are in progress the world over as a result of sociological and technological changes which, in no sense, are peculiar to fascism. But for the fact that so much publicity and credence has been given to absurd misrepresentation of the fascist philosophy about woman, it would hardly seem necessary to devote so much space to the subject.

The rôle of woman is a matter of biological and social necessity. This necessity is paramount to any social doctrine or personal preference. Problems involving women should not be thought of as presenting choices as to what to do for women to please women or men, but as presenting always, and only, a great series of exercises in making women play their rôles suitably in the given social scheme. More women will be pleased as a result of policies designed to enable them to play their indicated social rôles suitably in a rational social scheme than will be pleased by policies designed to satisfy individual and group demands.

A good deal of the nonsense about fascism and woman is expressed in questions like the following: "Will fascism put woman back in the kitchen?", "Will fascism end careers for women?", or "Will fascism end economic independence for women?" As for women and the kitchen, it need only be said that the majority of women have never left the kitchen, are not likely ever to leave it under any social order, and could not leave the kitchen without detriment to the community and themselves. Whether ten or forty per cent of all women remain outside the kitchen is relatively unimportant, and is likely to be determined by conditions over which governmental policy will exercise no positive control. Should fascism increase the percentage of women in the kitchen a few per cent, that fact would not warrant most of the wild charges made against fascism in this connection.

As for careers and economic independence for women, these phrases are used most deceptively by the critics of fascism and by the feminists. Marriage, of course, is, and remains, woman's chief career, a fact for which fascism is in no way responsible. Equally obvious is the fact that other careers and occupations have never been entirely barred to women, nor are they barred to women by fascism. Fascism believes in marriage as a career into which a large percentage of women should be assisted or guided, and into which all eligible women should be encouraged. Still, it cannot be said that liberalism has ever officially discouraged marriage. It would not be fair to liberalism to associate with it the absurdities of the feminism of twenty years ago. Liberalism has grown so feeble of late, however, that it has been allowing the most preposterous feminists to identify their theses with those of liberalism in a general attack on fascism.

There is no need to undertake a formal defense of marriage, child-bearing or the home. It is appropriate, however, to offer some explanations of the new emphasis on these institutions and the consequent decline of feminism.

We can well begin these explanations by pointing out certain false implications conveyed by the usual questions asked by the feminists about careers and economic independence for women under fascism. First, it is implied that employment outside of marriage is available for those who need it, that it is ordinarily well remunerated, and surrounded with satisfactory conditions. Second, it is implied that marriage is less generally satisfactory than employment and that, of all bosses a woman can have, the husband is by far the worst. The facts are that employment for women is not always, or even usually, available for those who need it most; wages, hours, and conditions of employment for women are far from satisfactory; the employed woman usually has an exacting boss, whereas the married woman is usually the boss of the man; and there is doubtless more unhappiness experienced by women in employment than in marriage, but of this there can be no scientific measurement.

From the point of view of pure self-interest for women, it seems obvious that, if a woman is looking for the best chances of finding wealth and power (the essentials of what is called economic independence) or simply personal happiness, marriage is her best bet. To confirm this conclusion as to wealth and power one has merely to look around among the rich women, who are a numerous company, and most of whom got their money through marriage.

Most of the absurd implications about careers and economic independence for women seem less absurd when worded more ambiguously or when considered in the light of special cases and individual comparisons. They seem plausible in terms of the comparison between the exceptionally bad husband and the exceptionally good job. They do not seem so plausible in terms of the comparison between the best marriage and the best job. But such comparisons are not made by the feminists. Then, again, during a period of heavy demand for labor, these implications seemed more plausible when certain women who needed an income, or who were unsuited or indisposed to marriage, found life's problems less difficult by reason of easily finding a good job. But it was not feminist propaganda or liberal doctrine which created those favorable conditions for woman's employment. Rapid industrialization, rapid increase in mechanization, a large migration from country to city, and the World War, drew large numbers of women into industry. Fascism is not now crowding them out but, rather, the decline of liberal capitalism and the necessity of readjustment to another order.

Today in the United States the number of women gainfully

employed is about equal to the number of unemployed men. A rational fascism for America would not proceed to drastic disemployment of women to create jobs for men. But, in the readjustments which have to be made, as well as in view of the fact that our potential output with the same number of man-hours can be further increased enormously, a large but gradual transfer of women from the office and factory to the home is clearly indicated. If the now unemployed men produced what the now employed women produce, the same output would be maintained and, in addition, the now employed women might be adding to the total social dividend their contributions to domestic well being to whatever extent they found happy adjustment into family life, chiefly through marriage.

Most of the now employed women could not, as a practical matter, be married in a year or two, and not all of them could ever be married. So there will be, for some time to come, a large number of women needing employment, and always some women needing life-long employment outside the home. There will always be jobs which only women can fill satisfactorily. These jobs should be made to take care of the women who need employment. But there is no reason to allow the number of women in employment forever to be determined entirely by the play of market factors, or to remain unmodified by state intervention to increase the percentage of the married and decrease the percentage of women competing with men.

Fascism clashes with liberalism as to whether the major stress shall be on the values of wifehood, motherhood, and the family, or on the values which women can achieve outside of wifehood and motherhood. No reasonable fascist will deny that some women, usually the exceptionally endowed, achieve desirable values outside of, and frequently in addition to, wifehood and motherhood, or that the family values are definitely out of the reach of a small minority of women. But the fascist insists on ranking far above all other values attainable by women those of good wifehood and good motherhood. He holds that the paramount objectives of public policy, so far as women are concerned, should be to make good wives and mothers and not to make as many soft berths as possible for old maids and thus to put a premium on the avoidance of marriage.

Liberalism does not exactly declare that subsidizing spinsterhood and sterility is one of the objectives of public policy. But it is evident from a study of the vital statistics of graduates of advanced institutions of liberal learning, subsidized by the liberal State, that one of the effects of liberal public policy is to encourage spinsterhood and sterility among the classes best suited to reproduce. Fascism says that it is one thing to provide training and jobs for women unable to marry and without means of support, or to provide training and opportunities for women of exceptional talent who have special contributions to make to the community outside of marriage; but that it is quite a different thing to allow educational and cultural institutions and leaders to exalt and promote spinsterhood and sterility.

It is too often forgotten that the vast majority of women in all callings, exactly like the vast majority of men, are mediocrities whose services or contributions are not unique. Most women gainfully employed, indeed, are doing less work and doing it less skillfully, less rapidly, and less well, than the average male mediocrity could do the same work. Most of these women get the job simply because their labor is cheaper. And their labor is cheaper because many of them are partially subsidized by their families or others. These women are doing ordinary work which could be done a little better by ordinary men, while they could be doing most essential and distinguished work as wives and mothers, or work which the most extraordinary men cannot do.

It is only fair to the feminists to say that they have asked only equality of work, pay, and opportunity in industry, and equality of opportunity for preparation for every career. Fascism finds it impossible to accept their thesis of equality between the sexes because fascism finds it impossible to escape the implications of sex and biological differences. Fascism can see no sense to discussing the sexes in terms of equality and inequality, not any more than there would be to discussing the forces of electricity and gravity in terms of such comparisons. Men and women are different, not equal or unequal to each other. Women must be thought of in terms of their relation to society and its implications, rather than in terms of the hypothesis that women are free persons who are at liberty to disregard the indications of their biological specialization to any extent their tastes may dictate.

The fact is that personal tastes in such matters are the products of social conditioning. And social conditioning is a process which the State must control in the public interest. If young women prefer jobs to marriage, where there are no extraordinary conditions indisposing them to marriage and pre-disposing them to a career, it is not to be supposed for a moment that such preferences are the spontaneous expressions of the will of free spirits. It is natural for women to prefer marriage and not to prefer to avoid it. If certain young women do not prefer marriage, most likely it is because they have been given by education and certain social pressures to suppose that a woman is better off in employment, or more to be envied and admired with a Ph.D., or pounding a typewriter, than with a baby or cooking her husband's breakfast. Feminism has not limited itself to championing the relief of the unfortunate woman who has needed employment to escape the tyranny of a brutal husband or the woman who has needed an opportuntiy to express her genius. Feminism has become a cultural force tending to bring marriage and child-bearing into disesteem among young women and to make them esteem more highly a career free of the responsibility and cares, but also bereft of the joys and compensations, of wifehood and motherhood.

Feminism is on the wane, not so much because its arguments have been refuted by fascist or other arguments, as because of the fact that nothing so far has happened under liberal capitalism to deliver women from the fate of being women. The so-called emancipation of women has left them still women and subject to all the necessities, spiritual and physical, of that quality. The feminist revolt against being women has won a series of wholly Pyrrhic victories. The men have made all the concessions demanded, but nature has not made a single concession, and the concessions of the men have not filled the cups of loneliness. Nature has rather handed some of the feminist rebels a few hard knocks, as only mental and physical examinations can adequately reveal. Fascism is the bane of feminism chiefly because fascism offers no deliverance for the woman who seeks escape from her sex. On the contrary, fascism makes a virtue and a glory of the necessity for women to be women. In this respect fascism combines some features of traditionalism and most of the indications of modern science.

An American fascism would involve no change in the political status and rights of women, either as voters, property owners, or parties to domestic relations. It would, however, undoubtedly find it necessary to initiate important changes of policy in respect to the encouragement of marriage and the discouragement of employment by women which is against the public interest. The employment of women would be made subject to a social control requiring for the qualification of every employable woman proof that the employment sought was in the public interest and, for the admission of women to advanced courses of specialized or professional training subsidized by the State or institutional funds, evidence that the applicant was exceptionally well suited for, or needed in, the field for which preparation was sought. Fascism would enforce some measure of vocational guidance equally on men and women. But it would not apply to both sexes the same standards of eligibility, for the good reason that both sexes are not the same.

The following qualifications could be recognized as entitling a woman to qualify for an employment license: (1) Need by the particular applicant of an earned income; (2) need by the community of a woman for the particular job; (3) need by the community of the special qualities or talents of the particular applicant; (4) and absence of objection to her employment founded on considerations of public policy. Under such rules, all women who needed earned incomes would, ipso facto, be entitled to work where qualified and needed. Conversely, a woman who did not need an earned income, and who had nothing special to offer, would not be allowed to qualify for work a man could do quite as well, merely to provide herself with extra pocket money. On the other hand, a woman wishing to qualify for an employment for which a man would not be suitable, such, for instance, as a chorus girl or a matron in a woman's institution, would be subject to no State-imposed disqualification.

In cases of women who asserted a right to work at a given job or career because of special artistic talent, there would naturally arise some disagreements with the public authority. The public authority might find that a woman ought not to be allowed to play a saxophone in a dance orchestra, unless she had no other means of support, though it would authorize her performance as a talented artist. Another source of frequent disagreement would be cases of women without children or heavy responsibilities who might wish to engage in extra-domestic activities for a salary or wage. In some cases such employment would be against the public interest, for it would involve the displacement of a family breadwinner from employment. In other cases it would not. In the cases of women who wished to engage in economic activities financed by themselves or their relatives or friends, there should be no objection to their doing so. Such economic activities would be no different from personal expenditures.

The net results of regulating the employment of women in the public interest would include the elimination from the competitive labor market of large numbers of women who do not need the money, or who have their labor at low rates partly subsidized by family, community, or other persons. If it is objected that social regulation and licensing of employment by women would involve considerable expense and administrative difficulty, it need only be said in reply that the relief of jobless heads of families involves quite as great administrative difficulty and more expense. Another objection can be disposed of by pointing out that nothing in employment regulation need prevent the mobilization by industry, in time of special need for extra workers, of as many housewives, actual or potential, as high wages could lure from their homes into factories and offices. During such an emergency the licensing policy would be modified to allow any desired number of additional women workers to enter industry.

Before leaving the subject of social control of employment, it is well to give a final word of emphasis to the point that free market determination of the number of women employed, of the jobs on which employed, of their hours and conditions of employment, lays on the community a concealed set of charges which it is nearly impossible to calculate with exactness, but which it would be hard to exaggerate. Classical economics claimed for free market determination of employment conditions a set of advantages which are wholly illusory today. When the head of a family is thrown out of work by a girl living in a hall bedroom on next to starvation wages, or by a girl living partly on her family, a slight economic gain may be netted thereby for the employer and his branch of production, but the taxpayers have the costs of relief for the unemployed head of the family. Moreover, in such cases, the taxpayers have also added costs for the health and welfare of the girl who has been lured from a comfortable country home or small town home, where most of her problems were economically and fairly well taken care of, to the large city, where she is apt to become a public charge or a social menace the day after she loses her job, or even while she holds it.

It is in regard to the training of women, however, that fascism is likely to work the most sweeping changes in this country. These changes will take two principal forms. In the first place, greater stress will be laid on training for wifehood and motherhood and, in the second place, training for both sexes will be given with greater regard for social needs than at present. Training for wifehood and motherhood will begin in the upper grades of grammar school and continue through all subsequent courses of instruction. There is a grotesque absurdity in present-day training of thousands of girls to be stenographers who have not the requisite intelligence quotient or basic knowledge for satisfactory performance of such duties. Many of them, of course, never hold steady jobs. It leaves these girls wholly untrained for the duties of wife and mother, for which they are suited and to which most of them are destined.

Correlating education with social needs is too large and technical a subject for extensive discussion here. Suffice it to remark that, at present, the ruling theory and practice of American liberal democracy is to try and give every one the kind of schooling he or she demands, whereas, under fascism, the attempt will be made to give every one the kind of education which corresponds to the national plan into which every one has to be fitted, both for his good and the good of the community.

This educational theory does not mean an entire disregard for personal preferences, and certainly not any disregard for personal aptitudes. It does mean, however, that if ten times as many women apply for training for law or stenography as there are places for them in these employments, all the applicants will not be given the training they seek, partly or wholly at public expense, merely because they want it. It means, also, that if boys or girls without the requisite intelligence or cultural background for serious work in the higher studies still insist on having a try at it, or at wasting a few years in college, the admission standards will not be lowered to admit them, and the examinations in the courses will not be lowered to enable these unqualified ones to get passing marks.

There is no intention here to class women candidates for instruction with the mentally more deficient candidates, and it is fully recognized that the scholastic records of women compare favorably with those of men. It must be acknowledged, however, that any intensification of competition for places in educational quotas is likely to eliminate from the higher branches a larger percentage of the present number of female than of male candidates. And any correlation of training quotas with occupational opportunities is certain to reduce even more drastically the percentage of women candidates admitted. But such correlation of training quotas with social needs cannot be said to exclude women from careers or training for a career.

In conclusion, it remains only to generalize briefly on certain high points of the outlook for woman under a planned society in which human necessities are rationally provided for and the necessary provisions are duly dignified. Fascism is not creating or intensifying woman's biological specialization. Fascism is rationalizing and dignifying it, not trying to offer woman an escape from it. The results of attempting either an extreme economic equality, or an extreme equality in sex relations, are invariably bad for society and worse for women.

It is being discovered in communist Russia, where the feminists had pretty much their own way at the start, that the socialist State, like any other State, needs the family and all that it stands for; that if both sexes are allowed legal and conventional license to divorce and remarry as often as they please with a minimum of formality, the men will be getting most of the fun, the women most of the hardships, and the family most of the detriment.

Both in economic and domestic relations, the more equality there is between the sexes as regards special duties, obligations, and protection, or the more equal freedom there is for making and breaking contracts by both sexes, the greater will be the inequalities for the members of the two sexes, in the long run, in the matter of opportunities for realizing the good life. A satisfactory measure of distributive equality, so far as achieving the good life is concerned, can only prevail between the two sexes on the basis of some scheme of rights and duties which clearly recognizes sex differences. Such a scheme of rights and duties greatly restricts woman's freedom both in economic and marital contracts. But it also restricts the man's freedom.

The institution of the family is essential not only to the State but to the happiness of men and women. The family requires for its preservation a degree of State oversight, or the opposite of laissez faire, appropriate to the needs of the situation. If extreme economic laissez faire, or sex freedom and equality, be practised for any length of time, women will get the worst of the bargains in business and in sex relations, because men as a whole have an advantage in bargaining power in both spheres. Woman's biological specialization and peculiar physical and spiritual limitations handicap her both in the liberal free market and in the feminist's free sex mart. Man's chivalry and protective attitude towards woman is partly connected with property rights and partly connected with man's need of the family. Feminism makes the mistake of seeing in differential treatment of the sexes an insulting inequality, which it has sought to replace with a legal equality in economic and domestic relations. Fascism holds that, in making a good and great nation, it is essential to provide for the development of good and great men and women, not just good and equal persons. Feminism says that women are just folks. Fascism says that they are women. The feminists may want to be legal persons, but most women, who are feminine rather than feminists, prefer to be women.

CHAPTER XXI

THE FASCIST IDEA OF NATIONAL INTEREST IN FOREIGN RELATIONS

THIS book has been written as far as possible in terms of broad principles rather than specific details. This has been done because any discussion in terms of details would be sure to prove largely obsolete and irrelevant by the time the book got through the press. Thus, for illustration, one might have laboriously analyzed the N.R.A. and offered a set of concrete recommendations approaching the problem of industrial control along the lines there followed, only to find all one's detailed drafting rendered completely useless by the decision of the Supreme Court and the implications of that decision.

So, in the field of international relations, the discussion will be kept as much as possible in terms of principles so broadly defined as at times, perhaps, to seem almost evasive of urgent problems of details. But what is the use discussing details, except for the purposes of day-to-day decisions, in connection with matters like tariffs and trade policies or laws, neutrality laws and policies, treaties, the League of Nations, or the World Court, on the eve of war and world changes which will undoubtedly sweep away much or most of the factual groundwork on which one may painstakingly build a body of premises and long range recommendations? In these days, when discussing social reorganization and long range plans, one must build chiefly on general principles and on evaluations of constant factors or trends. A book of this kind is no place to discuss proposals which might have a chance of tiding over an immediate crisis, just as at least four crises within the decade before the outbreak of the World War were smoothed over, leaving, however, the fundamental issues unchanged and certain eventually to precipitate a world war.

The chief purposes of any discussion of foreign relations and fascism in a book of this sort should be to indicate clearly certain public order imperatives and certain more obvious fascist choices in the orientation of public policy related to foreign relations. Scientific evaluation of the probable consequences of each given policy should be the supreme criterion. This philosophical attitude towards the working out of a foreign policy may well be stressed as a distinctive feature of fascism, and a feature conspicuously absent from the liberal approach to the same order of problems. Liberal influence over the minds of statesmen leads them to try to reduce every conflict of national interests, and every possible choice of policy, to an issue of right versus wrong, legality versus illegality, humanity versus inhumanity, good business versus bad business, always in a way to give to the dictates of self-interest or the whims of preference an ethical, moral, legal, and economic sanction.

The choices are not ordinarily evaluated by the true liberal in the light of their probable consequences—given conditions as they are and not as he chooses to assume they are. Having unctuously postulated a series of high-sounding ethical and legal imperatives, with interpretations and applications appropriate to a given situation, the statesman, if he has any sense of honor or decency, has but one choice every time he has to make an important decision. The assertion during the late War of our legal doctrine of neutral rights, or the right of our business men to trade with the belligerents under conditions prescribed by our lawyers, could only have in that particular conflict the consequence of dragging us into it. But the drafting of State Department notes setting forth our legal position was always done by lawyers expounding a theory of law which we said was international law and common justice. Our notes were not drafted by statesmen weighing the probable consequences of their words.

Our foreign affairs are luminous examples of what is wrong with lawyers when allowed to determine public policy from a legal point of view. The trouble with lawyers is that, after passing a judicial sentence or giving a legal opinion declaring what is right, they leave to other branches of government and the community the problems of execution and the problems of the costs or consequences of execution. Judges who issue mortgage judgments do not look after evicted farmers and home-owners. Lawyers who write State Department notes defining justice or international law, as we see it, do not weigh military plans for upholding their legal opinions. The War Department has to attend to the execution, and the community to the costs.

The American doctrine of neutrality was entirely rational and suited to our interests and powers of asserting it at the time evolved. But it has since become not only unsuited to our interests but utterly impossible to maintain, due mainly to changed technological conditions. These changes render invalid all our prior legal distinctions between contraband and non-contraband, or between belligerent and non-belligerent. Every legal rule or ethical principle for the maintenance of which we fought in the last War is certain to be violated by both sides in the next war. Must we fight in every future war in a futile effort to uphold doctrines which technological changes have rendered obsolete and unenforceable?

In wars before the 20th century, the armed forces went to combat with a limited set of weapons and economic resources, while the rest of the people went about their usual business. In 20th century warfare, the entire nation is mobilized for the war effort, and almost every resource becomes essential to the destruction of the enemy. Every able-bodied citizen is a belligerent, and everything is contraband. For the lawyers, however, right is right and wrong is wrong. What was right in 1815 must be right in 1915. They cannot be expected to be aware of changes and the implications of changes, for their science is not concerned with the events of today but with the rationalizations of the events of yesterday. The moral, of course, is that our foreign policies must not be shaped by lawyers but by an executive statesmanship responsible for finding ways to meet the consequences of a policy.

From the viewpoint of the believer in absolutes, or the average lawyer or judge, there is little point to considering the consequences of public decisions. One has to obey certain high-sounding ethical . or legal imperatives, whatever the consequences. Indeed, consequences have little to do with the validity of ethical and legal postulates based on the transcendental premise that a given course is right and anything different is wrong. One has to do right, though the heavens fall. One has to defend at all costs one's national honor or one's vital interest, thus defined, not by rational calculation, but by some body of inspired truths, all of which usually means a holy war at the end.

Fascism differs from liberalism in its conduct of foreign policy by proceeding on the premises that the only authority which may usefully be thought of as exercising any measure of supremacy is the human will; that the supremacy of the human will is synonymous and commensurate with the force factors or might it exerts; and that the only norms for the rational control of the human will in its highest expressions are facts and scientific probabilities. If the facts conflict with the logic of a given law, or rule, or concept of right, the facts win out and the law, commandment, or eternal truth, loses out. This, of course, is what always eventually happens. Rationality says, the sooner and more easily it happens, the better.

Taking the human will as the source of authority and power, we are forced to recognize the national State as the highest organism expressing this authority, and the only organism so far proved capable of expressing the authority and might of the human will in a way to maintain social order. The nation is a social necessity which has no substitute.

In international relations there are only national interests to be considered. Strictly speaking, there is no such thing as an international interest in any useful sense of such a term. Of course, it is possible to define the sum of several national interests as constituting an international interest. But the trouble with this definition is that there will always be found opposed to the sum of any given number of national interests (thus defined as an international interest) the opposing interest of one or more nations. Then we have the sums of two sets of national interests opposing each other. To call the sums of two sets of national interests in opposition to each other two respective international interests is not a useful sense or meaning to give to the term international interest. If the term or concept of international interest is to have any useful meaning, it must apply to a unique, or common, or universal, interest in respect to a given matter.

Just such an interest is the eternal dream of the internationalists. Similarly, a body of law, to be called international law to any useful purpose, must be law accepted by all nations. The trouble with so much that passes under the name of international law is that it is the law of a nation or group of nations. And it does not serve any useful purpose to call a body of law accepted by nations X, Y, and Z, but rejected by nations A, B, and C, international law, because this body of law is as much a body of international illegality as it is a body of international legality. One should only say of it that it is the law or legality of nations X, Y, and Z, and the illegality of nations A, B, and C.

The dream of a unique international interest or a unique international law (for law is but an expression of a public interest or a set of private interests having found the might of a State to uphold it) can never be realized. Situations will always be developing in which it will pay one nation to wrong another nation, or in which one nation can get away with wronging another nation and also get something advantageous out of the wrong. Part of our national patrimony, as every one knows, was obtained by wronging Mexico, not to mention our exterminating most of the original inhabitants of our present territory by way of taking their lands.

It is possible to conceptualize a world of individuals in which there would be no wrongs, but it is impossible rationally to visualize a world of nations in which there would be no wrongs or in which no wrongdoer ever profited from wrongdoing. The great and powerful nations have all been built up on the wrongs they have successfully perpetrated on other nations to their own advantage. Of course, it often happens that the perpetrator of a wrong to another nation will force that nation to acknowledge that the wrong was right, which, for juridical purposes, makes the wrong right, but never in the feelings of the wronged nation.

Given nations as they are now constituted, and as they are constrained by the logic of their very being to behave, it is a sheer contradiction in terms to say that there could be a universal interest in a wrongless course of events in the world of nations. It is absurd either to suppose that the wronged nations will ever consider that their wrongs of the past have been made right, or to imagine that a situation can be created in which powerful nations having military superiority will never find it advantageous to themselves to wrong a weaker nation.

It is, perhaps, slightly less unreasonable to suppose a world of individuals so conditioned under the direction of one universal and supreme will as to feel a universal interest in having everything happen in a certain way. This supposition is still conceivable, though somewhat fantastic, because individuals might be reduced by a long process of purposive and selective breeding to such a degree of similarity of basic reactions that they would behave as much alike as bees or ants. But it is wholly absurd to suppose a world of nations so homologized as to have a set of universal or common interests about everything. It is absurd, because the fact of nationhood, unlike the fact of anthood, necessarily implies great inequalities in might and great differences in ideological and behavior patterns.

Most of the internationalists reason from the false premise that all nations have an interest in peace, or that peace is a universal or international interest. This premise is obviously refuted by history. In 1848, our interest was not peace with Mexico but war and annexation. It is undoubtedly a fact today that our interest is to hold what we have with peace, and that there is no good war for us on the horizon. The same may be said of Great Britain and France. Any war we get into is likely to be one of defense of what we have, rather than endeavor to get what the other fellow has. But the fact that we today have nothing to gain by a war should not be turned to support the *non sequitur* that no other nation in the world will find a good chance to win a profitable war. We have to see to it that our national defense or war potential never weakens to such a point that we might seem or prove an easy mark for some other nation, exactly as Mexico in 1848 proved for us. And we should, from time to time, balance the costs of buying peace with concessions against the costs of fighting to keep what we have without making concessions.

Here it should be emphasized that there is no point to the oft-repeated argument comparing nations with individuals and deriving from such comparison the conclusion that, as honesty can be made by municipal law and social convention the best policy for individuals living within the police power of a nation, honesty can be made by international law and universal opinion the best policy for nations living within a society of nations. The comparison and derived argument are totally invalidated by the simple fact that, whereas individuals within a nation can be deprived of the means of getting away with theft and murder on a large scale with personal profit, nations cannot be nations and kept deprived of the means of getting away with successful war to their profit. No degree of equilateral disarmament would deprive nations of their war potentials. If all nations were disarmed down to only policemen with night sticks, nations like the United States and Germany would still have a tremendous war potential in their ability to create on short notice vast armies and quantities of war supplies. Speed in rearming would be the decisive factor.

The power of a strong nation to get away with a war of conquest and annexation is inherent in the facts of nationhood and would not be terminated by disarmament. Under complete disarmament, the present war potentials would remain substantially unchanged except by reason of differences in the speed potentials. It would be no gain for humanity to slow up the starting of the war and thus prolong its duration. Under total disarmament, the chief difference would be that nations capable of the speediest rearmament would have greater advantages than they have under a régime of universal armaments. Thus, under total disarmament, Germany would have a greater advantage over France than under any régime of equal armaments, for Germany could rearm more quickly than France.

To minimize the frequency of wars and wrongs by one nation against another, the only historically validated formula is a fairly even balance of power in which the sums of different national interests are so evenly matched as to force factors that there will be a strong deterrent to starting a big war, and a virtual impossibility of getting away successfully with a small war except with the assent of the powers making up the balancing factors in the balance of powers. Standing armies and strong navies make it possible to maintain an effective balance of power and to insure considerable periods of peace. If there were no great national armies and navies, it seems certain, if history is any guide, that we should have the conditions of perpetual, petty private warfare which prevailed in Europe for over a thousand years following the collapse of the Roman Empire. A similar state of petty factional warfare has prevailed for decades in certain small Central American Republics too small to maintain a strong national army. And, of course, a similar condition prevails over a large part of China, whose territory is too large, and whose resources and organization are too deficient, to allow of the essential national army to eliminate bandits and private warfare.

And it should not be forgotten that it took four years of warfare by a national army of the United States to end one sectional war and to prevent a successful precedent which might have led to innumerable other sectional secessions and civil wars. The best contribution the United States can make to world peace is to maintain such a war potential as will enable us to rope off a large section of the globe included within this hemisphere as territory in which outsiders may not come and fight, without having to pay a higher cost for such an adventure than it is likely to seem worth.

Fascism is nationalist and opposed to anything going under

the name of internationalism which seems bad for the nation. In this connection it is well to emphasize the fact that much of the ideology of so-called internationalism is largely a matter of confusion of thought. Use of terms like internationalism or international, though made with dictionary correctness, may easily lead people to suppose that whenever the prefix "inter" is added to something national it means that that something has ceased to be national. The use of the prefix "inter" is thought to imply that that something which was national, but which also affects several other nations, by reason of its affecting other nations is transmuted into something which is no longer national and is quite different from national. It is by this process of reasoning that much national law and policy gets called international law and policy. In this way, institutions like the League of Nations are thought of as being the antithesis of nationalism and the nation, when, as a matter of fact, the League, in so far as it is an effective agency, is but the tool of some strong nation or group of nations.

Whenever the League of Nations essays to do anything important, which is not often, it becomes ipso facto, or in that essay, not a thing apart from nations but merely two or three nations making a joint gesture against another nation or group of nations. Undoubtedly the gesture is properly called international, but it is also essentially national. If one wants to get down to tangible persons or things in the matter of the gesture, one comes to intensely real grips with national realities like the British fleet or the French army.

In brief, the internationalism of the League of Nations never amounts to anything more or less than the internationalism of any three or four powerful nations making a joint démarche or a war as allies. The démarche or war alliance is an international reality only as long as it lasts. While it lasts, the nations making it remain nations and behave as nations. The gesture or the war always ends. When it ends, the international reality has ended, but the national realities which made it, go on as ever. Hence, it serves no useful purpose to try to think internationally and so to lose sight of the perennial national fact. The international fact always embodies several national facts. And the international fact is never an organic whole made up of national facts. The international fact is merely a passing phase or aspect of several separate national facts.

There is no conflict, as many good people like to suppose, between nationalism and internationalism. There are just conflicts between nations and between nationalisms. The simple fact that these conflicts necessarily involve more than one nation makes them international. Nor is there any international spirit or unity except as the passing phase of relations between nations, such relations, when important, usually being connected with war. That is to say, the only effective international coöperation of importance is that which takes place between nations allied in making war or with a view to making war.

The underlying idea or wish of much talk about internationalism is that the nation may be weakening, or entering a phase of dissolution into a something or other which will have absorbed all the nations. But that is exactly what is not happening. The more international relations there are—most of them related to the liquidation of past wars and preparations for future wars—the more vigorous become the nation, nationalism, and the national spirit. There is no indication, even, of a vague trend towards the laying of the groundwork of a superstate which would swallow up the existing national States. The nation was never more vigorous or sharply defined than in 1935, and nothing has contributed more to the fortification of nationalism than international gesture publicizing institutions like the League of Nations, peace pacts, and the World Court. There is no need here to expatiate on why it is that the nation is showing greater vitality and gives no signs of early dissolution into any sort of international unity. Suffice it to state the indisputable fact that the nation was never more vital or significant.

There is for every nation, however, an international problem, or a problem of foreign affairs, precisely because there are many nations, and because they have national problems which involve relations with each other. The international problem, therefore, is always the national problem of several States. Any human mind approaching the international problem of any moment must approach it as a citizen of a nation who is interested in having that international problem solved or dealt with in a way agreeable to the interests of his own national State. This is equally true, whether that person be a high official of the Roman Catholic Church, the League of Nations, or the Communist International. When a person says he is interested in international welfare he merely means that he is interested in the national welfare of his own country in some international connection. He may or may not also mean, though he will usually say that he does, that he hopes or believes that what he considers good for his own country will prove good for other countries.

American fascism will proceed in foreign relations with a clear recognition that our interest in international affairs is a national interest. In the formulation of the specific scheme of national interest to be followed from day to day, an American fascism will be guided by the dictates of the national will, by indications of facts, and by as scientific an evaluation of the probabilities as it is possible for the fascist leaders to make.

CHAPTER XXII

OBJECTIVES IN FOREIGN RELATIONS

WE MAY roughly divide the objectives of our foreign policy into those classifiable under the head of national defense, economic security, and special policies. As for the objectives of national defense, it seems clear that in order to maintain our position as a great nation we should maintain naval parity with the greatest power, a professional army of at least four hundred thousand men fully equipped, and universal compulsory military service. It may be asked why we need such a large armed establishment if we are not going to be the aggressor and if, with a much smaller establishment, we could probably raise enough forces in time to meet any attack and secure our defense. The answer is that if we have an inferior military establishment, we are more than likely to be challenged, inasmuch as we will inevitably insist on having a lot to say in the foreign field.

We cannot avoid war by being unprepared for it, as our experience in the late War demonstrates. And we cannot determine for ourselves the scale of armaments which properly corresponds to our size and pretentions. The scale of armaments which properly corresponds to our size and pretentions must, in the nature of things, be dictated to us by the rest of the nations. If they maintain armaments on a certain scale, we must observe, accordingly, proportions on that scale corresponding to our size and stakes. To have the interests of a first rate world power, to insist on interposing our word or will as such, and to maintain an armed establishment disproportionately small, is merely to tempt daring and desperate powers to risk an encounter with us. As for the costs of national defense, it need only be said that men are better off in the army than in the bread line, and the country is better off to have the idle producing the instruments of self-defense than to have them idle. National defense is one way of producing and consuming wealth. Unemployment is not a source of income but a true and tragic waste.

Every one, liberal, fascist and communist, including all the professional and sincere pacifists, wants peace, provided it can be had on his terms. In this respect it is difficult to see any difference between the so-called pacifists and the so-called militarists. No one, certainly not any one of the numerous types of pacifists, is willing to have peace on any terms whatsoever which the other fellow may dictate. In other words, no one puts peace first in his list of objectives. There are no believers in peace at any price. Those who talk most about their love of peace and other men's love of war and who ordinarily oppose most violently any adequate military preparedness for their own country will be the first and most energetic advocates of getting their own country into a war for peace every time an international conflict breaks out anywhere in the world.

Fascism has been denounced by the liberals, pacifists and socialists as a war breeder, yet, at the time this book went to press, it was the latter who, along with the international banking and pro-English interests and sympathizers everywhere, were on record in the Italian-Ethiopian situation as supporting sanctions which could only mean a world war. On the other hand, the organized fascists of England, under Sir Oswald Moseley, and of France, under Colonel de La Rocque, were constantly making public demonstrations in opposition to policies which the British Government was trying to have carried out by the League, policies which, as the responsible British statesmen well knew, could only mean a world war.

The fascist, being an enlightened patriot of his own nation, is ready to fight for its defense and supposed best interests but never for abstractions like peace and international justice, terms which, as a practical matter, mean the side in a conflict taken by the user of these terms. The fascist sees that the defense and best interests of his own land do not require it to become involved in every war that occurs. The internationalist, on the other hand, must try to draw his country into every war that breaks out, for he is committed always to fight for peace and justice, as something quite apart from the selfish interest of his own country, and every war necessarily presents a breach of the peace as well as an issue of justice. The real issue between the fascist and liberal view as to foreign policy is not one of Shall we uphold peace or permit wars? for no League or similar agency has ever prevented or can ever prevent war. The Italian-Ethiopian and the Sino-Japanese episodes of the past two years have added to the long list of historical proofs of the impossibility of international action, through the League or without a league, preventing war or terminating war except as wars have always been terminated, namely either by fighting it out or by compromise diplomatically, not judicially, arrived at, according to the existing balance of power or force factors, not according to any normative verbalisms or principles of law or justice set forth in League Covenants, treaties or other masterpieces of legal draftsmanship. The real issue, so far as internationalism or Anglo-League-ism is concerned, is whether every challenge to the existing status quo which England may find dangerous to her imperial interests and consequently may wish to have pronounced a crime and an unwarranted aggression shall be turned into a world war, by reason of a British monopoly of righteousness and a British supremacy in finance and propaganda used to line up most of the nations of the world in opposition to the challengers and in defense of what England desires.

The internationalists, of course, try to argue that lining up the whole world into two camps of the angels versus the war making devil or devils will prevent wars from occurring or quickly end them if they do break out. The argument, however, rests on nothing but wishful thinking. It will, of course, happen in practically every war or clash of national interests that there will be a majority and a minority both as to numbers of nations taking sides and as to their combined resources. But it will not happen that the majority on the side of England and the angels will always be so overwhelming as to prevent a resort to arms. If the coalition on the side of the angels does not prevent the war starting, it is a travesty on words to call it —a coalition to make war—a peace-making measure. It will not always happen that the majority will side with England and the angels. And it may even happen that a majority with England and the angels will some day get licked by a minority fighting against peace and justice as defined by England and the League. Then there is strong reason to suppose that some nations will remain on the fence in a holy war between justice and injustice or England and the Devil, thus complicating military calculations or any program of joint coercion against the Devil.

The internationalists, most of whom are subsidized spokesmen of the bankers and their peace foundations, colleges, press and other cultural institutions, have a profound and understandable reverence for bankers, international finance and business men generally. This naive awe of trade and finance leads these internationalists and theorists to attribute to finance and trade a power to exercise deterrent pressure on political leaders which money changers and traders have never been able to exercise against strong men in the saddle. Alexander, Julius Caesar or even as recent a conqueror as Napoleon were never subject to restraint from making war by any possible action of money-lenders and traders, not any more than Hitler, Mussolini, Stalin or Araki are today. Money-lenders and tradesmen can support governments under which they live in making war on a Caesar or a Napoleon or a Mussolini, but they are effective only as auxiliaries of the men behind the guns in actual war, not as forces to prevent a war. The money lenders and tradesmen of the country of a political leader who wants to make war, of course, will always have to do as they are told quite as much as conscripted soldiers.

Economic sanctions without waging armed warfare are always certain to prove a farce. Economic forces can be mobilized effectively only to help make war, never to prevent it. The reasons are obvious on analysis of the factors which determine war making. It is hard enough ordinarily to hold together for any length of time in an effective measure of loyal and efficient cooperation any large coalition of nations allied in making a war. This feat was achieved by the Allies in the late World War only by virtue of the ten billion dollars of goods and services which the American people donated to subsidize the Allied effort. What holds a war making alliance together or what enforces a workable measure of solidarity, loyalty and efficient cooperation in a war enterprise is one thing: a strong and ever present sense of danger from a common foe. To expect a large number of allies to maintain such solidarity and cooperation in applications of economic pressure when no such paramount motivation operates to impose it is utterly naïve and unrealistic. Every member of such a preposterous coalition of peacefully coercing nations would have unlimited opportunities and inducements to cheat with safety and advantage. And it would be technically impossible for the alliance, as a whole, to act as an inquiring policeman, a judging magistrate or a disciplining force. Nations and large groups of individuals can only be disciplined by emotional drives from within. Legal verbalisms which they may adopt as norms of conduct have validity only to the extent that the inner drives in the majority of persons uphold the enforcement of these norms. In war time there is a majority group will to self-defense and defeat of the enemy in arms. In sanctions time there could be no majority group will to uphold measures which would operate to national economic disadvantage and which would be indicated by no imperative of immediate safety. The notion that war, in the abstract, is a public enemy against which all nations can be permanently united is the purest poppycock. Those who preach this absurd notion most are the first to refute it by rushing to embrace this public enemy war as a means to the desired end of peace.

As this book goes to press, the League is being manipulated by England in an attempt to force the rest of the world into an alliance to protect and further what those in power in England mistakenly consider to be Britain's best interests in the

Mediterranean. Any one would be rash to predict exactly what would be the outcome of a war involving most of the nations of the earth at the start in a war against Italy. But it is safe to predict what would not result from any such British or League war. For one thing, it would not long remain a united enterprise. For another, it would not succeed in its alleged undertaking to lay the foundations of a lasting peace and scheme of justice. It would begin by making a small war large. How it would end, no one can say, except to guess that it would end in the triumph of communism or chaos.

No Englishman is to be blamed for wanting to fight Italy or any other country if he believes such a war in the best interests of England. Nor should he be censured for trying to secure as many allies as possible for his country in that war by the use of the most unscrupulous propaganda, the most absurd exploitation of moral issues or the most barefaced lies. All is fair in love and war. Likewise, no Italian should be blamed for wanting his country to follow the illustrious examples of conquest and territorial aggrandizement which have made the United States, Britain and France great and powerful. But any American or Frenchman who would have his countrymen duped into fighting another nation's battle, be it that of Britain or Italy, when it is not the battle of his own country, should be deemed a poor patriot or a poor thinker or both.

It is absurd to argue that a battle against every aggressor nation is always the battle of all other nations, the argument now being advanced by Britain as the ruling principle of the League. Such an argument is historically and rationally untenable. The nations of the world did not combine to avert, defeat or even mildly censure a ruthless and unjustified American aggression against and conquest of Mexico or similar British and French aggressions, conquests and annexations too numerous here to mention, yet the nations of the world, as a whole, have never felt or had reason to feel the fear that America, Britain or France would go on from one conquest to another until the entire world had been subjugated by one or the other of these great powers. As Mr. Frank Simonds has so aptly pointed out in the Italian-Ethiopian conflict, it is absurd for the winners at the national game of conquest, having themselves acquired by conquest about all they feel able or disposed to manage, if not more, suddenly to go righteous and try to enforce on the entire world for all time a code of morality, the first commandment of which "Thou shalt not follow our examples."

Under the heading of national security, we must not only maintain adequate armed forces, but we must make sure of the exclusion of European powers from further extension of their influence in this hemisphere, as well as secure our control of the Panama Canal. To maintain our paramount strategic position on this hemisphere and prevent an extension of European influence, it is not necessary for us to repeat or continue the stupid and unnecessary adventures of Presidents Theodore Roosevelt, Taft, Wilson, and Coolidge, and Secretaries of State Root and Hughes, in dollar diplomacy, loans, military interventions, financial interventions, political meddling to insure fair elections, sound financial control, or protection, of American capital in the Caribbean republics. To keep Europe out of those republics is all we need aim at.

To do that, all we require is naval supremacy and appropriate bases in these areas. We do not need to insure good government, sound financial administration, or special protection for foreign capital, in the Caribbean republics in order to keep European governments out. We could not insure such ideal conditions there if we tried. We do not have them at home and certainly they do not prevail in most European countries today. Nor do we need to have any such ideal conditions in the Caribbean republics in order to make it possible for our citizens to exploit the resources and peoples of these republics. Nor ought we to attempt, through intervention in these republics, to afford American interests there a degree of security which business in the United States does not enjoy from gangsters, tornadoes, business depressions or high taxes.

The only interest in Latin America about which our government need be concerned is that of our security. That interest we can safeguard only, but easily, with an adequate navy. By disavowing the rôle of a purifier of Latin-American elections, finances, and police administration, and allowing our interests there to take their chances under local government, we can earn the friendship and goodwill of these countries for respecting their sovereignty, independence, and autonomy. At the same time, our fleet can dominate these countries as regards a European intervention, and our capitalists can dominate them economically as long as they choose to maintain extreme laissez faire. Should they abandon laissez faire and turn socialist, or extreme economic chauvinists, as Mexico has done and other republics are showing signs of doing, we should let them freely go their way as long as they make no move to invite European intervention. And if, as is most unlikely, they make such a move, we should check it by bringing to bear our diplomacy, backed by our potential armed might, against the European party to such possible intervention.

About twenty-five years ago, our statesmen, naïve in diplomacy and world politics, conceived the small-town idea that the Caribbean nations had to be good to avoid European intervention and that, because of this moral imperative, we had to make them good with financial and military interventions. As any worldly wise person ought to know, world powers intervene when, where, and because, the intervening is good, and not when, where, and because, the intervenee is bad and might, on that account, be deemed to merit a foreign intervention. About everything bad that a nation could conceivably do to the detriment of foreign interests, the Russian Soviet Government has done. But no foreign intervention has been made, or even seriously contemplated, for the excellent reason that, in Russia, the intervening would not be so good.

On the other hand, in Morocco, Manchuria and Ethiopia, the intervening may be called good and easy—or in Haiti or Nicaragua, for that matter. What makes the intervening good is not weakness of their morals or financial probity, but the weakness of their power of armed resistance, and the absence of opposition by the great powers to an intervention. We no longer need to mention officially the Monroe Doctrine. We might even expressly renounce it by way of flattering our Latin-American neighbors. The size and efficiency of our fleet will say to Europe all that the Monroe Doctrine was ever meant to say. And a big fleet will say it with a delicacy which will not offend Latin America and with an explicitness which will not be misunderstood in Europe. The Monroe Doctrine, after all, was but a crude substitute for a big navy in the days when we could not afford a big navy. What made the substitute work in those days was the big British navy.

As for economic security, here again we find our imperatives largely dictated by foreign powers and not our own choosing. The world has in prospect an era of increasingly closed economies. Why this is true, why the counter arguments of classical economics and free trade are wholly irrelevant and are being disregarded by prevailing public policies, and why we cannot change this trend, could only be explained in another book the size of this one. But an explanation of the inevitability of this trend today seems about as superfluous as an explanation of the inevitability of old age. The thing for nations or elderly people to think about today is adjustment in the most satisfactory manner to inevitable changes.

Adjustment to the imperatives of increasingly closed economies the world over, fortunately, is easier for the United States than for any other nation, because our import necessities are fewer and our near-monopolies in exports like cotton, tobacco and certain manufactures, are more important than those of any other country. With our resources for domestic needs and for export, we can feel reasonably confident of always being able to sell abroad enough to pay for our necessary imports of commodities like coffee, tin, rubber, silk, jute and tropical fruits which we cannot economically produce ourselves.

The making of these new adjustments will involve a series of barter arrangements and quota agreements, under which provisions will be made for the exchange of given quantities of

American exports of specified commodities for a countervalue of given quantities of imports of specified commodities. Within the framework of such a system of agreements, or controlled exports and imports, private interests in this country will have scope for considerable competition and initiative. The governing principles will be procurement of necessary imports; provision for necessary exports to balance the international accounts; protection of domestic industry, that is to say, of the domestic wage scale and the domestic investment; the relative immunization of the national economy from external disturbances, especially those incidental to large wars; and the achievement of a diversified national production affording the maximum economic self-sufficiency obtainable without unreasonable economic costs and sacrifices.

The ruling liberal, laissez-faire principle for foreign trade, namely that of dumping in order to stimulate domestic production and increase the nation's holdings of foreign investments, must, obviously, be discarded in a world of increasingly closed economies. Our present foreign investments, especially those in foreign securities or credits, must be counted as largely lost under the régime of closed economies, except in so far as countervalues of foreign-held investments in this country make it possible for American investors in foreign securities to collect foreign credits, or except in so far as Americans residing abroad are prepared to take payment in kind.

The American Government should do nothing to impair the foreign obligations held by its citizens. But it should do nothing involving the slightest national economic loss or inconvenience to enable the holders of foreign investments to collect. The economic relations between nations in the future must be on a pay-as-you-go basis, with the yearly international accounts or payments in even balance by the movements of goods and services. We do not want our national economy to collect goods from abroad in return for no corresponding exports of our goods or services, but merely in return for the cancellation of American claims against foreigners. We want a goods-or-service dollar exported for every goods-or-service dollar imported, excluding interest as a service item.

It seems unnecessary to attempt here an explanation of how State control of investment will operate. Obviously it will not be one hundred per cent effective or inclusive. But it can easily be made effective enough to reduce capital exports to a negligible quantity, which is all that is desired.

The reasons why foreign loans can never be repaid were explained at some length in my *Is Capitalism Doomed?*, so I shall not restate them here. The repudiation of War debts and the wholesale defaults on foreign bonds since the writing of that book in 1931 should make it unnecessary to give added proof of this obvious fact. Foreign loans are good as long as the lending countries re-lend each year the amount of interest income, as England has done consistently (except during brief periods of temporary misfortune, like war) during her entire history of foreign lending. It is clearly absurd from the point of view of national interest to export goods and services for foreign paper which can never be redeemed in goods and services. With communism and wholesale repudiations the current realities, it can no longer be held that a foreign obligation or property right, represented by a piece of paper, is the equivalent of a domestically-located piece of property. The nation is not the richer for its physical wealth held abroad, and the individual American is not the richer for his savings exported for a foreign piece of paper, the value of which is likely to be cancelled by repudiation, default, communism, or excessive taxation.

By way of justifying public policy in not making sacrifices of national interest to secure or facilitate payment on foreign investments, it should be pointed out that to sacrifice national interest to enable an American investor to collect a foreign loan is not a whit different in any essential respect from taxing the people to make good any ordinary business or investment loss suffered in this country.

It seems superfluous to undertake a lengthy refutation of the liberal argument that any restriction placed on international trade by public policy makes for international friction and war. To refute briefly that argument, it need only be said that trade competition is always a warfare between private economic interests of different nations competing for each other's markets, and that such private economic warfare is more provocative of warfare between the respective governments involved than a process of adjustment of international trade exchanges by direct agreements between governments. It is far less likely to contribute to a war between governments to have the United States government inform various groups of American exports-producers how much they can export and get paid for, than to have them either suffer or inflict a crushing defeat in free international trade competition.

It remains only to discuss briefly the subject of what is here called special foreign policies. Of these, fortunately, we have fewer than the European powers. Our Asiatic immigration exclusion policy is one of these policies. Our open-door-in-China policy is another. Most European colonial policies and military alliances may be classed in this category. Such policies are not strictly necessary for national defense or economic security. These are the policies which furnish most of the immediate causes of war. And these are the policies in respect to which it is possible to make most concessions or concessions with the greatest of ease. At the same time, it is extremely easy to inflame public opinion to violent self-assertion in respect to these policies.

It is a curious insensibility to reality, or a gross insincerity, which has made professed peace lovers since Versailles confine their pursuit of peace mainly to endeavors at concession-seeking in the fields of policies deemed by their champions essential either to national defense or economic security—about all the pacifists talk about is disarmament and tariff reduction—while these peace lovers have completely avoided advancing any significant proposals about those special policies in respect to which concession could easily have been made by the privileged. Indeed, such concession would have served to save the under-privileged from a desperation which, sooner or later, can only produce war. The United States is fortunate in having few of these special policies. Oriental exclusion and the open door in China are about the only important examples. The Monroe Doctrine is no longer to be considered a special policy but rather an accepted imperative of our national defense and of the existing balance of power.

In respect to the special policy of oriental exclusion, it is not to be expected that American opinion will tolerate any fundamental concession. But this intransigence might easily be compensated for in fact by rational and gracious acquiescence in Japanese expansion in northern China, and in renunciation of our open-door policy for China. We should thus be conceding little that is not already lost, or little that is worth much to us. At the same time, we should be giving something of great subjective value to the Japanese.

The diplomacy of the great powers of Europe fairly bristles with special policies which could be modified almost to any extent without involving any impairment of the national defense or economic security of the cession- and concession-granting great powers. England, for instance, though she could not make disposition of territory or economic advantages affecting vitally the self-governing British commonwealths like Canada, Australia, South Africa or New Zealand, could easily and safely make enormous cessions of territory, and concessions of special privileges and opportunities, in her crown colonies, and in India, to help countries like Germany and Italy solve some of their problems, including particularly the problem of what to do with the out-élite. France has African colonies, one of which has far more Italian than French colonists, with respect to which all sorts of concessions could be made without detriment to French military or economic security. England and France, also, have special policies involving military alliances or understandings with countries in central and eastern Europe which are in no sense essential or even useful, for the greater part, to the national defense or economic security of either power.

France has little to offer or to receive in political, cultural or commercial intercourse with the Balkan, central and eastern European succession States of the old Austro-Hungarian Empire, or with Poland. Yet France insists on trying, more or less ineffectually, to maintain a military and financial influence over these countries paramount to that of any other great power. France, being herself a nearly self-sufficient agricultural country, does not want or need the agricultural products of these preëminently agricultural countries. And these poor and undeveloped States with a peasant economy (except for parts of Czecho-Slovakia) have no business importing heavily of French wines, perfumes, or luxury goods, and luxury French professionals.

France, having no surplus population for export, is not in a position to send to these backward nations the essential technicians and skilled mechanics which they need. If France were attacked by Germany, these new allies would prove more of a liability than an asset. In short, there are no substantial bases of mutually advantageous and complementary commercial, financial, military, or migration collaboration between France and Poland, or France and the central and eastern European States making up the Little Entente. Yet France foolishly pursues the objective of a political hegemony over these States, instead of orientating French diplomacy towards a series of mutually advantageous deals with Germany which might lay the foundations of a prolonged European peace.

Germany, on the other hand, having an industrial surplus and an agricultural shortage, as well as surplus business enterprisers, technicians, and skilled laborers, for export, has every condition needed for a series of useful commercial, financial, and demographic relationships with these succession States over which French influence aims to be dominant. Germany needs these countries, and they need her. The political formulas for permitting the satisfaction of these needs have yet to be worked out. The chief objective of the liberal statesmanship of the Allied countries since the War has been to prevent the realization of any such formulas, which is just another one of the many reasons why liberalism is doomed.

Briefly, then, England and France could easily make cessions and concessions to Germany and Italy, but England and France could not, jointly or separately, win a war against the fascist governments of Germany and Italy, for the excellent reason that England and France cannot possiby restore liberal government where it has fallen, or where it never existed and where its chances of coming into healthy being are less today than ever before. If an Anglo-French military expedition were to be entirely successful in a military way against Mussolini and Hitler, it would be faced with the dilemma of having to maintain a perpetual military occupation or else make peace with, or relinquish the occupied territory to, the communists.

Liberalism and international finance are no longer in a position to finance a liberal régime anywhere with a stream of foreign loans. Besides, the temper of possible liberal leaders and of the people about such leaders in the now fascist countries can be said to render any liberal restoration well nigh unthinkable. The choices everywhere are fascism or communism, and an Anglo-French démarche in Europe which put communism in power could hardly be considered by those in power in England or France today as a victory for their side.

What is needed in a near future to save western civilization from communism and chaos is the coming to power in England and France, as well as in the United States, of fascist-minded leaders, who will change the entire orientation of foreign policy in those two leading European countries. The bases of long peace and helpful international relations must be laid in a statesmanship and diplomacy of realism, rational calculation of costs and probabilities, and honest recognition that there is no right which is not enforced by might.

Are the rights of the privileged nations of England and France, and the States which depend for their existence on the protection of these two powers, worth the costs of attempts at their maintenance in another war which only communism and chaos stand a chance of winning? Or is a new deal, based on a more accurate adjustment to the force and need factors, indicated? Here fascism and liberalism join issue.

An early fascist trend in the United States is needed to save us from being drawn into another wild adventure by the decrepit statesmen now at the helm in England and France, ostensibly to uphold certain rights of England and France and their dependent States of Europe, but actually to plunge Europe into world revolution and chaos. Our Anglophile and Francophile American liberals should recall, in their present reactions to events in Europe, that some twenty-odd years ago they got us into a fifty-billion-dollar war to deliver Germany from Kaiser William and prepare it for Adolf Hitler, who is much farther from the green pastures of liberalism than any Hohenzollern.

These same misguided, emotional, irrational, and frequently hysterical, American liberals with ideas on foreign affairs are now about ready to try to lead us into another crusade to oust Hitler to make place for a communist, who will be still farther from liberalism than Hitler. Liberal leadership everywhere in the world today is flogging the same dead horses of liberal issues which have been definitely lost. Liberalism had its great holy war under Lloyd George, Woodrow Wilson and Clemenceau. The holy war has been lost. Surely there is enough common sense among the peoples (and, more particularly, among the in-élite of the liberal nations of America, Britain and France), to turn from liberalism before it drags the world into another holy war to uphold certain principles and a status quo, which, incidentally, are inseparable, and which the trend of social forces moving in flood tide since Versailles has been steadily undermining. Only the fascization of the now liberal great powers can save us from another holy war to make the world safe for liberalism, or, rather to hand it over to the Red army of Russia, which is the largest and most fanatical military force in the field.

CHAPTER XXIII

THE PARTY: ORGANIZATION FOR ACTION

As WE pointed out in the first chapter, those who feel the poet's impulse

> To wreck this sorry scheme of things entire
> And mold it nearer to the heart's desire

are confronted first of all with the problems of a social system which does not work and the tasks of conceiving, inaugurating, and operating a successor system which will. Whatever else they may wish to accomplish, such as special types of social protection and social security, this they must first achieve and maintain, namely, an orderly functioning social order. Translating the poet's desire into an enterprise of social action, therefore, must be the work of leaders and followers, or a party of persons, with a will to power and will, through the use of power, to change what they may find intolerable and to conserve what they may find desirable. Such an association is a political party.

In this enterprise government is the principal tool or instrument to be used by efficient group or party organization for desired ends, which may be considered good or bad from different points of view. Contrary to liberal assumptions, government is not a neutral machine like a ship, of which public agents are the crew and the majority vote the owner. Nor, to use another simile, is government to be thought of as a sort of slot machine which will play any tune called by a majority vote. Nor, again, is it useful to consider government as a sort of divinity to whom prayers or petitions may be addressed. Government cannot be completely controlled by periodical exercises of the ballot and it responds to pressure more than to petition. Modern government controls public opinion more than public opinion controls government. Here I include within the meaning of the term government the powers who rule the chief agencies of opinion formation.

Government can either be conducted by a political party having certain social objectives or, as happens under liberal capitalism, it can be conducted by the resultants of innumerable contradictory but efficiently applied force pressures of minority groups. In the one case, that of a planned society, the objectives make up a plan of national interest which has to appear rational and good to many people. In the other case—the liberal type of government, for instance—the plan of national interest resulting from the blind play of minority group pressures in the pursuit of individual and small group interests has to be assumed to be both rational and good. The chief object or good of this liberal scheme is to play that type of game. If millions go unemployed indefinitely or suffer needlessly, these facts are regrettable but unavoidable incidents to playing the game.

If any number of people, even the largest majority, find themselves so dissatisfied with the results of this game that they want other results, they cannot achieve their wish by voting changes in the rules of the game. They must, more or less, outline the results they desire and set out to achieve these results. This means that they must capture control of the government machine, keep control of it, and use it efficiently for the ends they desire. If a majority of the people share this desire and join this enterprise, it would seem fair to say that their party and the resulting government are quite as democratic as any other. The fact they no longer will to uphold a game which suits our big financiers, promoters, and their batteries of lawyers, the fountain heads of exposition and definition of Americanism, the American system and the American Constitution, is not tantamount to saying that the people no longer wish liberty, law, order, and security, or that government has ceased to be representative of the people.

The chief aim of this chapter is to emphasize the logic and inevitability of a disciplined political party organization for

effective and responsible action through the instrumentalities
of government by any large association of people having a set
of common social purposes and not having the advantages for
action in self-interest commanded by combinations of small
numbers of the wealthy and economically mighty. The chief
point of this final emphasis on the mechanics of party organization for action—not protest or petition—will be found to
dispose of most of the objections to fascism as being chiefly a
thing of shirted armies and their violent acts. These objections
usually go with a failure or refusal to see in liberal capitalism
the realities and meaning of existent uniformed legions of the
state and private corporations.

Combinations of small numbers of the economically mighty,
nowadays usually of large corporations and banks, for specific
enterprises of self-interest, are exceedingly effective and disciplined in action. A popular movement of several hundred
thousand or several million people for some idealized scheme
of national interest has to have a discipline and technique
somewhat military or hierarchical in character in order to be
able to cope with the effective uses of money and power made
by these minority group combinations of the rich and mighty.
The old liberal idea that law, justice, and court rule enforced
by executive action will suffice to enable the people to deal
with minority combinations exercising power for private gain
is absurdly false, as has been pointed out throughout this book.
A score of great corporations can raise ten million dollars for
anti-social purposes of price-fixing or public-opinion manipulation more easily than the Republican or the Democratic Party
can raise a million-dollar campaign fund. As for the chances
of an incipient socialist, reform or populist party of the frustrated and discontented raising a million-dollar campaign fund,
they are not worth talking about. And the combine of a small
number of vast economic interests can use its funds more efficiently and more unscrupulously than any popular movement.

The shirted legions of fascism are the answers of the popular will to correspondingly effective uses of power by economically mighty minority groups. The liberally conducted parties

of reform or socialism in various countries at various times
have captured political offices. They have even captured the
titular headship of the government. But they have never captured power. Only Lenin, with the aid of the soldiery of a
nation in arms, has been able to capture power for Marxian
socialism. And only the fascists, with the aid of their disciplined legions, have been able to capture power for an effective
scheme of national collectivism.

It is incorrect to say, as do many liberal and socialist critics,
that control of the machinery of government rests with any
one person, group, or clique of persons or groups. Wall Street,
the big bankers, and the heads of the great corporations, no
more control government than the gangsters and exploiters of
gambling and prostitution. No group or coterie of groups controls liberal government or could control it. And no group
acting for a minority money-making interest would want to
control government. Such control would impose all sorts of
obligations and cares and yield none of the financial rewards
so generally coveted and so often obtained either from legitimate business or illegitimate rackets. Any two-by-four bank
operator or speculator will, with a little luck, make and salt
away a fortune such as no fascist leader would ever dream of
acquiring. No; the interests, legal and illegal, which are often
incorrectly said to control government in America, wish only
to control the making of certain specific decisions of government affecting them. And in return for these particular exercises of power they are willing to allow and aid other predatory
interests to do likewise. Thus, an interest opposing a given tax
will support any public extravagance in return for support of
the tax reduction sought.

In this connection, it should be remarked that a party
seeking political power or control of government must have a
large mass following, such as no group of private interests
could long command, and such a political party is never likely
to be initiated by a group of individuals on the make. For the
latter, liberalism is the perfect system. It allows power and
control only when and where power and control can be exer-

cised momentarily for private interest and it exempts those who thus use power from any real responsibility to the people.

But, playing the liberal game prevents any reform, socialist, or popular party from ever being able to do much about serious social problems. The fundamental reason why the party receiving a majority mandate to clean up a city government or to effect some large social or economic reform on a national scale cannot exercise political power or control adequate for these purposes is this: Such an organization or party, including its candidates elected to office, lacks the only type of organization and group discipline with which political control can be acquired and exercised.

As an eminent English economist on a recent visit to this country has so aptly put it, one cannot legislate successfully beyond the ability of administration to execute. And administration requires the right personnel and the right technique of using personnel. Reform, socialism, or a really new deal cannot be effected by passing laws alone or by law enforcement by officials unsympathetic with the new program, or by law enforcement under the rulings of a judiciary loyal to legal and constitutional theories incompatible with the new program.

To accomplish its purposes, a reform or socialist party must take over control of government quite as thoroughly and masterfully as an invading army of occupation. This the liberal mandatories of the people cannot do, for the excellent reason that they have not an army or do not constitute an army. The liberals who undertook to set up and conduct a liberal republican government in Germany after the war were doomed by the fact that, having no army of their own, they had to rely on a hostile army for the execution of their policies. An organization of mere joiners, button-wearers, membership-dues-payers, party-meeting-attenders, and straight-ticket-voters is not an organization with which anything important of a governmental or constructive character can be done. The button-wearers and dues-paying members neither constitute an army nor can they hire an army, something which, not only a billion-dollar industrial corporation, public utility, or bank can do, but something which even any first-class gangster is able to do.

It is, however, a great mistake to infer from the arguments for a disciplined party organization that, if it includes some semi-militarized units of men, the chief reason for this type of organization is to enable the leaders one fine day to seize power by a violent *coup d'état*. The gates to power were opened to the fascists in Italy and Germany in perfectly legal ways, not because the government had reason to fear an armed fascist attack on the government (for, at that time those in charge of the government could have liquidated the fascist organizations with a few whiffs of powder), but because the titular head of government felt that the fascists alone were able to exercise political control once they took office.

It is strange how people who regularly sing "Like a mighty army, moves the Church of God," and who regularly drill and parade in the uniform of one or more fraternal orders, will see in fascism only militarized organization for violence. The chief end of disciplined organization is not violent overthrow of government. For, in any country or moment, except a conjuncture like Russia just before the communists made a violent seizure of power, a disciplined fascist party would naturally seek to come to power in the easiest possible way, which would be a legal or conventional way. The chief end of disciplined organization is the efficient and responsible exercise of political control after it has been obtained.

Considerations of mass responses indicate disciplined organization. Men and women of the sort who are useful in any constructive undertaking prefer a political party or an organization of any sort to be orderly and disciplined. There are, of course, many people who prefer disorderly associations and meetings in which there is no real leadership, authority, or order. Such people merely want organized mass gesturing and argument. They make up the rank and file of the socialist, populist, and reformist parties. But the vast majority of people prefer group behavior patterns which are orderly and seemingly effective to some end other than that of merely blowing off steam. The fact, of course, is that more than half of our working population, in their daily occupations, are subject to an organizational discipline which differs from that of an army only in unessential respects. Our large city political machines have been disciplined organizations with hierarchical command for generations, facts which explain why they frustrate, defeat, and survive reform mayors and administrations.

Then there is the consideration that only through a type of organization in which there are appropriate units for administration and the transmission of orders is it possible to make efficient use of the resources of men, just men, for whatever the ends may be. The usual trouble with a party and leader elected to office on a reform, square deal, new freedom, new deal, or socialist platform is a failure to fill up the lesser executive posts of government with sympathizers with the new ideals. And this failure is due, not to a lack of such sympathizers qualified for these posts, but simply to lack of a type of organization which can make available personnel known to the chief and subject to direction by him. The liberal system tends to put personnel choice and management in hands like those of a Mr. Farley.

Another important consideration indicating the inevitability of disciplined organization is that only with such a type of organization is there likely to be clarity as to objectives and unity in action as well as an enlightened use of men and means for a given end. It would be easy to enumerate absurdities in personnel and policy choices as means to announced ends of liberal administrations. If policy decisions and governmental orders have to be formulated with a view to the needs of orderly administration by a disciplined party organization, most of the futilities and contradictions of liberal reform or liberal socialist parties in office will be averted.

The realistic political party machines of liberalism, such as those of Tammany Hall or the old Republican Party National Committee had rather more order and efficiency in action than the reformist leaders. After all, these machines had considerable organization discipline and clarity of aims, for the chief aim was spoils and the means of obtaining and retaining power in order to get more spoils. In the city and state governments these machines can still operate fairly well by simply passing the buck to the national government on all serious social problems, be it the war on organized crime and abusive monopoly, or be it unemployment relief. But the political machines of both the Republican and the Democratic Party of old are now doomed by the need for drastic social solutions. They can no longer side-step social issues, and maintain party unity and discipline on the central issue of getting and holding power as a means to spoils. The farmers of the West or the unemployed anywhere are going to force the issues on those in charge of government or running for office.

The imperatives and controls of a hierarchical party organization are now needed as never before, and they can no longer hold together an organization built around spoils. In groping after drastic social solutions, a political party must have the guiding and controlling forces of a disciplined organization, operating through members of a party council who are exercising governmental powers and who are constantly at grips with current problems. The guiding and controlling function of a majority vote, recorded every two or four years, was always largely mythical. Today, administration cannot be guided or controlled by majority votes every two or four years. The majority vote, for instance, cannot decide in between elections whether government should follow a policy leading to war, declare war or maintain neutrality. The majority vote cannot control the day-to-day decisions of government about economic policies, nor can the majority vote indicate a body of legal rules which can possibly bind government to any fixed course on the uncharted seas of economic control in which government is now everywhere navigating. Only the party council, constituted more or less as the general staff of an army in war time, can guide or control public administration in these vital matters. The most dangerous and vicious possible guidance for public administration is that of a vote-catching opportunism or that of a defensive mechanism trying to make day-to-day adjustments to minority group pressures.

Control of public administration is not a matter of having public debates and organized group manifestations, culminating in periodical majority votes. This is true today as it never was before on account of the potentialities of propaganda and the command of such potentialities by minority interests which have no genuine concern with public interest. One could go on indefinitely elaborating reasons or supplying concrete examples showing why a disciplined political party organization is essential to the orderly conduct of government in the present world crisis. Once his thought is directed along this line of inquiry, the reader's knowledge of conditions and imagination should enable him to develop this thesis to almost any length.

It remains to discuss briefly the question of how many political parties are possible or desirable. It may be said briefly that a planned economy, such as either fascism or communism must achieve, precludes most of the features of a multiparty system or even a two-party system along liberal lines. A good part of the case against a plurality of political parties and a periodical rotation of parties in office would be a repetition of much that has already been said about planning, the inevitable uniqueness of a national plan and the evils of minority group pressures which are necessarily irresponsible, anti-social, or anti-national and utterly incompatible with the successful pursuit of any possible scheme of national interest or public welfare. A plurality of political parties, no one of which can ever exercise responsible control, can only mean a plurality of irresponsible minority group pressures, the chief objective of which will be spoils and never the realization of a scheme of national interest.

One can never prove by science or philosophy which of several parties has the right or best scheme of national interest, for the decision or selection in such a matter must express an emotional attitude and depend on the ultimate values preferred and the premises taken for granted without proof. One can, however, sustain in a scientific or philosophical discussion the contention that a country has to make effective one scheme of national interest in order to avert chaos. And one can argue rationally that a country is better off with any one of many possible schemes of national interest efficiently pursued than with the anarchy of innumerable powerful minority interests operating in ways to render any effective social control impossible and, thus, to make any scheme of national interest unattainable. Such an argument would be largely a restatement and explanation of the historical trends and forces which brought order out of medieval chaos on the continent of Europe through the rise of nationalisms during and since the Reformation.

Granting that all government, like all human nature, is full of imperfections, there is no good case to be made out today for insistence on periodical changes from one bad government administration to another. Improvement would not seem to be best favored by periodical rotation of parties in government. One does not seek improvement in the management of Ford Motors or the Standard Oil Companies by changing administrations every four or eight years. The best answer to the argument for periodical party changes in administration is that such changes are not changes in anything vital or important to the masses and that such changes prevent the development of competent and responsible leadership. Personalities in administrative offices change, but the dominant interests and the system remain unchanged.

To the question How might an American fascist party, called by another name, of course, arise? it would be idle to attempt a precise reply. The right answer, which only future events can furnish, must depend on a combination of adverse conditions, the reactions of the adversely affected *élite*, the dynamic personality of a great leader and the opportune moment and set of circumstances for his dramatic emergence from obscurity to leadership.

The objective conditions and the probable reactions of the adversely affected *élite* we have discussed. The personality of the leader, the point in time of his emergence, and the nature of the circumstances of his emergence we cannot usefully discuss, for these are unpredictable factors. The French and Russian revolutions could be and were predicted. But Napoleon and Lenin could not be and were not predicted.

The fields of analysis and synthesis and, also, of useful speculation in which preliminary work can be done, are those I have attempted to explore. In this concluding chapter I have attempted no discussion of the techniques of disciplined party organization in the United States, because these are matters in which we have already abundant skill. In discussion of the question whether or not a country should prepare for or make a given war, there is no need to discuss the art of war. In arguing for or against the construction of a proposed canal which is admittedly possible, there is little need for an engineering treatise on the building of canals.

The real issue for discussion is whether those who want a different social order with the conservation of many of our present values should organize for the capture and use of government to this end, or whether they should merely go on protesting and petitioning without occupying themselves with the tasks of creating and operating the kind of social order they desire.

Preparatory thinking and discussion at this time can be most useful in exploring the possibilities of uniting a large number of the right people for successful action around a scheme of objectives. In this connection it is important to lay a major stress on the imperatives of order and the possibilities of choice in making up a new program. A successful party might get started with a set of promises to satisfy every interest. But it could not carry on long if it seriously undertook to keep all these promises. We may well get a fascism through a party making and breaking innumerable promises. It will be a better fascism to the extent that enlightened opinion, formed somewhat in advance, forces the new movement to be intellectually honest.

Undoubtedly the easiest way to unite and animate large numbers in political association for action is to exploit the dynamic forces of hate and fear. The most dynamic persons in any new political movement are those in whom frustration and defeat have generated most hate and fear. Obviously, the only way to avoid hates and fears is to prevent frustrations and remove dangers.

If liberal leadership succeeds in doing this for the underprivileged nations and the underprivileged members of the *élite* within nations, fascism will not triumph over liberal leadership. If, however, liberal capitalism is doomed, we must expect its successor to be largely the work of angry and frustrated men with a will to power. Preparatory thinking, nevertheless, can bring into alliance with these men the less frustrated and embittered and bring to the new movement their contributions. Only a body of enlightened and sympathetic opinion will be able to impose on an emergent fascism counsels of moderation and avert the extremes of a bitter class war.

INDEX

DATE DUE
